Clear,
Precise,
Direct

Clear, Precise, Direct

Strategies for Writing

Duncan Koerber
Guy Allen

OXFORD
UNIVERSITY PRESS

OXFORD
UNIVERSITY PRESS

Oxford University Press is a department of the University of Oxford.
It furthers the University's objective of excellence in research, scholarship,
and education by publishing worldwide. Oxford is a registered trade mark of
Oxford University Press in the UK and in certain other countries.

Published in Canada by
Oxford University Press
8 Sampson Mews, Suite 204,
Don Mills, Ontario M3C 0H5 Canada

www.oupcanada.com

Library and Archives Canada Cataloguing in Publication
Koerber, Duncan, author
Clear, precise, direct : strategies for writing / Duncan
Koerber and Guy Allen.

Includes bibliographical references and index.
ISBN 978–0–19–900640–3 (pbk.)

1. English language—Rhetoric. 2. English language—Grammar.
3. Report writing—Problems, exercises, etc. I. Allen, Guy, 1947–, author
II. Title.

PE1408.K62 2014   808'.042   C2014-902628-5

Cover image: Atomic Imagery/Digital Vision/Getty
Chapter 5 Photos: *city*: ©iStockphoto.com/celin; *dog*: ©iStockphoto.com/Wislander;
car: ©iStockphoto.com/victorhe2002; *Winnipeg*: ©iStockphoto.com/Arpad Benedek;
Collie: ©iStockphoto.com/DebbiSmirnoff; *Ferrari*: ©iStockphoto.com/Sjo

Oxford University Press is committed to our environment.
This book is printed on Forest Stewardship Council® certified paper
and comes from responsible sources.

MIX
Paper from
responsible sources

FSC
www.fsc.org   FSC® C103567

Printed and bound in Canada

1 2 3 4 — 18 17 16 15

Contents

From the Publisher

Oxford University Press is delighted to introduce *Clear, Precise, Direct: Strategies for Writing* by Duncan Koerber and Guy Allen. This text provides a concise set of strategies to help students improve their writing and includes the following features:

- Conversational tone and easy-to-follow chapter structure that will engage and motivate students
- Detailed explanations of enhancing factors and interfering factors that help and hinder writing
- Inspiring quotations from professional writers that acknowledge the rewards and challenges of producing writing that audiences want to read
- Boldfaced key terms that are defined in the glossary
- Boxed writing topics that analyze the application of writing strategies in published writing
- Peer writing models for students to analyze and emulate, including academic writing and personal narrative
- Exercises that ask students to find and analyze various types of writing both within and outside of the academic environment
- Assignments that give students the opportunity to apply each lesson to their own writing and that encourage them to revise previous assignments according to each new strategy learned
- Chapter summaries and further reading lists
- An appendix of documentation styles

A companion website provides podcasts, additional helpful material for students, and an instructor's manual.

Preface

Our Philosophy

All people have a desire to express themselves. People want others to hear and read their ideas and experiences. However, written expression doesn't come easy. People struggle with starting to write, with finding the right words. They fear judgements of their writing—often their own judgements.

People who turn to writing books for help often feel lost. Hundreds of grammar and style points glare back at them. Mastering those hundreds of grammar and style points looks daunting as a result—and there is no guarantee that mastering every single one of them will help writers express themselves easily and engage readers. They may become more correct writers, but not more expressive or engaging ones.

Our philosophy is different.

We think writers need a clear path to expression. That's why this book contains just seven major lessons about writing. Students find this short list of lessons provides clarity. The lessons teach students how to become more comfortable as writers and how to improve their work through editing and revising.

We also think writers need models to emulate. Not masterpiece models, however. As you'll see in the aphorisms sprinkled throughout this book, famous writers do everything we describe but their writing intimidates beginning writers in its depth and complexity. We believe that beginning writers should emulate the best work of people at the same stage as them. That's why this book includes peer models from students who went through our lessons.

We also believe in focusing on the positives in students' writing. We're taught in schools to be critical and negative. Students find it easier to find faults than to find strengths. In our classrooms and in this book, particularly with the peer model writing, we focus on the positives. We respect each student's effort.

Writing should also connect with readers. The reader can put down the book or article or the professor can award a D grade to a paper. With this in mind, writing becomes about expressing ideas and experiences comfortably to bring readers in, to engage them. Good writing is not about glorifying egos or showing off. It is not about trying to hide from, attack, trick, or confuse readers. Nor should readers have to guess at what a writer is trying to say—if they have to guess, the writer's connection with them is lost.

Good writing, as we emphasize throughout this book, should seem completely natural—for the writer and for the reader.

Our Approach

We developed the lessons, exercises, assignments, and general approach of this book out of decades of experimentation in our writing classes. Looking at the classroom like a scientific experiment, we tried out various exercises and assignments year after year, testing their efficacy before settling on this set.

The major finding of this long-term classroom experiment was that writing lessons worked best when combined with personal writing assignments within classroom writing communities. Students found content in their own lives and then applied the lessons willingly to their life stories. They took editing and revision seriously. Inspired by classroom editing sessions, our students spontaneously formed smaller editing groups outside of the classroom. Our courses were intense but rewarding: lessons, exercises, assignments, and regular revision led to writing that many students published in professional publications during or soon after the courses ended. Students applied all the lessons to their academic writing as well—this book provides peer models of the most successful ones.

To help beginning writers express themselves in a *Clear, Precise, and Direct* way, we have put together a set of strategies or lessons that we call **enhancing factors** to increase writing's effectiveness. The factors allow writers to cut through the confusion and difficulty of writing and make expression that's fresh, creating writing that readers intuitively enjoy. Writers who can apply these lessons—economy, strong verbs, active voice, strong nouns, original phrasing, parallelism, and sentence variation and sound—will develop a greater facility and precision with writing. They will express themselves as they want to, in a way that readers will enjoy.

The enhancing factors help writers take control of their sentences because they provide signposts—a frame for looking at writing objectively. When looking at writing, we also see seven **interfering factors** that cause communication to break down: wordiness, dead verbs, passive voice, vague pronouns, clichés, faulty parallelism, and monotonous sentences. These seven factors are not the only problems in writing, of course, but they are the Top Seven and, as such, they give students a tangible and manageable set of targets for revising and editing. Students who remove these interfering factors through regular revision improve their writing dramatically over a short period of intense work.

This book also asks writers to create samples of the major forms of professional and academic writing: the personal narrative, the research paper, the interview-based article, and the personal essay. Personal narrative tells the writer's direct experience. The research paper relates indirect experience from scholars. The interview-based article retells the experience of another person. The final assignment, the personal essay, allows students to write about their observations of trends and activist causes in their communities. We consider each assignment a natural extension of, not a departure from, the previous ones. Indeed, all the strategies apply to all the forms of writing we describe in this book, and in particular we show how they apply to academic writing in each chapter. We encourage you to see additional connections.

Benefits

Our approach to writing teaching helps students connect their inner and outer worlds. They don't remain inside themselves. Typical academic courses do not make this connection. The subject matter is often so far outside students' experience it could be on the moon.

In our courses, students who write about issues that matter to them take ownership of their experience. They care about writing and editing because their subject matter is so personal. With our list of micro-level enhancing and interfering factors in mind, they begin to see sentences objectively. They also develop an awareness of other writing issues that we don't even talk about in this book (the lesson on parallelism, for example, tends to prevent the dreaded run-on sentence). That's the spill-over effect of specific, targeted lessons. Students produce writing that says what they want to say—in their own voices. Students control the language instead of feeling controlled by it. They feel the urge to write more and more. That's fluid expression.

When starting with personal narrative, students can relax—the content is inside them—and focus squarely on the issues professional writers face. After gaining confidence in personal narrative writing, student writers then turn to academic writing ready to tackle difficult, often abstract content. Academic writing becomes manageable as a result. Students realize that rather than conforming to a false academic dialect and style, they have the authority to make decisions on writing; they have authority to speak in their own voices. After taking our courses, our students tend to improve in their other academic courses, sometimes by a whole grade category.

How the Book is Organized

We've ordered this book just like we order our writing courses: one chapter lesson represents one week of the course. Each chapter focuses on one major lesson with many examples. The examples help students see the good and the bad of writing. The chapters include peer writing that reflects everything we teach. Students read the peer models—written by students who went through these lessons in our classes—and immediately understand what we expect.

Each chapter includes exercises developed in the classroom. The exercises ask students to try out the lessons in novel ways.

Each chapter closes with suggested writing assignments. Topics are open—we want students to take control of the topic and go where they want to go. Writers write well when they write about topics they like.

How to Use This Book

For Students

This book provides a proven, tested set of strategies to help improve facility with writing. The students who improve the most work their way through the book in sequence. The chapter on strong verbs, for example, leads topically into the chapter on active voice. The exercises and assignments at the end of each lesson help students to build writing skills.

We remind you throughout the book to revise earlier assignments using the knowledge gained in latter chapters. It's a repetitive and recursive process.

Each chapter, however, is a self-contained unit, and so you may choose to focus instead on targeting problem areas. In this case, you can sample some of the chapters based on your own needs.

No matter which approach you take, merely *reading* the lessons will not help you improve as a writer. We implore you do all the exercises and the chapter assignment to gain the most from this book. Reading is vital to recognizing good writing, but writers must eventually write.

It's also important to continue to apply the lessons even after you've finished all the book's exercises and assignments. Learning comes from repeated application. Use this book as a reference as you're editing your writing or a friend's. Eventually, the lessons will become second nature. Writing is a performance medium, like athletics—the more you do, the better you get.

For Instructors

Instructors may use this book as the spine of a course. The lessons may also be used out of order, with instructors selecting chapters based on specific needs. Each chapter is organized in a similar way and stands strongly on its own.

Every class is different—judge your students' needs and assign readings accordingly. The most important point is that students must not only read, but also write and revise regularly.

ACKNOWLEDGEMENTS

In the summer of 1998, I took a writing course with Guy Allen that changed my life. Guy's refreshing teaching style fascinated me, and his unique lessons helped me see my writing clearly. I become a better student instantly—I went from earning Cs and Bs to earning As. Almost ten years later, Guy hired me to teach that same course, and naturally I dug out my notes from 1998. My experience on both sides of this writing pedagogy—as student and as teacher—informs this book. I want other students to experience what I experienced. Thank you for your mentorship, Guy.

Others helped greatly with this project. Robert Price always provided candid advice, and his notes on Guy's other class, *Specialized Prose*, added depth to the chapters. I'm glad my colleague Dominique O'Neill gave us permission to publish her handout on strong verbs in academic writing. This book also wouldn't have been the same without the peer models from my University of Toronto Mississauga and York University students. They applied the lessons and produced excellent writing for other students to emulate.

I'm grateful to Dave Ward at Oxford University Press for expressing interest in the project quickly and enthusiastically. Lisa Peterson and Leah-Ann Lymer at Oxford made this book a better one with their detailed comments during the revision stages.

I also want to thank the peer reviewers of the manuscript who provided positive feedback that made this book better: Laura Davis, Red Deer College; Deirdre Flynn, University of Toronto; Christopher Lee, Western University; Rebecca Menhart, Lakehead University; and Sheila M. Ross, Capilano University.

Two important people in my life deserve mention as well. I must thank my wife Ellie for her love and support during the many months of proposing, writing, and revising. She allowed me the time to get this project done. Finally, Kylie Aida was born after the peer review and, on many long nights, she slept next to me while I revised the manuscript. I hope she likes it.

Duncan Koerber
York University

Many people contributed to the development of the writing pedagogy outlined in this book.

Arnie Achtman and Margaret Procter took risks when these ideas felt scary and new. They tested this novel approach in their classrooms and helped me to see that these procedures had a life outside of my own teaching style.

Several administrators at the University of Toronto offered the secure space and administrative support that a pedagogical innovation requires. These include Richard Van Fossen, Cecil Houston, and Merl Wahlstrom, deans, and Marty Wall and Jack Wayne, program directors at the Transitional Year Program.

Keith Allen, Acting Director of the Transitional Year Program at the University of Toronto, nominated me for the 3M Teaching Fellowship in 1991. This seemed like an outlandish long shot. Winning the award gave me the credibility to come out of an academic silence where I felt timid about revealing unorthodox procedures. After this award, I publicized my experience with my evolving approach to the ages-old "writing problem." Thank you to 3M for supporting this kind of vulnerable and creative university teaching.

Thank you to the many colleagues who either adopted or experimented with parts of this pedagogy. These include Maureen Fitzgerald, Agi Lukacs, Duncan Koerber (co-author of this text), Denise Clarke, John Currie, Rahul Sethi, Robert Price, Laurel Waterman, Penny Verbruggen, Huamei Han, Tracy Moniz, Jean Mason, Keith Haartman, David Penhale, Ken Tallman, Geoff Lawrence, Penny Kinnear, and Carolyn Greco. Dialogue with colleagues stimulates and energizes thoughtful practice.

Laurie Kallis and John Dunford at Life Rattle Press provide support to writers who emerge from this pedagogy. Life Rattle provides students who feel inspired by expressive writing with a place to practice their new craft. Life Rattle publishes new writers and offers reading venues like *The Totally Unknown Writers Festival* in Toronto—no longer so unknown.

Karen Graham and Martha Ayim, whom I met as students, sharpened my thinking with brilliant writing and their articulation of the ideas they saw coming out of my classes.

Thank you to hundreds of students who have written their stories. You taught me how to teach writing. You taught me the things in this book.

Guy Allen
University of Toronto

Clear,
Precise,
Direct

Write Now

Start, Develop, Revise

> Convince yourself that you are working in clay,
> not marble, on paper not eternal bronze:
> Let that first sentence be as stupid as it wishes.
>
> —Jacques Barzun

WRITING MATTERS TO PEOPLE. We esteem those who do it well. We may feel diminished when we fail at it. Negative judgements by others about our writing may hurt us. Many people carry with them a cluster of bad experiences related to writing.

Our schools often expect us to write well—even though they may never have shown us how to do that. Writing in school often feels more like obedience training than learning. **Grammar** rules—like split infinitives and dangling modifiers—abound, and many teachers expect an elevated, formal voice.

Writing typically taught in school, such as the essay or research paper, seems formulaic in both structure and approach. Students replicate the "hamburger structure" of a general introduction, three body paragraphs, and a conclusion.

By the time students reach colleges and universities, many have accumulated scar tissue and fear and dread rooted in bad experiences with writing in school. They may turn away from writing to other subjects, such as math and science, to hide their scars.

Yet many of us, despite bad experiences, still hope to write well. We would like to engage and hold the attention of a reader. We would like to express meanings that reveal us to others and to ourselves. We want to tell a story about our past or speak to an important issue or even bring communities together. Our communities form through language, and we want to join, and sometimes lead, that conversation.

Writing is integral to our sense of being. When people learn how to write, their confidence grows not only in handling language but in other areas that don't seem directly related to writing. They become better thinkers. They speak more clearly.

While the "obedience training" method of writing may have left scars, you can find a way to heal. We and other writing scholars have studied the act of writing and discovered some basic principles about how people learn to write well. Those principles are as follows:

- People learn to write by writing. People learn best when they write often—several times a week. Frequency matters. People cannot learn writing by thinking about writing. People cannot learn by only listening to a teacher lecture on writing. They have to do it, and do it often. Think about exercise and your body: exercising once a year will not get you into shape. Exercising every day will.
- People learn faster by writing many short pieces than by writing fewer long pieces. While many beginning writers dream of writing novels right away, and many teachers assign long-form academic writing, these projects are difficult and ambitious for someone just starting out. In this book, we begin with short assignments. Master the short assignments before moving on to the more difficult ones.
- People can learn what they need to know to write good **prose** in two to three months. By "good prose," we mean writing that engages and holds the attention of a reader. You don't need years of writing instruction before you can become "a writer." A strong effort, regular writing, and focused lessons are all most writers need to improve significantly in a short time—even people who have never considered themselves writers. In two to three months, people can get to the point where they know how to handle language instead of feeling handled by it. Rather than feeling pressured by teachers' expectations, people can feel free and open. They can feel ready to express their experiences and ideas. Much of the peer model writing in this book comes from beginners who went through an intensive training course like the one this book describes.
- People learn the technical aspects of writing—sentences, paragraphs, techniques—more quickly when they first write personal **narratives** than when they first tackle **academic writing**. Typically the focus of writing in schools, academic writing can seem formal and prescriptive. Academic writing can easily fall into abstractness, which pushes readers off. Good personal narrative, on the other hand, pulls the reader along with chronological storytelling of concrete experience and vivid details readers see. Furthermore, few beginning writers seem interested in academic writing if the instructor chooses the topic. On the other hand personal narrative writing about subjects the students choose—in other words, writing that students want to do—seems straightforward and freeing. The narrative form is also familiar: narratives, after all, are all around us, in novels, in movies, in magazines, and so on.
- Writers who begin with narrative then find it easier to transition to academic writing. That's the path we will take in this book. The strategies you learn in writing narratives are directly applicable to writing other forms, particularly at the level of the sentence.

You have to realise that a lot of the time, you're going to be writing without inspiration. The trick is to write just as well without it as with.

—PHILIP PULLMAN

- Good writers learn by reading—that is, by watching and analyzing what other writers do. They read extensively the kind of writing they want to write themselves. It is often how they draw inspiration: by reading, writers learn by osmosis what works and what doesn't. Our advice to you is this: read the work of professionals, of amateurs, or of your friends—the distinction is irrelevant as long as the writing interests you. Study the peer models we have included in each chapter. But a word of caution: be careful not to turn to plagiarism, the advertent or inadvertent copying of another author's work without permission or attribution. You can find inspiration in another author's work and still avoid directly copying it.

- People learn to write best in positive settings. Writing makes people vulnerable. Writing is difficult enough without negative feedback; it becomes especially hard when disrespect and tactless criticism wreck the learning environment. Finding a community of respectful writers can improve learning. Positive communities inside or outside the classroom can provide feedback on what works in your writing and what needs editing. A welcoming community can become a comfortable testing ground—a safe place—for you to develop writing skills.

That's hardly all, but let's get writing.

Where to Start

Starting any piece of writing is difficult work. Does your drafting process look like this?

a) Write the first sentence
b) Look it over
c) Rewrite it
d) Take a break to check e-mail
e) Return to your word processor and write the second sentence
f) Look it over
g) Rewrite it
h) Repeat process for the next three hours

If you write this way, and many writers tell us they do, then it's time for a change. This time-consuming process makes writing more difficult than it should be.

A first draft of any piece of writing should be spontaneous, with no editing. It may look like a mess, and it will naturally violate many of the lessons of this book, but that's fine. Editing at the drafting stage only slows you down. It's better to get all of your ideas down quickly on the page, without judging them, without imposing order on them. This is called freewriting. You can impose order on your work during the revision and editing stage, which we will discuss later in this chapter.

You will learn to write by writing, and by writing a lot. Freewriting provides the opportunity you need to write enough to get better. Freewriting, a common practice among writers, goes by different names:

- journalling
- morning papers
- diaries
- free association
- automatic writing
- notebooking

These names describe writing writers don't intend for readers—other than themselves.

Freewriting stretches the writing muscles, providing a warmup for the brain and the fingers. Athletes know the value of warming up before a match, but sometimes writers forget this important preparation.

Without freewriting, you jump into the writing task cold. With freewriting, you knock off the rust without consequences or judgement. You just write and write and write about anything that comes to mind. You'll probably find that a short session of freewriting makes your brain and fingers work more smoothly on the next piece of writing. Many professional writers will freewrite for 15 to 30 minutes in the morning before starting their projects.

Freewriting gives writers a place to put thoughts and anxieties and fears and desires, somewhere to dump their clutter. It sometimes leads to nice surprises, ideas or passages writers can use in the writing they produce for other readers. Freewriting disregards plans or intentions, allowing those nice surprises to surface from the unconscious mind. On the page, it often looks like the outline of a "dream," a stream of consciousness piece. Freewriting flows from one idea or scene to the next, without the formality of stops and starts and introductions and conclusions.

Examples of Freewriting

In the following two freewriting paragraphs by two different writers, note the stream of consciousness effect, the apparent lack of organization. You'll probably also note mistakes. Neither one is better than the other. This stage of writing is about being comfortable with expression, not spelling or grammar or punctuation. These two writers weren't thinking about quality, just flow:

1. I went shopping today. I like shopping or maybe window shopping if you will. I like watching all the different kinds of people just hanging around the mall doing their business. I wanted to buy a pair of sunglasses. So I browsed through Sears and then various other stores while finding the right pair for me. I came across this store called Lush. It's a store where they only sell soap. I always used to pass by it but never really thought of stepping in. Since I didn't have much on my

hand today, I decided to check it out. This store was awesome. They had soap that looked like cup cakes and fruits. The store lady came over and asked me if I was looking for something specific. I just told her that I hadn't been in the store before and was looking around. She then asked me if a wanted to see a demo of a soap bomb. A soap bomb is the size of a tennis ball and foamy in texture. It was really colourful too. So I said agreed to look at what she was going to show me. She took me to one corner of the store and started to fill up a little sink with water. Then she dropped the soap bomb in the water after which it instantaneously disintegrated creating lots of fizz in the water. (By Nishkruti Munshi)

2. I have watched alot of movies lately but they all seem to be so violent. I haven't seen a movie that had anything heartwarming about it. I wonder if this is what people want in their movies or if they are just going to see anything. The movie I saw had police shooting gangsters and bodies torn apart and dogs eating the bodies. It was awful. But I still went to the movie, for some reason. I think movies today should be more heartwarming, but then I guess I'd be a hypocrite wouldn't I? the movie industry is a big business and if it was all happy stuff I guess nobody would show up. My favourite movie is Life of Pi, with the tiger and the boy on the boat. But even it has violence too, albeit between animals, but I think we cannot resist it now. I watch a lot of movies but I don't watch much TV. On TV I just watch sports and the news. I've gotten away from watching set programs at set times nowadays. It feels like I can't sit still anywhere anymore to watch programs. I only watch movies when I have friends over and we sit down on the couch and eat popcorn. I wonder if my attention is getting too divided when I'm alone. I have to check my phone all the time and can't stay focused on a sitcom or drama.

Neither of these pieces is edited, and it shows. Your writing may look like these in its initial stages. That's fine—many authors' initial writing looks just like these do, even though the final versions that you read look perfect. These freewriting exercises may lead to something better or maybe they're just a warmup, only to be deleted once they've served their purpose.

Many writers have high expectations for their writing. High expectations are natural—we want to produce the best writing we can. But it's unrealistic to expect to write a masterpiece every time you pick up your pen or go to your keyboard. It's unfortunate that we don't get to sit behind great writers and watch them work. If we did, we certainly wouldn't see perfection forming on the page in every sentence, without revision.

> If you want to write, you need to keep an honest, unpublishable journal that nobody reads, nobody but you. Where you just put down what you think about life, what you think about things, what you think is fair and what you think is unfair.
>
> —MADELEINE L'ENGLE

The masterpiece mentality will get you nowhere that you want to go. It may actually lead to debilitating paralysis. Perfectionism tortures writers. Comparing your draft writing to the published works of Hemingway, Salinger, or Faulkner is pointless. What were they writing at your age and writing stage? What did their first drafts look like? You don't typically get to see all the false starts, the words scribbled out, or the revisions their editors sent back. The so-called masterpiece authors also had time to develop. They often worked decades on their crafts, facing rejection after rejection from publishers until finally meeting success. To expect perfection from the start is unrealistic and doesn't represent the way writers actually work.

> Freewriting is the easiest way to get words on paper and the best all-around practice in writing that I know.
>
> —PETER ELBOW

Freewriting sidesteps the masterpiece mentality. Freewriting means writing without worrying about the quality of what you write, at least for now. Freewriting means putting words on paper, any words at all. Put away your grammar books and dictionaries—grammar and spelling don't matter here. Freewriting means not worrying about a teacher's comments or a reader's judgements.

EXERCISE 1 ▸ Freewriting

Produce seven pieces of freewriting: one a day for seven days. Start each entry in your freewriting journal with the date, the time, and your setting. Write as much as you can in 10 minutes, and at the end of each session, count your words. Enter your word count below your writing.

Advice:

- Write quickly. Write on a keyboard or with a pen.
- Try not to stop. Don't think; write. See if you can write more than 400 words in 10 minutes.
- Write anything. If you're stuck, write about being stuck. Write about what you did today, or what you didn't do. Write about how you want to start an academic writing project or some of its subtopics.
- Watch for The Judge. After you write your first line or two, The Judge, an internalized critic, may tell you that what you have written is stupid, irrelevant, or unacceptable. Learn to escort The Judge out of your writing room. You may need to do this again and again. The Judge will take advantage of your vulnerability. The Judge will try insults, profanity, reason, logic—anything to undermine your freewriting. The Judge may become ruder and more aggressive as you write more. The Judge can only prevail if you stop.
- If The Judge feels too strong, then turn off or cover your computer screen with paper so you cannot see what you're writing. This act may seem strange at first, but it allows you to focus on what you're thinking, not what you've already written. If you can't see it, you can't judge it.
- You succeed in this exercise by doing it.
- Try to increase your word count as the days go by.

After this freewriting exercise, think about how you felt. Our students have differing opinions on freewriting. Some find it, as intended, freeing. It allows them to open up and let out a torrent of experiences and ideas onto the page. They feel less inhibited. They want to do this exercise every day they write to help themselves get going. Some students have written rough drafts of academic writing in one 30-minute freewriting session (with much editing and revision to come after, naturally).

Other students feel uncomfortable. They want to stop and think. Students who turn off the screen or cover the screen with paper to avoid The Judge wonder whether what they're writing is good. They want to impose order and rationality as they write, not afterwards. They want to look back at their words and edit and revise on the fly. They try other ways of getting warmed up. How do you feel?

> There is no wrong way to do morning pages.
> —JULIA CAMERON

We believe that if you give it a chance, freewriting will improve you as writer. Freewriting helps develop the ability to move ideas and experiences from your brain directly to the page without hesitation, as if you were speaking comfortably to an old friend. Eventually, if you keep it up, you may find that you can sit down and write freely any time, focusing on the experiences and ideas you're putting down.

Freewriting may also benefit you in other ways. Numerous scientific control studies show that freewriting, or expressive writing, a close cousin, may improve health, both physical and mental. Freewriting enhances academic performance too. One 2010 study reported in *Science* demonstrated that people who wrote about their anxieties before taking a math exam achieved better results than people who didn't write before the exam.

Our advice: continue your daily freewriting. Writing will come easier, and you will probably get better results the more you do it.

Two Composition Approaches

The result of freewriting—big blocks of stream-of-consciousness ideas and opinions and stories—rarely reveals a clear direction, a direction that would lead to a polished piece of writing. Instead, it's up to you to impose some sort of order on this freewriting chaos. Taking this material all the way to a polished piece of writing is a detailed process.

People who study writing pedagogy identify two main ways to move forward with any piece of writing, one way involving a writing sequence and one way involving a writing recursion. In a writing sequence, writers work through a clear process: they begin with specific goals; they then think deeply about the topic; they plan and perform research and outline possible sections or parts of the work; they work up a draft; and finally they revise.

If you choose to work in a sequence, you have clear plans for the writing: a form, a story to tell, an argument, and so on. You understand well the form you're working with and the length required. You take time to consider possible plot or theoretical avenues, whether it's a scene or an academic theme. You plan out the parts of the story or academic writing using an outline—the outline represents a skeleton that will hold up the whole writing (scholars do this, and so do screenwriters and novelists and creative non-fiction writers in plotting out their writing—they want a map of where they're going with their writing before they start on that road). Furthermore, you spend an appropriate amount of time researching the topic or story (gathering details) until you feel comfortable with the material—comfortable enough to write about your own past or enter an academic conversation and have an original argument. You then write what is always going to be a *rough* draft. Finally, lengthy revisions polish the work for submission. This approach works well for writers who like logical, rational steps to achieving their writing goals.

For some writers, however, writing-as-sequence feels like a straightjacket. Alternatively, these writers take an approach that's more fluid and less formulaic. If that sounds like you, you might consider a recursive writing process. This means moving back and forth between writing and thinking. This is opposed to a sequence process where one thinks before writing and writing is a task of inscribing pre-developed ideas on the page. On the other hand, in recursion you freewrite random ideas until one sticks. You start writing the middle parts—the body—and leave the introductions and conclusions until the end. You chase any idea or plotline you want, when and as it interests you. You pause to re-read your sources and do new research right in the middle of the writing process; in that way, the writing comes into dialogue with new ideas as you go along, not only *before* you start writing. This approach works well for writers who prefer freedom and openness. More rational types find this approach too free—it may lack direction.

The above are two distinctly different approaches to the writing process. We encourage you to try both and recognize that writers can employ varied methods—including mixing the two approaches—to produce effective writing. For example, while outlining seems a natural fit for the sequence writer, particularly near the beginning of the process, it's also a valuable strategy for the recursive writer at the end of the writing. For example, recursive writers may draw up a skeleton outline of what they've written *after* they've written it to see if the writing has structure and flow. And even the sequence writer will realize a truism of any writing process: you will come up with new ideas—ideas you couldn't have planned—only by getting on with the hard job of drafting. You need to find what approach works best for you.

Now let's turn to some practical advice. If you've done freewriting and face a great deal of disorganized text, you may still wonder what to do with it. We have a few suggestions that may help you move forward:

- Examine what you've written to decide what's worth keeping. You may keep nothing and try freewriting again. You may find some goodness among a lot of waste. Take what works and discard the rest.
- In academic writing in particular, look for thematic clusters within what you've kept. Use the cut-and-paste feature of your word processor to move paragraphs that share themes together.

- Think only about the body of the writing at this point. Save the writing of beginnings and endings until you've got the body in place.
- Chunk the freewriting into smaller parts if it seems too extensive and unwieldy. Those smaller parts may eventually serve as sections and paragraphs. Or those smaller parts may end up each being a separate and distinct piece of writing.
- Add more detail (imagery, description, facts, statistics etc.) when you can—freewriting may have left your writing vague and general. That's expected.
- If writing a research paper (also called an academic essay), see how the thematic clusters may defend a specific overall argument or thesis. We often start academic writing with a general point in mind, but eventually we need to refine it and make it more specific. Refine the argument through more thinking and more reading of research sources. Finding a specific thesis at this stage may redefine your whole project or your goals—that's a positive.
- If writing a story, ensure that the developments in the narrative link together coherently. Add detail where needed to help readers see what you saw. Write some more in places that feel underdeveloped.

These strategies should help you mould your freewriting into a form that's ready for revision.

Beginning with Storytelling

In our courses, we develop writers by first showing them how to write detailed, precise stories (also called narratives). This chapter includes two full peer models of personal narratives to give you a strong sense of this important form before we introduce the first peer model of academic writing in Chapter 2. Read these two personal narratives carefully.

Stories offer a powerful tool to capture and hold the attention of readers or listeners. People have likely been telling stories since the beginning of humankind, even before paper and printing in the oral age. Those stories were passed down in speech from generation to generation thanks to memory and regular retelling. Don't underestimate the power of story, even in academic writing. People may forget everything else you say, but they rarely forget the stories you tell. Stories take hold of the human mind as no other form of writing does. Consider the tenets of the world's great religions: they come to life in stories—both printed and oral—that have survived for centuries.

No wonder then that people learn writing faster and more easily when they start with story writing, particularly personal narrative, before they tackle academic writing. When people write about a topic they know nothing about or in which they have no personal interest—one of the realities of assigned topics—they

Freewriting for Direction

By Duncan Koerber

When many academic writers sit down to write, they feel unsure of how to begin. They stare at their notes, and then at the screen, and consider their options. This is natural. Inspiration rarely strikes writers when they want it. Getting past this feeling of aimlessness is the first challenge.

Rather than staring at an empty screen, some writers choose to freewrite in the hope that ideas will eventually find their way onto the page. It may take 10 minutes, 20 minutes, one hour or even days of freewriting, but these writers believe that inspiration will come if they just work at it. Indeed, freewriting can be one way to tease out ideas without the fear of having to be complete or correct right away.

I faced just such a problem when writing my PhD dissertation, a document that the university expected to be around 200 pages (70,000 words). Obviously, a 200-page dissertation cannot be written the night before it's due. It's an intimidating target.

Once I'd completed two years of research, I looked over the pages and pages of handwritten notes and saw a jumbled mess of random ideas, undeveloped thoughts, and unrelated quotations. What to do?

I couldn't start writing the introductory paragraph, as some writers do. I couldn't write the first sentence, and then the second sentence, and then another. That approach seemed a daunting task, like climbing Mount Kilimanjaro. Even chunking the project into smaller parts—a common way of tackling big writing projects—would not help. No neatly defined topics for chapters came to mind. The ideas and quotations in the notes touched on many subtopics.

Finally, I turned to freewriting as a way forward. Each day I sat down with a page of rough notes, freewriting for an hour in any direction the notes sparked. No order, no plan.

Quickly, ideas formed. The ideas didn't necessarily connect. Sentences included grammar, spelling, and punctuation errors. But none of these problems mattered at the drafting stage. Rationality and order would come in revision. Most importantly, freewriting allowed me to finally see a direction. A month later, after freewriting almost every day, I had material to work with: seventy pages (around 21,000 words).

With the hardest part over, another difficult step loomed. Revising and organizing seventy pages of stream-of-consciousness freewriting presents its own challenges. Clear topics lurked in different places in the document—for example, a paragraph topic on page 2 connected with a paragraph topic on page 65. Bringing these pieces together—bringing coherence to the writing at the structural level—was the next step.

But how do you bring together bits and pieces of freewriting together across seventy pages in a Microsoft Word file? A problem with word processing programs is that you can only reasonably view about one or two pages at a time on the screen. In this situation, it's easy to forget where ideas are located and lose valuable connections between distant parts. Only one solution existed for such large structural revision.

I printed out all seventy pages, got a pair of scissors, and cut the pages into strips—one paragraph per strip. Then I found a large white wall in my room. I took clear tape and taped every piece of paper onto that wall—around 400 pieces. It looked messy but the process helped immensely. With the freewriting displayed completely in front of me, I saw the whole project in one glance.

Slowly, I read and then moved paragraphs from one side of the wall to the other, where they best fit with other paragraphs. After a week of un-taping and re-taping, the writing had order: I finally saw thematic clusters—although I still saw a great deal of redundancy.

I then sat down and looked back and forth from wall to word processor, slowly cutting and pasting the paragraphs in the new order in the Microsoft Word file. This new order of thematic clusters eventually became the seeds of clearly defined chapters, five of the final eight (I wrote the introduction and conclusion, plus another chapter, after this body was firmly in place). Now I found enthusiasm—I knew where to go next. Of course, that meant the need for another 130 pages, but this represented a major writing victory. Introductions and conclusions, topic sentences, and some additional research content filled out the chapters. The final page count, seven months later? A whopping 296.

Most importantly, this revision process became a creative, not just corrective, act. As clarity developed, new ideas and connections surfaced in my mind, ideas that hadn't arrived during the years of research and note-taking.

In this way, freewriting and structural revision sparked and developed ideas that weren't even born during the research process. These processes can move us away from the hesitation and procrastination that come with academic writing. Freewriting is one way to tackle an academic writing project that seems, at first, impossible.

Tip: If you feel aimless when freewriting a research paper, then create a simple outline of the paper's sections. The outline will help you see the parts of your paper and keep you focused. Nonetheless, you may still try freewriting each section of the outline to help you get started.

don't always care about the subject and thus don't always pay close attention to the act of writing. Writing becomes a task they must complete to earn a grade, not to entertain an audience. Yet when people write stories of their own lives, they have a stake in the quality of the writing. They care. They learn.

We have just a few points to say about stories here. You'll learn more about storytelling in the following chapters. You'll learn even more from reading the peer models in each chapter. The basic story form has a number of characteristics:

- a beginning, a middle, and an end
- a **plot**
- characters

The most basic story form is not

- an **analytical argument**;
- a **commentary**; or
- a random collection of thoughts.

Basic narratives tell a story in a straightforward way, from A to B to C. The best ones work like scenes in a movie, retelling events in a confined period of time in great detail. If you connect many short scenes with the same characters, you may have a book.

Some writers like to modify the order of events in a story, such as in a reverse chronology (that is, starting from the end and ending at the start). Some writers will also intersperse other narratives, here and there, within a narrative. At this point of this book, however, you should focus on the simple, short, focused chronological narrative. You can experiment once you master it.

Here is a peer model story, "The Stovepipe Hole," written by Elizabeth Clark, who was a relatively inexperienced writer when she wrote the story. She wrote "The Stovepipe Hole" in an introductory course called Expressive Writing. This story does everything we describe. And, like almost all published writing, it has undergone extensive editing and revision based on the lessons we present throughout this book. This is not a first draft.

"The Stovepipe Hole" depicts, among other things, child abuse. That sounds dismal and alarming—and it is. Many writers choose to write about difficult moments in their lives. Those difficult moments reveal humanity at its most real. Don't fear writing about such experiences. If you don't have such moments to write about, don't worry that your stories won't be interesting—we all have valuable experiences, both heartbreaking and joyful, that readers love to read. But watch how Elizabeth Clark handles her subject. Observe how you feel at the end of "The Stovepipe Hole."

Note: a stovepipe hole is a round hole cut into the ceiling/floor of a two-storey house above a woodstove. A sheet metal pipe goes from the woodstove through the roof to carry smoke and fumes out of the house. In this story, the woodstove and the pipe have been removed. The hole remains.

The Stovepipe Hole

By Elizabeth Clark

I stand on a chair and wash the supper dishes. My nine-year-old sister Mary dries. The kitchen window reflects my ten-year-old face. I shiver at the draft coming through the crack in the upper half of the window. In the day the window looks over the snow-covered cornfield in back of the farmhouse. At night the bare light bulb hanging over the middle of the big wooden kitchen table makes the window a mirror. A long red gash marks my left cheek. Mary's right eye swells shut.

Dad, surrounded by empty Molson Golden beer bottles, sits behind us at the end of the kitchen table. A butt-filled ashtray sits next to his elbow, and an empty pack of Player's Plain lies on the floor between his feet. Half-eaten spaghetti, pushed aside at supper, forms hard crust on the plate near his other elbow. He jams his hands under his chin to keep himself from pitching forward into the mess on the table. The air, thick with cigarette smoke and scents of beer, barn and spaghetti, upsets my stomach.

Katie and Lisa, the two youngest, eight and six, huddle together on the tattered red sofa on the other side of the room under the big picture window that looks over the three barns at the bottom of the hill. The lights from the Warkworth Prison on the other side of the dirt road cast an orange halo in the sky. The halo stretches from the Campbells' farm on one side of us to our grandfather's farm on the other.

Mom works late at the nursing home as an aide on Saturday nights. She won't be home till after midnight. Dad bolts up from the chair. He holds the edge of the table for balance. My body jolts. I watch him in the window reflection. Lisa and Katie huddle tighter. Mary dries the dish in her hand over and over and looks straight ahead.

Dad steps silently toward the living room, holding his body rigid, forcing himself to walk straight. He ricochets off one side of the door jamb, then the other, and staggers into the semidarkness of the living room.

Through the curtainless window in the living room, I see across the long snowy pasture to my grandfather's brightly lit farmhouse. Curses follow a thud as Dad stubs his toe on a chair. He bounces off the cellar door into the middle of the room. He staggers backwards, bangs into the door leading to the upstairs, and staggers back into the middle of the room again. He reels forward and hits the half-open door of his bedroom. The door closes with a bang behind him. Springs squeak and groan as Dad flops down onto the bed.

My sisters and I exchange silent glances. We look toward the back porch door at the other end of the kitchen. Above the back porch is our fourteen-year-old brother Sam's room. Ten minutes pass silently while we wait to be certain our father sleeps.

Loud snoring signals safety. I switch on the light in the porch and step under the round hole in the ceiling where the stovepipe used to go through to the upstairs. The two woodstoves are gone now, replaced by the oil furnace, but Dad hasn't filled in the two holes yet. The one that opens into Sam's room is just a big round hole.

"Sam," I whisper. "It's safe. He's passed out."

My brother's face, a huge bruise on his left cheek, appears in the hole.

"Does it hurt?" I ask.

"No, not too bad," he says. "What about you?"

I touch the gash on my cheek. "It's okay."

"I'm freezing up here," Sam says. "The old prick took my blankets."

Sam hugs himself. Mary tiptoes upstairs to the linen closet to get blankets.

"Do you want something to eat?"

"Yea, I'm starved."

"Okay. I'll get something."

Standing on a chair, I pass two thick blankets up the hole to Sam. I pass a bowl of cereal, a peanut butter and honey sandwich, an apple and a glass of chocolate milk. My sisters and I finish cleaning the kitchen. We do the dishes, put beer bottles in their cases, sweep the floor, and wipe the cupboards.

Sam whispers, "I'm done, Becca."

He passes the dirty dishes through the stovepipe hole to me. Mary takes them to wash.

"Becca, I got to piss something wicked."

"Piss out the window."

"Can't. Shit-for-brains nailed them both shut."

"Maybe I can get the lock open with a coat hanger or something."

"HELL NO! Don't even try. If you screw it up, we'll all get killed. Just find me something to piss in."

"Okay."

I rummage in the cupboard looking for something nobody uses. My hand falls on the pot my mother uses to poach Dad's eggs on Sunday. She never uses it for anything else, and only Dad eats poached eggs. I pass the pot up through the hole to Sam.

"Becca, this is the old man's poached egg pot."

"I know. Piss in it. I promise not to hurt myself scrubbing it clean."

We laugh wildly.

"Be quiet," Mary whispers.

I sit on the chair. I listen to the piss hit the metal of the pot.

"All done. Here you go. Careful, don't spill it on yourself."

I take the piss pot from Sam's hand. I walk to the outside door of the porch as though I carry something explosive. I reach the end of the porch and pitch the contents onto the snow. I give the pot a shake then run back inside shivering from the cold.

"Where'd you throw it?" Sam asks.

"Off the porch."

"He might wonder in the morning where it came from."

"He won't remember, Sam. He'll think he did it hisself."

We snicker quietly.

I put the pissy pot back in the cupboard without washing it. Mother will use it in the morning. I feel guilty. Then I think, this started over piss so it's only fair it ends pissy. This afternoon Lisa accidentally wet herself. Dad said, "I'll cure your damn pissing problem once and for all." He pulled the belt off his pants and swung the buckle end at

Lisa. Lisa cowered near the kitchen table. I caught the first swing of the belt in my hand before it hit her. Dad yanked it loose before I could get my balance. The second swing hit me in the cheek and cut a long gash. I screamed. Lisa and Katie bawled loudly. Mary grabbed Dad's arm from behind and took an elbow to the eye. The screaming and crying brought Sam in from outdoors. He lowered his head and charged Dad. Dad fell against the wall. Sam rushed him again. Dad caught him this time. Sam took a couple of punches to the face. Sam let Dad drag him upstairs and lock him in his room.

* * *

The next day, at breakfast Dad slops poached egg onto toast. Sam and I look at each other then down at our cereal.

Dad says to Sam, "Bet you're hungry, son."

"Yea, Dad," Sam says flatly.

"Well, let that be a lesson to ya then. Don't defy your father and interfere when I'm disciplinin' your sisters."

"Okay, Dad," Sam says.

"Let it be a lesson to you girls too."

"Okay, Dad."

"All I'm asking from you kids is a little respect."

(Clark 88–92)

Observations about "The Stovepipe Hole"

In each chapter, we ask you to critically analyze the peer model writing. Here, we'd like to show you how we (the authors) analyze "The Stovepipe Hole." Use this approach as a guide for your rhetorical analyses throughout this book. We could write a lot about the choices Elizabeth Clark has made in telling her story, but we will limit our discussion to a few essential observations:

- Clark builds her story around a single incident: the story of the kids' response to their father's drunken brutality. Her story tells us a lot about her family, but she sticks to this one incident—this isn't a novel. The story contains no unnecessary digressions. It's focused.
- Clark shows us what happens. Writers say "Show, don't tell." Details show. Clark shows by letting us watch actions and listen to what people say. We get a sense of unique people living out real lives in a fascinating setting of a farm. We can "see" everything that Clark saw in our mind's eye. Without such detail, we could not experience the incident the way Clark experienced it. Relevant details make the story seem authentic and true. They create a sense of immediacy, of being "in the moment."
- Clark avoids any kind of judgement or moral in her story, which are common approaches in expository academic writing but which can cloud the focus of a simple narrative. Instead, she leaves these judgements to

her reader. When the father says, "All I'm asking from you kids is a little respect," Clark lets the reader ponder the stupidity and irony of his comment. She does not push us there. We might resist if she did. Clark leaves to us to ponder the kids' revenge—and the treatment that preceded it. This means Clark resisted the writer's urge to comment on the story or use generalization. Rather than forcing the reader to see the story a certain way, Clark just tells the story as it happened. She leaves the interpretation to the reader, thus opening up the story to a wider range of readers who can make what they want of the story.

- The writer creates a **psychic space**. As readers, we move into that space, we look around, we listen, and we react to what we see and hear there. Good writing gets readers to move into this created space and become co-creators of the meaning in the story. We have to make assessments and conclusions about what's happening and the intentions of the characters because Clark doesn't make them for us. This involves the reader.

- Notice how Clark locates the scene at the beginning of the story. We learn what we need to know about these kids and their situation to make sense of the story that follows. With every story you write, imagine your readers being transported in a time machine to a certain place and time: when the time machine's door opens, readers need details about where they are and who is there. Without such details, the reader is lost. Too much could bog us down—Clark does it just right. After that locating, the story's plot may begin. This technique can be applied to academic writing, where a good introduction acquaints the reader quickly with the subject and argument before moving into the body of the paper.

- Finally, this story creates magic. The story details horrific abuse (and implies the abuse is not unusual). Yet the story surprises us with a smile at the little victory these sisters and their brother manage in their desperate situation. We can root for these kids even in their difficult situation.

Here is. another peer model story written in an introductory writing course like the one we describe in this book:

Cell Phone

By Peter Palladini

I wasn't happy with just a pager, so I bothered my parents for a cell phone. I wasn't happy with just any cell phone. It had to be a Motorola Flip Phone. My mother didn't like the idea of the 15 year-old son having a pager, let alone a cell phone. I knew I was in for some yelling, arguing, making up and kissing ass. At the end of it all, as usual, I got my way.

* * *

Even though I hang out with the same friends at the same pool hall every night, I have to have a cell phone. It's not that I need the phone, but how other people, mainly girls, treat you when you have one. I feel important, respected, looked up to and, most of all, wealthy.

At school I wear my phone on one side of my belt and my pager on the other. School rules don't allow pagers or cell phones because they disrupt class. I don't care. I have an image to uphold. I met a girl I'm quite fond of about a month ago. Her name is Mary. My best friend John dates Mary's best friend, Diane. Since I don't have the courage to ask Mary out, I asked John to do it for me.

Tonight John went to meet Diane and Mary downtown. He's gonna ask Mary if it would be okay for me to join them. John said he's gonna call me on my cell phone at 8:30 sharp. I dressed up in a pair of my least faded black jeans and a black T-shirt I pulled out of my hamper. I ran out of the house.

Now I sit in Coffee Time Donuts and wait for John's call. It's 8:20. If John gives me the okay, I gotta take a bus downtown. I'm nervous. What if she says no? My right hand rests on the cell phone while my left hand fidgets with my lighter. My palms sweat. My throat feels dry. I sip cold coffee. I eye my phone. I check the time. 8:28. He's not gonna call. Mary said no. John can't bring himself to tell me the bad news. I don't think I'll take it that bad. It's not the end of the world.

I look around me. A man and a woman sit at a table and play cards. Their eyes focus on their cards. The lady at the counter scratches her head and reads a newspaper. These people don't care that I wait for an important call.

RING. RING. RING.

It's him. It's John. I knew he'd call. My heart pounds. My hands shake. What will he say?

"Hello. Mom? Whadya want? No. I'm not being rude. I'm waiting for an important call. . . . Okay, okay, I won't be home late tonight. Yes, Mom, I promise . . . yes Mom. I love you too . . . okay bye."

Shit. John's not gonna call. What if he called while I was on the phone with my mom? He better try again if he got a busy signal. My mother can't leave me alone for one second. If John doesn't call, it's her fault.

A new customer comes into the donut shop. My eyes follow his sluggish, clumsy feet. He drags every step. Stains of what looks like dried blood spatter his dirty jeans. His grey hair looks oily and wet. His beard, untrimmed and uncombed, reaches halfway down his chest. The stench from his body reaches halfway across the donut shop.

He shuffles past the lady at the counter, who still reads her paper, and walks to the bathroom. He looks over his shoulder at the lady, then sets his eyes on me. I look away. His empty stare freezes my mind. He pushes the bathroom door open and goes in.

RING. RING. RING.

I jump. I almost forgot about John's call.

"Hello. Ma! I told you I was waiting for a call! No! No! Bye!"

I can't believe her. She can't leave me alone. 8:42. I stare at the clock. What happened to the guy in the bathroom? I wonder who's winning at cards. My eyes burn. My back tenses. My hands feel cold and wet. I don't even like Mary that much. I don't know why I'm making a big deal out of this.

RING. RING. RING.

"Hello. John! Why didn't you call me earlier? Yeah, I've been waiting at the donut shop. Well, what's the story? . . . Good news and bad news? Tell me the good news first. . . . Hello? . . . Hello? . . . John? Can you hear me? My battery's dying. . . . What? I can't hear you. All I hear is static. John? . . . John!"

My battery has died. John called me from a pay phone. He won't be calling back.

I think about my wasted night. The couple still plays cards. The lady at the counter still reads her newspaper. The man with the beard is still in the washroom. I light a cigarette.

(Palladini 77–79)

EXERCISE 2 ► Rhetorical Analysis

Write a rhetorical analysis of "The Cell Phone." Write your rhetorical analysis in a personal, informal style. This is not academic writing with a hamburger structure or a thesis statement. Just start writing—jump right into your analysis in the first sentence, the way you jumped right into your freewriting. This is not a "correct answer" exercise, either—each reader will have unique insights about the story. This exercise asks you to write out some your insights.

Consider responding to these questions, if they're helpful:

- Which strategies does Peter Palladini use to tell this story?
- How would you describe the psychic space Palladini constructs?
- What does the ending have in it? What does it not have?
- How does dialogue work in the story?
- What does the writer show us about the narrator's (the teller of the story) relationship with his mother?
- When and how does Palladini locate the story?
- How does Palladini show the setting of the story?
- What are some detailed phrasings Palladini uses?

The rhetorical analysis is a training exercise in appreciation. By reading the writing of others, particularly those at the same stage as you, you can understand what's possible. You may enjoy the writer's techniques or approach. Keep these models in mind for your own writing.

Assignment 1a

Note: In this book, 1a means the label of the first draft of the first assignment. The second draft will be labelled 1b. Every time you revise an assignment, advance the letter. This code will tell you how much revision you've accomplished over time. Many writers advance to "g" or "i" in a few months of focused revision.

Suggested Topics:

1) Write a narrative about a negative academic writing experience you have had.
2) Write a narrative about a positive academic writing experience you have had.
3) Write a narrative about an experience you've had working with another writer, either as co-writer or as editor.

Here are some suggestions for writing:

- Use everyday language. Do not use words and phrases you do not ordinarily use in conversation with your family or friends.
- Base your story on a single incident—something that happened at a particular time in a particular place. It helps to think of the story as a small slice of time in your past—5 minutes, 30 minutes, or a few days. Anything longer may become unfocused and generalized.
- Near the beginning of your story, include information on when and where it happens (we call this locating).
- Show what happens through specific details of actions and dialogue. Do not explain or interpret what happens. Just show it, and let the reader decide what it means.
- Fear not the short sentence. Short sentences often maximize clarity and impact. Readers find short sentences helpful because they present just one point or idea (long sentences, which we deal with later in this book, tend to confuse by presenting many ideas). Many people somehow get the impression from schools that long sentences show more sophistication than short sentences—not true. We talk more about this in Chapter 2 on economy.
- Make the story as long as you want: one or two pages will suffice. If you think it needs a longer treatment, that's fine.
- Word-process and double-space your story so you can easily make edits and revisions.
- Some writers will freewrite to spark an idea and also freewrite to produce a rough draft. Write your first draft as quickly as you can without worrying about spelling, grammar, or punctuation.
- Put your story away for a day or two before you revise it. In the heat of the writing process, we lose objectivity about our work. The distance that a day or two off provides will freshen your mind, and you'll come back with a more objective view of the story. Then read the story aloud. Your ear will help you revise.

- You don't have to come up with a title for your story, but you can if you like.
- Stay true to what you remember—don't make up anything. This is non-fiction. However, you cannot expect your memory to be perfectly objective. We are subjective beings and each person's account of a real-life incident will differ. If you think your memory of the distant past is poor, then write about incidents that occurred recently. Or you may turn to documentary evidence to jog your memory: old photos, videos, documents. You may even ask a person who was there to remind you about it. Consider this like research you'd do for an academic course.

Academic Writing

Throughout this book, we link personal narrative writing to academic writing. The lessons you apply from each chapter to personal writing assignments are just as valuable in academic writing assignments. At the sentence level, all the enhancing factors we describe in these chapters are indeed vital to any form of writing. Peer models of academic writing begin in Chapter 2.

Where we think academic writing differs is in its **discourse**. *Discourse* is a slippery term—it means many things to many people. We think of discourse as the expectations for how to think, speak, write, and act in any social domain. What's a **social domain**? Think of a community defined first by spaces and also by socially constructed meanings.

When you visit the opera, the **spatial** domain is the opera house. The opera house has its own rules and traditions that regulate your actions: be quiet while the show is on, wear formal clothing, and clap politely at the end of the show. The sports stadium, also a social domain, has a very different discourse: wear your team colours, yell, cheer, eat, and drink.

Written and spoken language disseminates the expectations of the social domain of higher education. The gatekeepers of the academic social domain—editors and professors—uphold these expectations. If you don't meet them, you fail. One way to have your work accepted in academia is to mimic or emulate good academic writing.

No one **academic discourse** exists, however. A great debate exists among professors about how academic writing should look. College or university subjects are diverse: history, chemistry, sociology, biology, and so on. Sociology papers are written differently than history papers, for example. This makes it difficult for us to explain definitively and completely all academic writing types.

Academic discourse—like any discourse in any social domain—is always constructed and contested. Expectations change over time. Professors will differ on some points too. For example, professors disagree on the use of the personal pronoun *I* in scholarly writing. You should always check with your instructor for specific requirements.

Regardless, an academic discourse does exist to some degree; there are some generally accepted elements across academic subjects. Academic writing's accepted discursive elements are

- an introduction,
- an overall argument or thesis,
- credible evidence,
- citations of sources, and a
- conclusion.

Let's take a look at each in turn.

Introduction

An introduction in good academic writing maps out the paper. It acquaints the reader with the specific topic fairly quickly in the first or second paragraph. The opening line should not be so broad that the paper could be about anything. Zoom in to the topic as soon as possible.

The mapping of the paper is a structural issue. In academic writing, the author tends to explicitly show the structure. Professor Jonathan Wolff explains on *The Guardian* website:

> Academic writing needs to be ordered, precise, and to make every move explicit. All the work needs to be done on the page rather than in the reader's head. By contrast, good literature often relies on the unsaid, or the implied or hinted at, rather than the expressed thought.

In personal narrative, the point or argument of the writing is implicit, if the writer has any point at all (many writers of personal narrative simply want to express themselves and entertain a reader). The introduction in academic writing is your chance to explicitly tell the reader what's to come.

Additionally, the body of any piece of academic writing must eventually live up to the promises of its introduction. Readers will feel let down if they find out that you never wrote about certain ideas described in the introduction. Promise and then keep that promise.

Overall Argument or Thesis

Academic writing cannot be a random collection of evidence. Good academic writing always contains some overall argument, also called a thesis, that links together every section, every paragraph, of the writing.

A major complaint about student writing from teachers is that papers lack an overall argument. Such a problem may reveal itself in questions from teachers like: *Why is this paragraph here? What does this paragraph have to do with the other points you've made?*

Part of the problem is that many students don't know the subject matter well enough at the early drafting stage to form a specific argument about it. Papers become a collection of data and quotations, nothing more. If you've failed to do enough research, you'll fall back on general statements: *This paper will examine the history of communication in Canada* or *I think the actions of Williamson had a great effect on political developments in the province* or *The media has been important to socialization in Africa*. These statements are vague (the first one doesn't even argue anything).

Some students have an argument in mind but don't come out and say it. Scholarly writing cannot be like a personal narrative that just lets the reader think what they want to think about the topic. Good academic writers never leave the reader to figure out the point.

Getting started on a specific, detailed overall argument that will direct your whole project is challenging. It may feel daunting to sift through large bodies of research and narrow down material into a few thousand words. At some point you need to focus, focus, focus. You must peel away the layers of the topic until you find a specific point you can argue.

At the drafting stage, you don't need a fully defined argument—just a point that guides you in the right direction. It need not be particularly controversial such as *I disagree with assisted suicide*. It could simply be a general statement like *I think race has been ignored in the study of historical newspapers*.

> A difficult truth is that those issues most worth arguing over almost never have all the evidence on one side or the other. Both sides have compelling proofs.
> —WENDY BELCHER

As you research and write down ideas, you may wonder at what point you have a specific argument. But just as a writer of a personal narrative would not try to tell their whole life story in 2000 words, an academic writer would not try to tell the whole history of the world—or sports, or music, or fashion—in 2000 words.

Professor Wendy Belcher of Princeton University provides an example of how to move towards a specific overall argument. Notice how the statements below get progressively more specific as Belcher zooms in on the argument:

1) The purpose of this paper is to analyze Jamaica Kincaid's novel *Annie John*.
2) This paper uncovers what we can learn about the postcolonial experience from Jamaica Kincaid's novel *Annie John*.
3) Jamaica Kincaid's novel *Annie John* is helpful to our understanding of the postcolonial experience.
4) Jamaica Kincaid's novel *Annie John* aids our understanding of the postcolonial experience by detailing how Annie John's British education increasingly alienates her from her mother. (85)

Statement number 4 finally reaches the level of specificity demanded of good scholarly writing. You may not reach this level in the early stages. Sometimes writers realize that kind of argument only after writing the body of the paper. But when completed, academic writing needs that kind of specific overall argument stated in the introduction.

Evidence

Evidence in academic discourse comes from research, which we discuss in more detail in the appendix at the end of the book. For now, recognize that academic discourse demands evidence for any statement you make. Evidence comes in many forms: statistics, studies, facts, direct quotations, paraphrases, summaries, and so on. Evidence is like the detail you include in personal narratives, although in personal narratives the evidence usually comes from your memory, not primary and secondary sources. In academic work, primary sources are pieces of evidence that were created by the participants in the period you're studying, including documents and artifacts. Secondary sources are after-the-fact materials built upon primary sources.

Statistics are particularly valued as evidence today in academic writing. State a number—"73 per cent of students have education loan debt"—and most people respect it. The problem is that numbers tell only part of the story. Sometimes numbers are missing their context. Consider this statistic:

25 million people are on welfare.

While the raw number seems large at first glance, it raises questions: What percentage of the population is on welfare? Is the number increasing or decreasing? How much do people get on welfare? What's the significance of this number? What's causing the problem? We also need to assess the credibility of the number itself: Who came up with the number? What was their method? Why are they releasing the number?

Many credible researchers and organizations produce credible studies that can be used as evidence in academic writing. Thousands of studies are published every day on any number of subjects. If you're writing about a social problem, you can probably find a published study that attempts to understand or solve that problem. Credibility means the methods and procedures are sound. Credibility means the individuals doing the study are forthright and ethical about their procedures and the sources of funding for the study. Furthermore, a credible study is usually peer reviewed—professors have vetted the study to make sure mistakes were not made.

Direct quotations from unbiased reputable sources provide strong evidence in academic writing. The reader hears the very words of the person you're quoting, often words that the writer couldn't have written any better. Quoting pure fact is pointless: *Dr. Smith writes that "6 in 10 people are obese."* Quoting scholars saying fascinating things in their own unique ways is interesting: *"If we don't treat obesity, millions of children will die before their parents do," warns Dr. Smith.* Academic writers must be cautious, however, not to over-quote. Over-quoting can lead to cut-and-paste pinball essays where the writer becomes only a moderator at a debate, leaving theorists to speak in long quotations page after page.

If the quotation isn't brilliant, don't quote directly. But if the information in the quotation is still valuable, you can paraphrase or summarize. Paraphrasing involves restating in your own words, without condensing, small parts of someone else's words in your own unique way. This can be challenging because re-using even a few words from the original without attributing or referencing them constitutes plagiarism. Sometimes students tell us it's hard to paraphrase as they can't think of alternative phrasings. The best way to paraphrase someone is to write that person's thoughts without looking at the original. Use words you use in everyday conversation.

Another aspect of academic discourse, summarizing the work of another author, is an important skill to master. Like paraphrasing, however, summarizing too can turn into plagiarism. One solution to avoid this can be direct quotation, but this can lead to over-quotation. As with paraphrasing, you may find it better to put the original source away and try to explain it in your own everyday words. Another way to avoid plagiarism here is to condense significantly—indeed, that's what the best summaries look like. If you describe an 8000-word journal article in 100 words, you shouldn't fall into verbatim transcription. With both paraphrase and summary, you want to try to capture the meaning of the author, but don't be a slave to the original. Indeed, the way you paraphrase and summarize may be your unique perspective on the source.

Perhaps the best-known aspects of academic discourse are citations: the Works Cited list (in MLA style) or the References list (in APA style). Citations aren't unique to academia—journalists use quotations and other information as well, often with the attributive *said*, as do personal narratives (by means of dialogue). One problem of academic writing, however, is over-citation, which is often caused by the fear of plagiarism. Remember that basic, accepted facts—like the year of the 1867 confederation of Canada—need no citation, nor do generally accepted ideas in a field. However, you do need to know enough about a topic to know which facts are common knowledge and which are original ideas or research that needs citation. We talk more about citations and research in the appendix at the end of the book.

> I once asked a young dissertation writer whether her suddenly grayed hair was due to ill health or personal tragedy; she answered: "It was the footnotes."
>
> —JOANNA RUSS

Conclusions

In personal narrative, a conclusion isn't a big production. You end your personal writing when you feel like it. In academic writing, the conclusion is more explicit. The conclusion signals the end of the piece.

The only rule with conclusions is never to introduce new material. A restatement or reminder of the point of the paper and what it has proven is usually good enough. Some editors and writers advise that the conclusion end on a poignant note. The goal is to signal artfully and elegantly that the paper is about to end.

Some writers signal the end of the paper with clunker phrases like *In sum, this paper has argued that. . .* or *I would like to conclude by saying. . . .* These are weak. Still, awkward closing statements are fine in rough drafts. Such phrases may actually help you write an ending. But when you're done, edit out these clunker phrases while keeping the points.

You will learn more about academic writing in the following chapters, and you will see academic peer writing models starting in Chapter 2.

EXERCISE 3 ▸ Introductions

Find an introduction to an academic journal article. In 250 words, assess its effectiveness in introducing the topic and mapping out the direction of the article. Write down the overall argument or thesis, if you can find it. If you find the introduction ineffective, explain why.

EXERCISE 4 ▸ Evidence

Using the same journal article as you used in Exercise 3, write down one example of each kind of evidence the author employs (statistics, studies, facts, direct quotations, paraphrases, summaries). Next to each example, note the source and the date of the source.

EXERCISE 5 ▸ Summarizing

Summarizing other scholars' writing is an important skill. It helps you digest the theories and ideas—if you can't summarize it, you don't understand it well enough. Summarizing is a sort of literature review, a vital element in the scholarly discourse. In this exercise, summarize the journal article you have in about 300 words. Don't copy or reuse sentences and phrases from the article. Use your own voice here.

▌ Revision

By this point, you should have completed a rough draft of one of the suggested topics for Assignment 1. You may or may not be happy with the way it turned out. That's fine. It may need a lot of revision, but that's what this book is primarily about—we teach you how to edit and revise. Starting to write is the hardest part of the writing process. Now you have something to work with: the draft in front of you.

Submitting rough drafts to teachers and editors will usually garner a poor reception. Revision is vital to developing a polished piece of writing that readers will enjoy. Writers must revise, revise, and revise again. Each time you learn a new lesson in this book, and each time you observe a quality you like in another writer's work, go back to your writing and revise with those lessons and qualities in mind.

> I have rewritten—often several times—every word I have ever published. My pencils outlast their erasers.
> —VLADIMIR NABOKOV

This recursive process means you will be continually applying what you learn. You cannot learn to write well simply from reading the lessons in this book. You must apply them completely and regularly. Ideally, you will apply the lessons by doing the exercises listed throughout these chapters. And then those lessons, practised in exercises, should find their way into your assignments. At some point, as some of our writers have noticed, you may find that these lessons become ingrained in your mind, and that you don't have to think consciously about them or refer back to this book—they just become a part of your style. We think of revision as creative and dynamic. Expect your writing to change dramatically during the editing process. In this way, revision should not be drudgery, like taking out the garbage. It should be a creative act and a second chance. We learn through revision.

Editing is the most rational part of the writing process. It secures the writer amidst all the other mysterious and threatening parts of writing. Editing means you don't have to get it right the first time—or even the second time.

No writing is published in quality publications without any editing. At newspapers and magazines, one, two, or even three editors may revise the work before it is published. In school writing, well-edited papers shine from the pile of last-minute first-draft efforts. If you can edit well, professional publications may publish your work; in academia, teachers and peer reviewers will give good grades to work that makes their task of reading easier. The way most school papers are often produced—without much time devoted to editing—is an anomaly in the writing universe. Not much other writing works this way.

All writers use editors, even if the editor is not a professional but a brother, sister, or best friend. That editor should be a trusted supporter and confidant. Do not work with editors who leave you feeling criticized and diminished. You are vulnerable when you show your work to someone. Naturally, all writers feel a bit concerned: *What will they think of me from my writing?* But recognize that good editors are surrogates for readers—good

> Revision is one of the exquisite pleasures of writing.
> —BERNARD MALAMUD

editors exist to help you massage a piece of writing into a final product that people will enjoy reading. Use editors. Heed their advice. You don't have to accept everything editors say, but that sounding board could provide suggestions to make your writing better or reassure you that you're on the right track.

Your teachers may have said that writing is a solitary endeavour—accusations of plagiarism may scare you away from letting others comment on or edit your work. Plagiarists take someone else's work without permission and reference—ideas, arguments, phrasings, sentences—and represent it as their own. But even with academic writing, it helps to have someone offer opinions and editing suggestions—this is perfectly fine and ethical. In this process, other people respond to your original work and offer helpful comments to make it better. As a result, your work comes into a dialogue with a test audience. This process always improves the writing. If professionals do it, students can do it too. Feel free to thank those who helped you in acknowledgements at the end of the work.

Reading other people's work as an editor can also help you develop your editing skills. If friends ask you to read their work, recognize their vulnerability too. We recommend that you do not look at the editing job as simply a chance to find mistakes. Instead, think about the editing job as finding positives and the opportunities in someone's writing. You're making them and their work better.

When you're done editing, first offer the writer comments about what you liked in their work: you might tell the writer that the piece moved you, or that the details brought the scene to life, or that the writing was clear. By telling the writer the positives first, you ensure that the writer won't remove those elements in the revision stage. You also put the writer in a good mood—writers will often accept edits more readily if you start with the positives. After providing positive comments, you can then provide suggestions for improvement or opportunities. Most writers will appreciate your careful, positive response.

Some editors have a tendency to change the writer's work for unnecessary reasons. Sometimes the editor—whether your buddy or a professional—seems to want to reshape your writing so that it reads the way they'd write. Be careful when revising someone's work that you don't simply edit for editing's sake or impose your style or image on the writing. Any revisions you suggest need clear justifications. Talk with the writer about the changes and see what he or she thinks. Sometimes you'll find that the writer wondered about the same problem but wasn't sure how to edit it.

If you're on the other side of the relationship, consider seriously the editor's proposed changes. It's easy to be offended even by positive, constructive criticism. Keep an open mind. Editors should be there to help you. In our experience, writing almost always gets better after this process. Comments from an editor can help you catch mistakes you didn't see, make plots tighter, add details, and determine completeness.

But if you genuinely feel the editor doesn't have your best interests in mind, then you don't have to accept those changes blindly. It's your story and you have the right to preserve the original phrasings of sentences or the original choices of words. You can, at the very least, explain why you think those elements should remain. In this way, you have carefully considered the edit, and the choices you have made are deliberate, not haphazard or a coincidence. If you and the editor ultimately don't agree, you may need to find another, more suitable editor.

If you don't have someone to read your writing, read it out loud. In our print-dominated world we've moved away from reading our work to audiences, the way people in the oral age shared their stories. Now, our eyes tend to fill in the missing words. When you speak the words written on the page, however—as if reading a TV or radio script—your ears will hear gaps and problems that your eyes don't see. Chapter 8 deals with the importance of rhythms of writing; one way to feel those rhythms is to read the writing aloud.

Types of Editing

Editing occurs in two main ways and in a certain order. Prose editing looks at the big changes such as plot, character, location, introductions, and conclusions. Copy editing looks at the smaller—but no less important—details such as grammar, spelling, punctuation, interfering factors, tense, and sensory details. It's best to begin with the prose editing. Otherwise, if you start with copy editing, you may find yourself editing sentences that won't even remain after you make the big changes.

Some call prose editing "structural" or "substantive" editing. In this stage of revision, you look at large issues with the piece of writing. At this stage, worrying about grammar, spelling, and punctuation is pointless—you may end up cutting out the very sentences that have errors. You may decide to introduce a new character or place. You might consider the coherence of the piece—make sure that each part belongs or else remove it. For papers or essays, check that the writing has an overall argument or thesis. If you're editing someone else's work, offer these points as suggestions to the author—do not go ahead and make changes yourself.

Once the prose editing is done, a copy editor takes over. The copy editor specializes in the rules of writing. These rules have a long history and reflect writing norms. These norms are expectations—most readers expect you to use words in the right ways and punctuate properly. Standards of writing depend on these rules. However, always keep in mind that the end goal is not simply grammatically correct writing. The end goal is to produce writing that people want to read. By this stage, copy editors hope the writing is engaging.

The copy editor is responsible for seeing that virtually error-free copy (text) goes to the proofreader for a final check for typos before it goes to the printer. A copy editor assumes that the prose is in good shape, that everything that the author wants to say has been said in the order the author wants to say it. Copy editors do not want to make big changes at the final stage, as unintentional errors may be added—one finger slip on the keyboard can introduce an error that the writer never made. The best copy editors obsess over small details.

How and Where to Edit

With the process of revision described above in mind, we have some tips for working through the editing process. These tips apply to all forms of writing.

- Edit the big elements first. Consider whether the writing moves people, makes them laugh or cry, makes them think about a topic in a new way. People don't yearn to read just grammatically correct writing and proper spelling. They yearn for writing that affects them in some visceral way. Consider whether the writing is fresh and new.

> That's the magic of revisions—every cut is necessary, and every cut hurts, but something new always grows.
> —KELLY BARNHILL

- Do the plot, characters, and tone make sense? Is there coherence to the story or the overall argument? Or does it have digressions that do not matter? You are in control of what to include and what not to include. You are not required to relate to the reader every single part of a story or a topic.
- Does the introduction locate and situate the story in time and place or introduce the overall argument or thesis in a specific way?
- Is the ending satisfying? Does it need more development or does it drag on too long? Michael Ondaatje gave *The English Patient* a new and completely different ending as a result of his dialogues with his editor. That's a major revision. Endings are notoriously difficult to find. When editing, you may want to see if the piece of writing could end either sooner or later. Sometimes the best ending is a few paragraphs before the one you have. Sometimes the best ending has yet to come—continue writing.
- Most writers overwrite their drafts. Most write fast and write more than they want to see in the final draft. Go through your draft and cut out redundant sentences and paragraphs. Sometimes editors cut as much as 30 to 50 per cent of the writing, depending on the writer. Ask yourself, "What can I cut without moving anything around?" After the cutting stage, it is often possible to arrive at a clearer view of the piece.

> The more you leave out, the more you highlight what you leave in.
> —HENRY GREEN

- The next task is redrafting. Ask yourself, "Where is new writing needed? Where is the sensory detail insufficient? What needs to be moved? What needs to be added? Is more research needed? What patches of the overly familiar writing need to be replaced with original thought?" Move towards the strength, the "soul" of the piece.

Let's look at one example of one of the larger-problem points above—not spelling or grammar—and see how it could be revised in the context of a personal narrative. In the following sample introduction to a story, consider the importance of locating and situating.

Original Introduction

I looked at Samuel and smiled. He knew why I'd come.

"I'm so glad to see you, Sammy," I said. Samuel jumped from his chair and wrapped his arms tightly around me.

"You've grown so much," he whispered into my ear. He kissed the side of my cheek and then let me go.

"Grab a seat! You must be tired from your trip. Here, I'll get you a drink. Water is okay? Or would you like your green tea? I still remember, see."

I asked for green tea and Samuel jumped towards the kitchen, disappearing through the doorway.

In the above excerpt, the reader observes a simple interaction between two characters who clearly know each other well. However, the reader might feel lost. Where are we? The story could have happened anywhere and anytime. It could be in a house, an apartment, or even a workplace (workplaces have kitchens, after all). It's also not clear if this story occurred in the 1950s, the 1980s, or just recently. Without an early indication of place and time, readers may feel something is missing. They may feel they are disoriented. A simple revision solves the problem:

Revised Introduction

In May of 1975, 10 years after the breakup, I strolled up the steps of my parents' old Victorian house on Church Street hoping Samuel was still there. I quietly turned the doorknob and stepped into the living room. It smelled as always, like lavender. Samuel sat in the corner reading a thick, worn-out novel. I looked at Samuel and smiled. He knew why I'd come.

"I'm so glad to see you, Sammy."

Samuel jumped from his chair and wrapped his arms tightly around me.

"You've grown so much," he whispered into my ear. He kissed the side of my cheek and then let me go.

"Grab a seat! You must be tired from your trip. Here, I'll get you a drink. Water is okay? Or would you like your green tea? I still remember, see."

I asked for green tea and Samuel jumped towards the kitchen, disappearing through the doorway.

In the revised introduction, we get an immediate, but not overly drawn out, sense of place and time. We feel more comfortable knowing exactly where we are. This locating is enough to help the reader get oriented. The introduction then jumps right into the scene—this isn't a long setup or back story. The scene begins at the first steps up to the door and continues to where the "action" is, with Samuel inside the front door. Whether working on narratives or scholarly papers, you need to dive right into the piece in this way, with enough specifics, or else you'll lose a reader.

This is just one example of one possible larger revision beyond the level of the sentence—other chapters in this book deal with more revisions on a broader scale in stories, research papers, interview-based articles, and personal essays. The peer model writing in this book provides examples of such big picture revisions—it's helpful to look beyond the individual words and sentences to see these larger points. Apply what you have observed in your revision process.

When you're happy with the large revisions, and you feel everything is in place, you can turn to the smaller revisions. Author William Zinsser calls this process weeding (15). The metaphor goes like this: you may have a garden full of beautiful flowers (engaging content), but if weeds (writing problems) crowd them out, you can't see their beauty. Many writers have weeds lurking in their writing but they can't see them objectively (another reason to have a friend or colleague read your writing). Attend to those in the copy editing stage and your readers will see your beautiful flowers.

The major lessons of the rest of this book—starting with Chapter 2's lesson on economy—work on the sentence level. We call these major lessons enhancing factors—factors that look small-scale at first but have a big impact in the end. A good, careful edit at the sentence level across hundreds and hundreds of words can transform a piece of writing by removing interfering factors. We describe interfering factors in each chapter of this book. Interfering factors get in the way of good writing—each enhancing factor has its opposite interfering factor. Revising this way on the small scale will also help you develop precision—the ability to see sentences, down to the word, more objectively. As you develop these editing skills, you may find that your writing on subsequent assignments is more precise—from the start.

Here are a few general approaches when revising any kind of writing at the micro level:

- Ensure that you use enhancing factors and remove interfering factors. Many of the enhancing factors reflect the expectations of editors, teachers, and readers. They reflect the demands of the professional writing discourse found in books, magazines, newspapers, and academic journals. If your writing eventually resembles that discourse, you'll find it easier to achieve high grades or get published, whatever your goal.
- Check that your verb tense is consistent. Choose either past or present tense in a sentence and stick with it. Most stories are written in the past tense. Warning: the one difficulty with present tense is that it's easy to fall out of it into the past tense, particularly if you're not concentrating. Then you'll be breaking usage rules. Choose which tense feels most comfortable for you. We recommend the simple past or present for now. Other tenses may complicate your writing at this learning stage.
- Turn generalized phrasings into specifics. Writing in a detailed way is difficult work, and sometimes we take the easy route of generalizing. Instead of writing "The book was wonderful" you could write "The book contained an engaging set of characters and a strong sense of place." Readers enjoy specific details of any sort.

We recommend the process outlined here for revising your assignments. You may develop additional steps on your own. The point, however, is to understand that you need to find some way to get past doubts and paralyzing fear about writing. Once you've found a way to get your experiences and ideas down on the page, then you should spend a good deal of time on the vital revision process. It should take longer to revise the rough drafts than to write them. Revision will help you express yourself more clearly and engagingly. Readers will, in turn, appreciate your clarity and precision with language as they enter your world of experience.

CHAPTER SUMMARY

In this chapter we recognized that many people have had bad writing experiences in schools. The way writing is taught in school—as obedience training about grammar and spelling—has turned many people off writing. People come to dread mandatory writing after escaping high school drudgery. Yet writing is also a vital human experience, as writing heals. Success in writing can give people confidence.

To become a good writer, one must write often and regularly. It's best to write many smaller pieces when you're starting out. Master the single scene or incident, and then move on to longer pieces. Writers should begin style lessons with personal narratives before turning to academic writing. Nonetheless, a writer will not develop without reading. Read peer, professional, and academic writing for inspiration and emulation. Model your writing after those you respect. Finally, we encourage you to join writing communities and share your work.

Next we examined the difficulty of starting to write. Freewriting acts as a way to get the writing engine started. Freewriting can be messy—it is a draft stage, after all. The point is not correctness, but getting comfortable with writing. Otherwise, writers tend to expect perfection and this can be disabling. Try to forget about The Judge in your brain when you write rough drafts. You'll have time in the revision stage for correcting any perceived faults.

The chapter then looked at two possible writing processes: a sequence approach and a recursive approach. In a sequence approach, the writer works through a logical set of steps in producing a document. The recursive approach is more fluid and free, allowing writers to start at different points in the writing process and also stop writing to reconsider points and do more research. We then provided some tips on working with freewriting material.

The chapter presented the basic principles of stories as a way to begin writing. A story has a beginning, a middle, and an end—in other words, a chronology. It has a sequence of events called a plot. It has characters. We then presented an outline of academic writing discourse, which includes an introduction, an overall thesis or argument, credible evidence, citations, and a conclusion.

Next, we considered revision. Revision is not just about cutting—revision is a creative act where you may discover new ideas and new ways of thinking. Revision gives you multiple chances to get your writing into publishable shape. We then encouraged you to let friendly people read and comment on your work, functioning as editors. If you edit a friend's writing, talk about the positives not just the negatives. You should also frame the negatives as "edits" or "opportunities." When negatives are positioned this way, writers accept them more readily.

Finally, we considered revision as a process: prose editing (the big changes such as plot, character, location, introductions, conclusions) and copy editing (the small changes such as grammar, spelling, punctuation, interfering factors, tense, and details). Start with prose editing and finish with copy editing to maximize efficiency in the editing process. You don't want to worry about the small details when the big things are bound to change.

Further Readings

For more about freewriting:

Cameron, Julia. *The Artist's Way: A Spiritual Path to Higher Creativity*. New York: Jeremy Tarcher, 1992. Print.

Elbow, Peter. *Writing with Power: Techniques for Mastering the Writing Process*. New York: Oxford University Press, 1998. Print.

For more about writing stories:

Clark, Roy Peter. *Writing Tools: 50 Essential Strategies for Every Writer*. New York: Little Brown, 2006. Print.

Rhodes, Richard. *How to Write: Advice and Reflections*. New York: Quill, 1995. Print.

For more about psychic space:

Wood, James. *How Fiction Works*. New York: Picador, 2008. Print.

Economy

> When your story is ready for rewrite, cut it to the bone.
> Get rid of every ounce of excess fat. This is going to hurt;
> revising a story down to the bare essentials is always
> a little like murdering children, but it must be done.
>
> —STEPHEN KING

IT IS A WELL-KNOWN commonality that written communications of all sorts have a propensity to descend quite deeply into a kind of approach imposed very often unwittingly by the author that absolutely ensures the fact that the desired message is not, for the most part, uncomplicated, a stylistic habit that, unless regarded with utmost concern and consideration—an attentiveness boasted by merely a few writers—can turn into an obstruction to fulsome understanding.

Take a deep breath.

When you read that 73-word sentence, you probably felt a mental weight lowering on your mind with each successive word. As you processed the sentence, you slowly understood its points, but it wasn't easy (the double negative in particular requires a mental leap). You felt challenged to decipher the author's meaning, the way a spy slowly deciphers an enemy's codes. Maybe you had to reread parts of the sentence just to be sure.

The wordy sentence above is not great writing, despite its use of big words and a challenging grammatical structure. Good writing can certainly challenge a reader with big ideas. But the worst kind of writing challenges the reader simply to decipher it. In that case, readers struggle not with the ideas but with the style. The style of effective writing—shown in the peer models in this book—doesn't challenge the reader in the way learning Spanish challenges a beginning student. Writing style should look deceptively simple, even in academic writing.

The 73-word sentence above violates all the rules of our first sentence-level enhancing factor for good writing: economy. Economical writing uses the fewest number of words to make meaning. Following the rule of economy does not mean writing like a child might. Long sentences can be clear and precise too.

It does mean, however, editing out the interfering factor of wordiness. **Wordiness** means saying something in more words than you need. You know you've achieved economy when you just cannot pare down a sentence any further without altering the meaning.

> The most valuable of all talents is that of never using two words when one will do.
>
> —THOMAS JEFFERSON

Editing out wordiness is important for making your writing more focused and direct, both worthy goals. Economy gives readers a good return on their investment in reading your work. It means fewer words for readers to process. It means less work for them. In addition, writers who can identify wordiness develop a sense of precision in their writing. Writers who can look at the meanings of words more carefully will express ideas and experiences more precisely and carefully.

The word *economy* was not born out of the study of writing. According to the *Oxford English Dictionary*, economy first meant the management of finances. The word eventually gained the positive connotation of *good* financial management. That is, someone who was economical in his or her financial management was prudent, measured, and careful with money. An economical *writer*, we suggest, is someone who is prudent, measured, and careful with words.

Many print journalists are particularly conscious of economy for practical reasons. Print editors may assign a word or column-inch count to articles, the space around the large advertisements on the page. Time limits the words a TV or radio anchor can squeeze into a newscast. Subtract the time of the advertisements from the typical hourly nightly newscast and just 45 minutes remain to present the major news of the day. You can see how these practical limitations condition journalists to write articles and scripts economically.

In some cases, the Internet has reduced such pressures—a web page, for example, can be as long as the writer wants. Yet people who use text messaging or applications like Twitter know the pressure of economy too: texts and tweets are limited to 140 characters, forcing writers to cut their ideas down to size. All sorts of short forms (for example, LOL or BRB) have developed to help users squeeze in as many words as possible. Still, tweeters and texters know to keep it simple—one idea or two per message.

Advertisers and marketers recognize economy too. Advertisements, product labels, brochures, and pamphlets are costly printed real estate—having too many words adds up to higher costs. And verbose writing in these forms can turn off customers, who want information quickly and easily.

Student academic writing—even published academic writing—is not always known for its economy. One academic journal, *Philosophy and Literature*, ran a contest about ineffective academic writing to highlight the problem. The 1998 contest "winner" wrote this paragraph in a journal article:

> The move from a structuralist account in which capital is understood to structure social relations in relatively homologous ways to a view of hegemony in which power relations are subject to repetition, convergence, and rearticulation

brought the question of temporality into the thinking of structure, and marked a shift from a form of Althusserian theory that takes structural totalities as theoretical objects to one in which the insights into the contingent possibility of structure inaugurate a renewed conception of hegemony as bound up with the contingent sites and strategies of the rearticulation of power. (Butler 13)

Some may argue this passage is perfectly fine if you understand the concepts of structuralism, hegemony, convergence, rearticulation, and temporality. Certainly distinct academic fields have their own **jargon** that you must understand to enter the academic conversation; indeed, college and university students must learn that jargon to understand the theories of their chosen fields. However, the writer above combines and compresses a large number of difficult concepts into one short passage. It feels thick and heavy even to someone with a PhD. This writing is the complete opposite of economical.

At the post-secondary level, however, writing like this example remains a problem. It is emulated and thus perpetuated, not just by undergraduate students but also by professors. The captive audience of academic writing rarely can demand better as the academic writing market isn't dependent upon competition in the way that the fiction market is. For example, most schools buy access to academic journals for their students regardless of the writing quality: no incentive exists for these authors, then, to produce clear writing.

Athalya Brenner describes some other, more subtle, problems of academic writing:

It is supposed to be factual and dry, "objective," or at least relatively clean of personal influence. It is supposed to contain extensive references to previous and current chains of learning. It is supposed to display the writer's knowledge to advantage. Notes are expected, and the more the better, so that a text and a subtext run concurrently. A certain degree of originality is demanded, even when it is the result of hair-splitting, but it should not come at the expense of "depth." Literary style, when too personal, is frowned upon. A clear distinction is made between "literary" discourse and academic or scholarly discourse. And thus, and increasingly so, academic/scholarly so-called research, in its written forms, is becoming more and more boring and less and less aesthetically pleasing. (99–100)

We don't think the accepted format of academic writing gives students a licence to write poorly. Most other writers—aspiring professional writers, journalists, novelists, business writers, just to name a few—need to write clearly to succeed in the competitive and difficult writing market. Similarly, students should write clearly to succeed in the competitive and difficult market of the classroom, where the clear, direct paper stands out from the rest.

The number one goal of writing is to communicate ideas, experiences, and information effectively to key audiences. We want to connect with as many readers as we can in the clearest

> Never use a long word where a short one will do.
> —GEORGE ORWELL

possible way. Increase the power of your writing by cutting words and sentences down to size. Avoid the tendency to think big words and long sentences make you sound smarter.

If wordiness comes between the writer and reader, it's the writer's problem, not the reader's. Faced with poor writing, readers can often turn to other writers for satisfaction—select another book from the library, subscribe to another magazine, or click on another website. The teacher-as-reader can award a poor grade and move on to the next paper. In the end, the wordy writer is left without an audience.

For most casual readers—not those trained in writing as you are—the effect of wordiness, as with other interfering factors, is a visceral, not always conscious, negative reaction. Wordiness leaves readers with thoughts like *I just didn't understand what she meant* or *I didn't like the book.* Readers may not know why they don't like the author's writing, but chances are wordiness plays some part in their feelings.

Obviously you want to avoid this reaction if you want to gain as many readers as possible for your work. Look at it a different way and think about your favourite writers: you probably like them because their writing is clear and precise. They break down that wordiness barrier.

Most writers we know who have learned to be alert to wordiness are able to see it in their writing and the writing of others.

Furthermore, in addition to improving preciseness, an attention to economy can help a writer become a clearer thinker. Students have told us that when they attend to clarity in their writing, they start thinking more clearly.

EXERCISE 6 ▸ Bad Academic Writing

You've probably come across some ineffective academic writing in school. Deciphering it was likely a challenge. It wasn't your fault that you couldn't understand the concepts—it was the writer's fault. Find a passage of badly written academic writing and think about how it violates the principles of this chapter. List a few points about what it is doing wrong.

EXERCISE 7 ▸ Good Academic Writing

Find a piece of writing by an academic author you enjoy. The writing could be a journal article or a scholarly monograph or a book for a general audience. List three examples of particularly clear and direct passages.

▌ The Morality of Wordiness

Novelist and journalist George Orwell, best known for his novel *1984*, draws our attention to the issue of economy. In the 1940s, Orwell wrote a number of essays, the most famous titled *Politics and the English Language*, about how English had degenerated. At the time many politicians deliberately employed verbose and long-winded sentences (a practice that continues today). They used a difficult style to hide facts and avoid responsibility for unsavoury actions. Orwell valued economy and railed against wordiness. "If one gets rid of these habits," Orwell wrote, "one can think more clearly, and to think clearly is a necessary first step towards political regeneration" (157). Orwell connected economical writing to politics: economical writing was vital to democracy.

As Orwell noted, politicians may use wordiness as a deliberate strategy to trick the public or avoid blame. Citizens may feel confused or perplexed as a result. In the worst cases, citizens may accept political action that isn't in their best interests. They may be tricked by big words. Or they may become overawed by such **elevated language**.

For some writers, wordiness is **jargon**. In every field, there exists a set of key words everyone must know. Scientists, professors, politicians, and business leaders know their own fields' languages. Jargon becomes a form of shorthand, a way of evoking meaning quickly and easily—the meaning is shared among an expert community and codified in words and phrases. But in writing intended for the general public, jargon can alienate readers. Experts may in fact use jargon to keep readers out of their communities—the readers just cannot gain entry, metaphorically speaking, to the field without knowledge of this language. If this book talked about *the way in which human beings are interpolated as constructed subjects in the discourses of fields,* our readers would be alienated. Without a clear and detailed explanation—or even with it, some may argue—that language has no place here.

Most writers don't employ wordiness as a strategy the way a politician or businessperson might. They may not see their writing as wordy at all. Instead, wordiness creeps up on writers, just like dandelions pop up on your lawn in the spring. And there are many degrees of wordiness—from the verbosity of the first sentence of this chapter to less obvious examples in our own work. Regardless of degree, we must weed out wordiness to keep a pristine view of the "green grass" that is good writing.

Some writers, particularly students, use wordiness to achieve a given word count. Students are often required to produce words and words and even more words. A word or page count always looms. Under stress and deadlines, a student's main goal becomes length, not effective communication: *If I can just churn out 2000 words by tomorrow, I'll be done.* In this light, economy may seem counterproductive: *If I'm economical, I'll never meet the word count.* Word counts concern all writers to some degree. But the solution to the lost words is simple: add more pertinent content—ideas, scenes, quotations, data, and so on.

A Report Like No Other:
The MFP Financial Services Scandal

Business and legal reports are not known for wonderful language. At best, the writing is dry and bland. At worst, the writing confuses and complicates the content. One case, however, shines out as a positive example of the possibilities of the business and legal report genre.

In 2005, after over two years of public hearings, Madam Justice Denise E. Bellamy released her 1123-page report about Toronto City Council's computer leasing scandal, which saw the city enter into an agreement to buy new computer technology from a private company, MFP Financial Services.

In a short time, the cost of the contract had ballooned from $43 million to $84 million. Councillors soon demanded an investigation into why. The hearings called in 156 witnesses, including bureaucrats, solicitors, administrative assistants, lobbyists, politicians, and business people. In great detail, Bellamy's final report outlined lies, ethical breaches, bribes, and improper lobbying that led to financial benefits on the deal for insiders.

Beyond the content, the report is most interesting for its style. Councillor David Miller, who pushed for the investigation, said that the report was not "a dry academic exercise," and said it "reads like a novel" (Barber). "Only the title—Toronto Computer Leasing Inquiry/Toronto External Contracts Inquiry—is bland," wrote the *Globe and Mail* in an editorial. "Her unflinching four-volume, 1123-page report could easily have been called 'Liars, Liars, Pants on Fire' ('Let's Follow Through')."

Let's look at Bellamy's style to understand how she wrote a different but still effective report.

First, Bellamy includes enticing headings that encourage readers to read on: *A Small Crack Reveals a Big Problem*; *MFP Hires a Hunter*; *More Bumbling: Extending the Leases from Three Years to Five*; *The Makings of a Mystery*; *An Intimate Relationship by Any Other Name*; *Hockey Night in Philadelphia*; *Caught in a Web of Lies*; *A Hint Over Breakfast*. These attractive headings read like the chapter titles of a fiction novel, pulling readers along to see what's next.

Next, Bellamy shows a skill for storytelling. Consider this excerpt of her story about an MFP salesman's connections with a prominent Toronto city councillor involved in the agreement:

> In the early evening of May 2, 1999, six passengers gathered in a private hangar at Toronto's Pearson International Airport and boarded a small jet belonging to Skycharter Ltd. The captain and co-pilot noted the name and citizenship of each passenger and signed the flight manifest. Soon the jet was airborne for the short hop to Philadelphia. . . . The Philadelphia Flyers were playing the Toronto Maple Leafs, and the Leafs were one win away from advancing to the second round of the playoffs. They had not been so close in five years. Much-publicized bad blood between the two teams, especially between popular Leafs enforcer Tie Domi and Sandy McCarthy of the Flyers, heightened the tension.

continued

> The host of the evening had even more reason to eagerly look forward to the game. He was Tie Domi's older brother. Dash Domi had made the arrangements for the trip. It would all be paid for by his employer, MFP. . . .
>
> The Leafs won, but Dash Domi scored that evening, too. The City of Toronto was his account at MFP. The City had recently bought millions of dollars worth of computers. . . . For months, Mr. Domi had been cultivating close relationships with potentially influential people at the City. One of them was a politician, and Mr. Domi had persuaded him to come along on this clubby, exclusive boys' night out. Who was Mr. Domi's prize political catch that night? The chair of the Budget Committee and veteran City Councillor Tom Jakobek, a Leafs fan who had his own gold seats at the Air Canada Centre. . . . When Mr. Domi filed his expense account with MFP for reimbursement, on the back of the receipt in his handwriting was his claim for "Ont. Gov. & Tom J., City of T.O., Vince." "Tom J.," he said, meant Tom Jakobek. Councillor Jakobek knew at least four of the passengers very well. Yet later he would adamantly, repeatedly, and publicly deny that he was on that flight to Philadelphia. Some of his fellow passengers would either swear he wasn't there or wouldn't be able to remember his presence. (Bellamy 171–2)

One of many stories in the book, this one is written in a clear and direct style—Bellamy avoids the wordiness common among those in her profession. Bellamy resists the urge to generalize. She includes great detail about each step of the trip. She shows rather than tells. The detail about the councillor's denial adds mystery to the story—was he or wasn't he on that flight? Columnist Jim Coyle of the *Toronto Star* praised Bellamy's "yarn-spinner's sense of pace and narrative drive. . . . Like many a novelist, Bellamy knows where the heart is, where the ribs are, and precisely where the blade goes" (A01).

In her report, Bellamy hints at the reason for, and significance of, her novel-like approach. She mentions a city report about the computer leasing agreement that raised suspicion in one councillor and sparked the investigation:

> Little about photocopiers arouses interest, much less excitement. This routine report promised to be dry reading; a predictable step in buying standard office machines. Surely, in the colossal pile of reports, impossible to get through before the Council meeting, there were many documents with a far more compelling claim on a councillor's limited preparation time. (33)

Bellamy shows that she knows her report must go beyond the routine to interest the public in its findings. Well-written, detailed, concise, clear narrative, not a basic exposition of facts, entices readers. The report packages the details in a form that regular readers want to read, a form they recognize.

Bellamy's report reminds us that conventions of a particular field sometimes need to be set aside, not emulated. The business and legal report should consider the needs of the audience, needs that may be satisfied by adapting other forms of writing to the project.

Some writers may believe that elevated language will make their writing sound better. They think they'll get better grades or impress superiors if they use big words and flowery language. Perhaps some teachers and bosses *do* favour students and employees who write in this way. But in the professional writing world, wordy writing fails in the market. It turns people off.

Finally, a psychological issue promotes wordiness. Writing is a psychologically unnerving experience since people judge our writing. Writers wonder what others will think of their writing and of them. Writers find it tough to make meaning when they are solely responsible. We react to that harsh world by distancing ourselves from it. The stress causes us to react by clothing ourselves in a cocoon of words, the way a child clutches a blanket.

These concerns are valid. Yet it's rare that good editors and teachers praise writers for wordiness and criticize for economy. Good editors and teachers may criticize simple thinking—thinking that does not develop an idea or experience—but that's a different problem. Economy of writing style does not necessarily need to result in overly simplistic thought.

Forms of Wordiness

So far we've made a case against wordiness. We want you to write economically in all your work. But you need to know what wordiness looks like—what are you looking for exactly? A copy editor will take care of wordiness and other problems in your final draft. But how can you eliminate it from your early drafts?

All writers produce wordy first drafts—particularly those who freewrite. As we explained in Chapter 1, trying to write economically as you draft inevitably slows you down and inhibits creativity. We know it's difficult, after reading this chapter, to avoid thinking about economy as you write, but it's best to leave the editing of wordiness to the revision stage.

Wordiness occurs in many different forms; it is beyond the scope of this chapter to list them all. But the following examples of the worst culprits will help you at least to understand and recognize the problem. As you work through the lessons and exercises, you'll identify unique examples from work that you read (maybe even this book—wordiness lurks everywhere).

The goal of editing for wordiness is not simply to cut and cut and cut anything you come across, like a villain in a slasher film. Rather, the goal of editing for wordiness is to develop awareness of the problem and substitute less wordy options. If you cut out the following four main types of wordiness, you will find that your writing communicates more effectively.

1. Redundancy

Teachers often present redundancy as a problem on the level of the idea. Students may repeat an idea in a term paper, each time with slightly different phrasings (another strategy to increase the word count).

Redundancy also exists down low, at the level of the word itself. Redundant words serve no purpose—they just take up space like a couch-surfing friend. Removing redundant words is one way to pare down a piece of writing to fit space or time limits.

Here are some sentences with examples of redundancy. You'll think of your own as you get comfortable with the idea. Before looking at the answers below, consider the words you could remove without changing the essential meaning of each sentence:

a) The board was long in size.

b) The plane circled around the airport before landing.

c) He dashed quickly across the busy road.

d) My invention is a great new innovation.

e) Jakob is a personal friend of mine.

f) Our company is currently involved in advance planning.

g) We share in common a love for baseball.

h) Amir told a deliberate lie to the teacher.

i) His wife Sarah gave birth to a beautiful set of twins.

j) I think our effort on the project is adequate enough.

k) Holly's dress was green in colour.

l) The food was hot in temperature.

> I believe more in the scissors than I do in the pencil.
> —TRUMAN CAPOTE

Editing for this kind of redundancy doesn't mean rephrasing or recasting the sentences, as this can alter the author's intended meaning. Rather, we want to determine first whether we can clarify as much as we can without rewriting the sentence completely.

The edits in the answers below show that we just needed to delete some words. We explain our reasons for the change below each sentence.

a) The board was long ~~in size~~.
   Explanation: The adjective *long* implies size.

b) The plane circled ~~around~~ the airport before landing.
   Explanation: The verb *circled* implies going around. When one circles something, one goes around it.

c) He dashed ~~quickly~~ across the busy road.
   Explanation: The action of dashing is done quickly. One would not, for example, dash slowly.

d) My invention is a great ~~new~~ innovation.
   > Explanation: An innovation is, by nature, new. The word comes from Latin. In Latin, *in* means *into* and *novus* means *new*.

e) Jakob is a ~~personal~~ friend of mine.
   > Explanation: Friends are personal. If they are not, they are acquaintances. We would never say *She's an impersonal friend*. A wrinkle comes thanks to Facebook. On Facebook, many people "friend" others whom they don't know personally. But in common usage, the adjective *personal* is redundant.

f) Our company is ~~currently~~ involved in ~~advance~~ planning.
   > Explanation: First, the verb form of *to be*—is—denotes the present tense. The meaning of *currently* exists in the verb. Second, all planning occurs in advance. No one would say they're planning after the work is done.

g) We share ~~in common~~ a love for baseball.
   > Explanation: The verb *share* means "in common."

h) Amir told a ~~deliberate~~ lie to the teacher.
   > Explanation: Any lie is inherently deliberate. If it's not deliberate, it's not a lie. We know of no accidental lies.

i) His wife Sarah gave birth to ~~a~~ beautiful ~~set of~~ twins.
   > Explanation: Naturally, twins are a set, so there's no need to say so.

j) I think our effort on the project is ~~adequate~~ enough.
   > Explanation: The adjective *enough* connotes adequacy.

k) Holly's dress was green ~~in colour~~.
   > Explanation: Readers would know that green is a colour.

l) The food was hot ~~in temperature~~.
   > Explanation: The adjective *hot* implies temperature.

Redundancy also occurs in dialogue **attributives**. Most writers use *he said* and *she said* to attribute quotations to people in narratives, research papers, interview-based articles, and personal essays. Consider the redundancy in these attributives:

a) "You're the worst person I've ever met!" she raged.

b) "The medium is the message," emphasized Marshall McLuhan.

c) "Do you have the car in cherry red?" he inquired.

In all three examples, the attributive verb repeats the meaning of the speech. Most readers would judge the speech in the first quotation as full of rage even before the attributive calls it rage. In the second, it's clear that he's emphasizing something. And in the third, a question naturally is an inquiry. *She said* and *he said* would be fine attributives for these quotations. In story writing, sometimes you don't even need the attributive. The reader can figure out who is talking if only two people have been introduced in the story.

Students say *Can't I use redundancy for emphasis?* Redundancy doesn't always work for emphasis. It waters down the point. Short, distinct, clear sentences emphasize a point. But we'll deal more with this question in Chapter 7 on parallelism.

In all of these cases, the redundancy occurred because the meaning of one word already existed in the meaning of the other. None of the edits alters the essential meaning of the sentence. The edits simply make the writing more concise and focused. Why waste space on words that sit around and do nothing?

> Vigorous writing is concise.
> —WILLIAM STRUNK JR.

2. Phoney Intensifiers

Phoney intensifiers are small fortifying words, often adverbs ending in –ly. Speakers or writers who use them seem to be straining to appear confident. We use them in speech when we're unsure of ourselves or to fill dead air. They don't add new meaning and, paradoxically, they often detract from what you're saying.

Here are a few examples of phoney intensifiers. You may think of others. Identify and cross out the offending words:

a) I am absolutely confident in my abilities.

b) We are basically good students.

c) David certainly needs to water the garden today.

d) I really want to go to the store.

e) The dog is very ugly.

f) She is quite beautiful.

g) I'm totally sure I submitted the test.

> Substitute "damn" every time you're inclined to write "very"; your editor will delete it and the writing will be just as it should be.
> —MARK TWAIN

In the first example, the introduction of *absolutely* suggests some doubt—is the speaker unsure about his or her confidence? Why else would she or he intensify the meaning? One is either confident or not. "Basically," in the second example, raises one key question—are the students fully or always good, or are they sometimes bad students? This needs explanation. If David needs to water the garden, he certainly does. What benefit does the *certainly* provide? It's also not clear why the person *really* wants to go to the store. Next, if the dog is ugly, describe its ugliness to the reader—the reader cannot visualize the difference between ugly and very ugly. Similarly, if the woman is beautiful, describe her beauty don't just tell us. Finally, you're either sure you submitted the test or not; *totally* doesn't add any meaning. Lazy writers fall into such constructions.

Some academic writers use phoney intensifiers like *naturally, of course,* or *it is obvious that* when the idea isn't always that natural or obvious. Consider these sentences:

a) Of course the solution is simple: lower taxes.

b) It is obvious that Hart meant something quite different.

c) Naturally, no one wants to sacrifice that much.

This kind of language doesn't allow readers the option to disagree with or dispute the point. Indeed, the writers of these sentences seem not to want the reader to question their opinions. In personal essays and research papers, phoney intensifiers can close down debate. Eliminating them will open up your points for debate and invite the audience's opinions. Make a strong case and let the reader decide what is obvious or natural.

Here's an example of a paragraph containing phoney intensifiers. Can you see them? Cross out the offending words:

> Basically, Terry cycled down the street, passing the cars totally stopped in traffic. He felt very excited to visit his mother on the other side of town for Mother's Day. But up ahead, police totally blocked the intersection. Driving right up against the curb, he squeezed past the absolutely stopped cars and neared the blinking lights and blaring sirens. He jumped off his bike and stood and watched as a procession of black limousines slowly passed by. Somebody really important was in those cars, he thought.

Here's the edited paragraph without the phoney intensifiers:

> Terry cycled down the street, passing the cars stopped in traffic. He felt excited to visit his mother on the other side of town for Mother's Day. But up ahead, police blocked the intersection. Driving right up against the curb, he squeezed past the stopped cars and neared the blinking lights and blaring sirens. He jumped off his bike and stood and watched as a procession of black limousines slowly passed by. Somebody important was in those cars, he thought.

In the revised paragraph, the removal of the phoney intensifiers hasn't in any way changed the essential meaning of the paragraph. The intensifiers did not add to our experience. They performed no function expect to make sentences longer, prolonging the reader's work. We argue that writing becomes more forceful when you remove phoney intensifiers—the useful content shines more brightly as a result.

We'll discuss in greater detail the problem of adverbs in the next chapter. For now, identify these words in your writing and remove them. You might also notice that you're peppering your speech with phoney intensifiers. Consider why you do this.

3. Stretchers

Stretchers are combinations of small words that add only quantity, not quality. Think of these like fillers added to ground beef or chicken nuggets by unscrupulous food companies. You don't want them in your food or your sentences. Hard to see at first, stretchers fill space but add no meaning. They force the reader to spend more time finding the essential meaning of your sentences.

Here are sentences with a few common stretchers. Can you identify what's stretching out these sentences unnecessarily?

a) In order to get to the store we have to cross the railroad tracks.

b) At this point in time, let's read the book.

c) Hemingway's use of economy is his hallmark.

d) William persuades by means of logic.

e) Sandie started to stop crying.

f) The fact that music is a big business is well known.

g) Kunal began to punch.

In each of these examples, the stretching phrases can be edited out with no change in meaning. *To get to the store we have to cross the railroad tracks* means the same as the original. Saying simply *Now let's read the book* reduces the sentence by four words while retaining the meaning. The other sentences are much more focused without the intensifiers: *Hemingway's economy is his hallmark. William persuades with logic. She stopped crying. That music is a big business is well known. Kunal punched.*

The following paragraph contains many stretchers common in academic writing, as well as some new ones. Identify the stretchers before reading the edited version:

The fact that Marshall McLuhan presented his work in a unique way, through the use of probes, garnered a great deal of attention from both the public and the scholarly world. McLuhan seemed to be interested in fame. In order to gain even more attention, he coveted the public spotlight. Surprisingly, in his later years, his fame started to fade and his theories became less important.

This paragraph is not the worst example we've ever encountered but it does contain a number of stretching phrases doing no valuable work. The reader is led along a longer and more winding path than is needed. Why let these "sentence freeloaders" in? Notice how the revision is tighter, more forceful, than the original:

That Marshall McLuhan presented his work in a unique way, through probes, garnered great attention from the public and scholars. McLuhan seemed interested in fame. To gain even more attention, he coveted the public spotlight. Surprisingly, in his later years, his fame faded and his theories became less important.

With the stretchers removed, the revised paragraph is 17 per cent shorter (editors and page designers will appreciate this reduction). The meaning, however, remains the same. The benefit comes in enhanced clarity. The point of each sentence arrives sooner than in the original. An added effect is that the valuable content that remains gains impact by emphasis—readers focus squarely on the points the writer makes. No weeds crowd out the ideas.

> If it is possible to cut a word out, always cut it out.
> —GEORGE ORWELL

4. Thickeners

Writers or speakers may employ thickeners—unusual, often archaic words—that make them sound like a lawyer or a member of a royal family. If you're a lawyer or the Queen of England, feel free to use them; otherwise, delete them.

Some student writers feel the need to thicken their writing to sound important or smart. In fact, teachers may reward students who use elevated language because it mimics a certain kind of academic discourse. Students in turn may believe that certain audiences, like teachers or officials, expect such language from them, or they may use it simply to show off. Whatever the reason, good editors and smart readers feel these words drop like boat anchors into the middle of sentences.

One simple test of whether a word is a thickener is this: ask yourself if you would use the word in conversion with your friends or family. If you wouldn't use a word in regular conversation, then don't use it in your writing.

Here are a few sentences containing thickeners. Can you identify them?

a)   Therefore, it is clear that we must not study after the party.

b)   It has been heretofore mentioned that Shakespeare's work is significant.

c)   Herein lies the key point.

d)   Sarah found the means whereby she could cheat on tomorrow's test.

e)   John likes ice cream and Joe likes popsicles. The former also eats deli sandwiches while the latter eats subs.

f)   I am speaking to you of language practices about which much has been said.

g)   The road to the store, which wound around the forest, was closed.

Let's look at the case against each thickener:

- *Therefore* is a heavy word. If you write well and use proper evidence, you don't need *therefore*. You certainly don't need it when talking about studying and partying. Some students may find a reason to use it in academic writing, but always look for alternatives first before choosing it.
- Would you use *heretofore* while talking to your mother? Only if she were the Queen Mother, perhaps.
- Lawyers and medievalists have good reasons to use *herein*, but the rest of us do not.
- The writer could easily change *whereby* to a more common phrasing: *Sarah found the means to cheat on tomorrow's test.*
- *Latter/former* is a particularly awkward construction born out of a fear of repetition (we talk about this in more depth in Chapter 7). The problem is that the reader must hold the names of the men in mind until the second sentence and then relate the two words, *latter* and *former*, back to the appropriate names. Tired or inattentive readers may forget the names or misread the sentence. Make it easy on your readers and simply repeat the names John and Joe: *John also eats deli sandwiches while Joe eats subs.* We'll talk more about this when we argue for strong nouns in Chapter 5.
- In the next sentence, *which* sounds pretentious. Nobody uses *which* in this way in regular conversation. Look out for other cases of prepositions combined with whiches: *of which, by which, through which, in which, over which.*
- In the final sentence, a *which* clause interrupts the flow of a sentence. If the sentence needs the information in the clause at that exact spot, keep it. But consider removing the information and creating new sentences: *The road to the store wound around the forest. The road was closed.*

▎ Editing Wordiness in Academic Writing

There is no excuse for wordiness in academia. Big words and difficult sentences don't impress well-read readers or help them understand the subject any better. Effective academic writers see beyond the big words and difficult sentences—they focus instead on the deep and interesting ideas they've developed. The content itself, rather than the form, is allowed to shine through.

> Knowledge that is not accessible is not helpful.
> —GLORIA STEINEM

Stretchers are exceedingly common type of wordiness in academic writing, as seen in these examples:

a) The chemical substances were mixed in order to create the reaction.

b) The fact that media history is a burgeoning scholarly field is undeniable.

c) McLuhan's use of probes confused many people.

   d)   In the study of communication, the effects of media are a prime concern.

We can easily remove these useless stringy phrases. Don't these sound more straightforward and focused?

   a)   The chemical substances were mixed to create the reaction.

   b)   That media history is a burgeoning scholarly field is undeniable.

   c)   McLuhan's probes confused many people.

   d)   In communication studies, the effects of media are a prime concern.

Thickeners are also found in academic writing. One described above, *therefore*, is fairly common, particularly in philosophy. It has a purpose, and we don't want to avoid it completely. But sometimes a simpler phrase like *As a result* works better and sounds a bit more natural. Before you use *therefore* or other thickeners in academic writing, try to find an alternative. If none exists, keep the thick word and ensure the rest of your sentence is economical.

We know that many scholarly subjects have a jargon that writers must use or reference. In the field of communication, for example, all scholars must understand words such as interpellation, semiotics, epistemology, hegemony, hermeneutics, media ecology, and so on. The problem comes when writers use these words in sentences directed towards non-specialists and combine them with difficult syntax, awkward phrases, wordiness, and so on. If you must use jargon, ensure that you explain the concept for those unfamiliar with it.

> Order and simplification are the first steps towards mastery of a subject.
> —THOMAS MANN

Economy makes difficult concepts digestible for readers. In the following example, Guy Allen writes about a psychological theorist and human development:

> According to Winnicott, an important event in this potential space is the infant's identification of a transitional object. This is some object, like a toy or a blanket, that becomes the infant's first "not-me" possession. As separation between the "good-enough" caregiver and the child begins, the child uses the transitional object to create the illusion of the comforting caregiver. (151)

This paragraph isn't a collection of too-simple or too-short sentences. The sentences are a reasonable length and each deals with an important psychological theory. The paragraph cannot be edited down further. Allen explains an important, abstract concept in a clear, direct style. Readers cannot misunderstand Winnicott's theory after reading this excerpt. Allen has done the hard work for readers—digesting

> If you can't explain it to a six year old, you don't understand it yourself.
> —ALBERT EINSTEIN

the theory and translating it into something clear, concise, and straightforward. Whenever you write about difficult concepts, choose a concise style. This also forces you to completely understand the concept—you cannot explain it succinctly otherwise.

EXERCISE 8 ▸ Wordiness in Professional Publications

Editors of quality publications are conscious of wordiness and remove it during the revision process, but sometimes wordiness remains. This exercise requires you to find a patch of wordy writing in a newspaper or magazine. Photocopy your example and then edit it right on the page, crossing out the unnecessary words. If you want to make this exercise easier, find an article in a sports or celebrity publication; these are not known for their economy.

EXERCISE 9 ▸ Wordy Writing

Write two paragraphs of about 100 words each of wordy writing (yes, we want you to be wordy this time). Each paragraph should be on a different topic. Use examples from all four of the categories discussed above. Have fun with this. Read them out to your classmates for laughs. After completing the exercise, never do this again, unless you're writing comedy.

EXERCISE 10 ▸ Economical Writing

As a contrast to Exercise 9, this exercise requires you to write two economical paragraphs of about 100 words each on any topic. To help you become as economical as possible, we have two restrictions: do not use words longer than six letters or sentences longer than 10 words. Most students find this a challenge, since many everyday words are longer than six letters and many everyday sentences are longer than 10 words. One tip to make this exercise easier: write in the present tense (verbs won't need the –ed ending in present tense).

Nobody expects you to write in this extreme economical way all the time. But you'll probably find moments in your writing when short, declarative sentences with simple diction work best. Exercise 9 and 10 represent the opposite ends of the economy↔wordiness continuum. Over time, you'll find a comfortable position, hopefully closer to the economy side.

Many students tell us that after applying the economy lesson in Exercise 10, they see wordiness everywhere: in their friends' essays, newspaper articles, their own speech, signs alongside the street. Becoming more aware of wordiness helps them see their sentences with a more critical eye.

Other students worry that an adherence to economy, as in Exercise 10, will remove all rhythm from their sentences.

But rhythm and economy are not mutually exclusive. We'll deal more with rhythm in Chapters 7 and 8. In particular, we'll show how repetition (some call it planned redundancy) improves writers' communication with readers. Often in the classroom, for example, teachers will repeat ideas so students encounter them at least twice—that reminder helps with comprehension and memory. You'll notice in this book, too, that we repeat ideas at times. Think of these as "reminders with a purpose." Planned redundancy has a strong defence—the repetition reminds the reader of key points. Unplanned redundancy has none—it just takes up space and prolongs reading.

We hear another concern about editing for wordiness: *This is picky stuff. How is removing a few words here and there going to make a difference?* It's true that when working at the sentence level you are looking at micro-level issues. We argue, however, that removing all four main types of wordiness from your writing makes a significant difference when done across hundreds and thousands of words. No one instance of wordiness undermines your writing, but a lot of it can lead to a larger overall readability problem.

Some of the edits you make may reduce the length of your work by 20 per cent or more. If you cut down your drafts by removing redundancy, phoney intensifiers, stretchers, and thickeners, you'll have a tighter, more focused piece of writing that readers will intuitively enjoy. You'll develop a keen eye for detail too.

Readers will have no idea what you've done in the revision stage (this can remain our secret). They may just think *I understand this writer well* or *I want to read more by this writer.* That's the kind of reaction you'll get when you pay attention to the enhancing factor of economy.

Peer Models for Emulation

In Chapter 1, you read two stories from beginning writers. Each piece of peer model writing in this text has gone through substantial revision, including removing wordiness. The authors, their classmates, and editors keenly edited the models, looking out for redundancies, phoney intensifiers, stretchers, and thickeners.

The next peer model story presents the experience of a child living in the suburbs, a reality many of us have lived. Read this story for pleasure and then reread it for the lessons we've described so far.

My Mom and Bramalea

BY JULIE MICHELANGELO

I live in a new house in Bramalea, in Section J where street names all begin with J. I stand at the end of Jeffrey Square and wait for my yellow school bus to arrive for 7:45 a.m. Old leaves from last autumn drift in short gusts of wind across the twenty acres of field, cleared for development and more J-named streets.

The bus squeals and stops in front of me. I mount the steps. I see faces that I do not know. Each face, like a picture on a page in a book, looks flat.

"Last stop," the driver calls.

I leap from the last step and follow wooden planks over mud to my portable classroom. I start grade two at Saint Jean Brebeuf in May, two months before grade two ends. Ms. Pickles, a tall woman with a long face and pale skin, peers at me as I step into the portable. I move from the door to the desk added when I came on my first day. Ms. Pickles talks about a story book I have not read. I lay my head on my desk, turn away from Ms. Pickles, close my eyes and sleep.

"Julie, you need to sit up."

I hear Ms. Pickles' voice over my head, open my eyes, and focus on the buttons on her skirt, level with my desk. I forget for a moment that I sit in a chair at school. Twenty students stare.

"I want to go home," I tell Ms. Pickles. Tears well in my eyes.

"Go out and wash your face."

I stand up, press my arms close to my body, and walk to the door. Four more portables separate me from the office. Mrs. Diggles, the secretary, sits in her chair. Her head scrunches over her desk, and her fingers extend above typewriter keys.

"Mrs. Diggles? My teacher said I could go to the bathroom. I don't feel good."

"Go ahead."

Warm water from the sink fills my hands. My hands move toward my face and wet my skin. Two fingers from my right hand reach inside my mouth, find the back of my throat, and press down on my tongue. My fingernails scratch warm, soft flesh. Acid juice from my stomach reaches my mouth. I spit the orange mixture on the floor. Pink, red eyes look back at me in the mirror above the sink. "I threw up!" I yell out from inside the bathroom.

I hear Mrs. Diggles' chair roll across the portable floor. Mrs. Diggles comes in the bathroom and glares at me, then my vomit.

"Go sit down, Julie," Mrs. Diggles says. "I'll call home."

My heart beats through my throat and out of my ears.

"Mrs. Michelangelo? Julie threw up again today. No, I looked for myself. Yes, she is right here."

Mrs. Diggles passes me the phone.

"Mom?"

"Julie-I-do-not-have-a-car!" Mom says.

Mom tells me to go back to class and wait for the end of the day. I pass the phone to Mrs. Diggles and walk out of the office and to the three wooden steps that lead to my grade-two portable. Ms. Pickles peers at me. I sit at my desk.

The bus drops me at the end of Jeffrey Square. I follow the house numbers until I reach number eight. The front door opens and frames my dad's face. My dad's chin clenches and tightens around his lips. Muscles in his neck show when he swallows.

"Wait here," my dad tells me. "Stay out of the living room."

The phone moves into my dad's hand and receives words from my dad's shaky voice.

"Julie, I want you to go to Shirley's."

An ambulance siren gets louder and stops outside our house.

"Right now, Julie."

"Dad, where is Mom?" I cry.

"She's okay. Just go!"

"Okay, Dad."

I walk to Shirley's house in the P section in Bramalea. Shirley, Mom's friend, spoons corn and ham onto a plate and puts it down on the table in front of me. My stomach feels hungry when I smell the corn. My throat feels sore when I swallow a kernel. I work up to ten kernels and feel full. A car engine outside interrupts the silence. I stand up to answer the door.

"Hold on, Julie, I'll get it," says Shirley.

My father clears his throat, speaks to Shirley, and clears his throat again. He looks past the doorway to the kitchen where I stand, half hidden behind the wall.

"It's okay, come here," my dad tells me.

I stand beside my dad and hear him swallow.

"The ambulance had to bring your mom to the hospital," my dad says.

"Is Mommy coming home?" I ask.

"Not now, Julie. Later, when she feels better."

Two months pass before my dad brings me to see Mom at Peel Memorial Hospital. People in their pajamas fill the waiting room. A lady with a steel brace around her head and neck stands by the back wall. Mom walks into the room and sits down beside Dad.

"Hello, Julie," Mom says.

Mom looks above me and out the window and covers her legs with the housecoat she wears.

I look at Mom's red hair and the soft white skin of her face.

"Hi, Mom," I say.

Dad talks to Mom while I sit on a chair.

"Say good-bye to your mom, Julie," Dad says.

"Bye Mom," I say.

"Good-bye Julie," Mom says.

I ask Dad when I can see Mommy again. He stares ahead.

Mom came back to our home in Bramalea in August. Years later, I learned that Mom had suffered a nervous breakdown. At 26, Mom had tried to take her life.

Dad listened when Mom asked to move back to Toronto. We picked a house close to my mom's mom on Juliana Court.

I started grade three in March at Warren Park Public School. On my first day, after the lunch bell rang, I walked to the fence at the end of the school yard, swung my body underneath the metal wires and followed the sidewalk to 46 Juliana Court. Alphaghettis, bread and butter, and a glass of milk waited for me inside our new home. My mom and I sat on the couch and watched The Flintstones until one. "Come home right after school," Mom said.

"Okay," I said. "Bye Mom."

(Michelangelo 10–13)

EXERCISE 11 ▸ Rhetorical Analysis

Write a rhetorical analysis of "My Mom and Bramalea." Write it in the same personal, informal style as your rhetorical analysis in Chapter 1. (See our sample analysis in that chapter if you've forgotten how to do it.) There's no correct answer here, just your unique analysis. You may consider these points, if you like:

- What role does place play in this story? How does Julie Michelangelo develop a sense of place and locate the story?
- The story includes a lot of dialogue. What role does dialogue play in the story? Talk about the nature of that dialogue.
- Describe the phrasing of some details Michelangelo includes to suggest the era or time period of the story.
- Describe the relationship between the mother and child, and provide specific examples from the text of how Michelangelo shows that relationship.
- What is the most important scene in the story? Explain why.

Keep your insights from this exercise in mind during revisions of your own writing. All writers borrow approaches and techniques from writers they admire.

Personal experience can still play a role in your academic writing. Emilia Di Luca developed the following student research paper from her own experience with pets. She contextualizes that experience in a number of ways. As you read Di Luca's piece "The Pet Owner's Burden," think about how it blurs distinctions between personal topics and academic topics.

The Pet Owner's Burden

By Emilia Di Luca

Like many pet owners, I strive to provide the best life for my dog, Amber. On Amber's third birthday, I rushed home with a "chocolate" bone that read "happy birthday." Upon jamming a lit candle into the treat, I clasped Amber firmly in front of the bone as my family sang an awkward rendition of "happy birthday" until a growl interrupted the song. I blew out Amber's candle. Instantly, I felt ridiculous, and thought, "Why would I light a candle that Amber, a dog, cannot blow out?" The extinguishing of the candle ignited another burning question: why do owners treat pets as humans?

Gourmet treats, cute clothes, and birthday parties attack a pet's essential nature as an animal. When people give human traits to their pets, they humanize animals. The humanization of pets occurs in various forms: pets can look human, act human, or be treated like humans. Although the humanization of animals seems unnatural, people naturally attribute human characteristics to other species. Various forms of human nature—people as imperialists, narcissists, mothers, and consumers—cause humans to seek control and belonging from others. The humanization of pets seems harmless. Pet owners tell themselves that they treat pets as family members out of love, but the humanization of pets merely masks itself as affection. As well, "[pets] have been made to suffer indignities and humiliation" (Tuan 4). Despite humans' belief that their actions benefit their pets, humanization does not yield happiness in anyone but the owner. Thus, as selfish beings, people humanize their pets to satisfy their need for power and affection.

Since primitive times, humans commandeered nature, specifically animals. Domestication illustrates one of the earliest forms of animal humanization. The terms "domestication" and "domination" connote similar meanings: "the two words have the same sense of mastery over another being—of bringing it into one's house or domain" (Tuan 99). By bringing animals into the domain of human culture, people modify animals to suit human needs. For example, people bred animals as livestock and hunters. Yet, after people abandoned a nomadic life, created leisure time, and developed recreational activities, domestication prepared animals for a different purpose (Fox 26).

Domestication created the pet. The poodle provides a striking example. Initially bred for hunting, the poodle received a "lion clip," a haircut resembling a lion's mane, which enable the lion to easily move through bodies of water while hunting. During Louis XIV's reign, however, poodles grew immensely fashionable in France. Consequently, people bred poodles as pets, and poodle barbers became trendy. Barbers shaved patterns and even monograms on the poodles; the dog became a canvas for art the way people tattoo their bodies (Tuan 104). Similarly, the Chinese bred goldfish as pets to suit an unusual aesthetic taste—perturbing eyes and array of patterns (Tuan 96). Although the poodle and the goldfish do not resemble humans physically, people still humanized them. Humans adopted these pets into a culture that altered their appearance to suit humans. Eventually, people not only bred animals to distinguish pets from wild creatures, but also to resemble humans. Some dog breeders dock the tails of such hunting breeds as the Cocker Spaniel. As a result, the dog appears to lack a tail; humans of course lack a tail. Thus, domestication allowed "man [to create] the dog in his own image" (Beck 167). Once pets visually resemble humans, people easily transfer their culture upon their pets.

Indeed, humans strive to dominate others; the best example stems from the Age of Imperialism. Failure to *help* strangers by ruining a unique culture and implementing unwanted social systems would impose a burden upon the poor unselfish Europeans. Whether fear or sheer egotism motivated them, Europeans sought to relieve themselves of the "white man's burden." Europeans believed that their superiority obliged them to impose their culture on the less fortunate. While people stopped using the phrase "white man's burden" because of its racist implications, domination of the "other" remains a central notion.

Humans possess an imperialist desire to dominate and project values onto not only humans, but also other species. Like nineteenth-century imperialists, pet owners bear a burden—"the pet owner's burden." Pet owners feel obliged to provide animals with the human experience. After all, how can one tolerate the sight of a cat sleeping on the cold tile floor? Such a sight appears uncomfortable, unfair, animalistic.

The pet owner's burden targets owners of all sexes, ethnicities, and religions. Some Jewish households, for instance, celebrate a youth's coming of age. A Jewish boy has a Bar Mitzvah, a Jewish girl has a Bat Mitzvah, and a Jewish dog has a Bark Mitzvah. Both the 13-year-old boy and the young dog wear kippahs. Lee Day performs Bark Mitzvahs and thus encourages the practice among furry friends: "I really believe that animals have a right to a party and a religion" (Deninno). Day observes dogs' entitlement to religion, unlike many other rabbis who believe Bark Mitzvahs degrade the Jewish tradition (Deninno). An animal's right to religion only emerged with domestication. People desire to impose religion, a human construction, on animals. Animals do not desire to participate in religion. Yet, people's sense of superiority centres on owners' concerns about relieving the pet owner's burden through animal humanization. Humans civilize animals to feed their own egos.

Because of human narcissism, people extend their identities onto their pets. Narcissism, excessive interest in oneself, transforms a pet into the image of the owner. Pet owners, therefore, indulge themselves through their animal companion. Animals, for instance, undergo medical treatment—hip replacements and cancer treatments— once solely available to humans; owners see themselves in animals, and thus, pets deserve prime medical care (Pets for Profit). In the short documentary, "Pets for Profit," Lisa, an eccentric pet owner, confides that her animals give her a lot of pleasure (Potter). The pleasure occurs because she treats the animal the way she treats herself. As Lisa describes her spending habits—she purchases expensive doggie clothes regularly—the frame highlights Lisa and her Chihuahua, Bellini. Just as pale blonde hair frames Lisa's tiny face, and a frosty pink sweater hugs her bony body, pale blonde tresses frame Bellini's tiny face, and a frosty pink sweater hugs her bony body. The repeated image startles viewers.

As in cartoons, the pet mirrors the owner, an image originating in the ancient notion that "people and animals can share identity and change one into another" (Beck 63). Since early humans feared themselves transforming into barbaric animals with threatening teeth and vicious claws, they exercised dominance (Beck 63). Fearing another species, people integrated human traits on animals to familiarize the "other." Egyptian gods, for example, "wore the head of a dog or a hawk on a human body" (Beck 64). Whether urged by indulgence or fear, humans' narcissism projects the owner's identity onto pets. Specifically, pets reflect the owner as an infant (Beck 71).

Pet owners humanize animals since they recognize the pet to be themselves as infants. As a consequence, pet owners indulge in birthday parties that resemble children's. Many dog birthday parties include eccentric cakes, party hats, and loot bags. Owners relive their childhood experience through their pet; but, to reinvent their childhood, people humanize their pets by dressing them in princess tiaras and singing happy birthday. The costumes and rituals project human traits onto the animal. Fittingly, the treatment of pets as infants positions the owners as mothers.

A mother ties a bow in her two-year old daughter's hair. A mother ties a bow in her two-year old Shi-Tzu's hair. Pet owners mother their pets as parents mother their toddlers. Since owners see pets as representations of their infant selves, the owner becomes a parent. Pet-keeping parallels pseudo-parentism (Perin 78). Some young couples—they hesitate to start a family—own pets to substitute for children; some retired couples use their free time and money to dote on pets like grandchildren. Nonetheless, both instances of pseudo-parentism evoke a common language—"motherese."

Pet owners speak to their pets not only as humans, but also as babies. Katcher defines "motherese" as a type of "baby-talk" mothers employ to address young children (Tuan 53). For example, Lisa reveals that "[Bellini] is ready for her walkies" (Pets for Profit). "Walkies" is "motherese" for "walk." Talking "dumb" to pets, establishes an adult–child relationship, making the pet a child subject to the owner's parental authority. Moreover, although "motherese" appears innocent and goofy, the language represents affection. Affection occurs in relationships of inequality, such as between an adult and a child (Tuan 5). Upon the creation of the pet as a child, some owners demonstrate superabundant love toward their pet, or surrogate child.

Like any good parent, pet owners shower their pets with unrelenting love. The love owners feel for their pets often challenges rational love. With pets, owners can express unnatural amounts of love without the fear of rejection. In fact, people humanize pets because they love the animals like children; and thus, they treat animals like children. Pet owners purchase goodies and speak "motherese." In addition, pets fulfill humans' emotional needs, especially in contemporary culture. Presently, social medium and fast-paced urban lifestyles discourage casual physical contact and they further isolate people (Tuan 112). Most people demonstrate their human-like love of their pets by talking to them. Many more people demonstrate their love materialistically; capitalist culture encourages owners to spoil their beloved companion with treats.

Contemporary consumer culture compels owners to humanize their pets by purchasing human-like products for their animal companions. Such pet products as dog food resemble human food. A brand name food manufacturer, *Caesars*, sells "Mediterranean Chicken Casserole" described as "gently cooked in gravy" (Pets for Profit). Owners' mentality suggests that if the food appears edible to humans, it suits their pets. Similarly, pet owners can access designer fashions for animals, although pets do not recognize the value of brand names. Gourmet food and designer clothes instill pride and satisfaction in pet owners—they give their companions the best products as a token of their love. Furthermore, designer doggie fashion prompts dogs to model in Harrod's annual dog fashion show. Hence, this cultural tradition imposes itself upon animals and causes dogs to function as models. In addition, pet boutiques provide such specialty items as crystal studded collars and sports jerseys for pets (Pets for Profit). Such goods carry cultural significance. The pink collar imposes gender construction on animals—it feminizes the pet; the jersey imposes cultural practices on pets—it suggests animals engage in sports. The humanlike goods extend to humanlike services for animals.

Pets experience human culture through amenities typically provided for people. Today, a simple grooming fails to satisfy pet owners; pet spas provide animals with a luxurious experience. Many doggie spas offer such treatments as pawdicures, all-natural flea baths, blueberry facials—I wonder how they keep the dogs from licking the substance off—among many others. With the plethora of spa treatments, one might wonder how dogs managed before domestication. Similarly, pet hotels have sprung up in major cities and now many hotels offer pet packages. In New York, for instance, one animal hotel, "The Ritzy Canine"—the name suggests a five-star rating—caters to animals through humanization. A luxury suite costs the owner $175 per night; a television and orthopaedic bed complete the suite (Pets for Profit). Through amenities, people treat animals humanly, and elevate their status.

Animal humanization occurs because people desire power and love. Humans' imperialist and narcissistic nature provokes pet owners to control and thus humanize their animals. Similarly, people function as mothers and consumers to demonstrate love for their pets; as a consequence of mothering and consuming, people make pets humanlike. Pets assume human appearances and practice human rituals since people treat animals as children and people. An animal assuming human status seems innocent; dressing a cat in a tiara or a dog in a sweater harmlessly amuses pet owners. Yet the humanization of pets may yield consequences for both humans and animals. Humanization fosters an unnaturally close bond between animals and humans. Thus humanization of animals can instill violence or separation anxiety in pets. Some pets do not fare well with other animals because they are not socialized properly—they have been raised as humans. Likewise, people may develop sub-par socialization skills among their own species or financial issues because they fund pets as though they were children. Humans humanize pets because they want the best for their animals; as Lisa tells viewers, "If you have a pet you must take care of it" (Pets for Profit). However, ignorance and egotism blind Lisa, like many pet owners. Animal owners ought to care for pets not as humans, but as animals.

Works Cited

Beck, Alan, and Aaron Katcher. *Between Pets and People*. United States of America: 1996. Print.

Deninno, Nadine. "Dog 'Bark Mitzvah' Revived as Latest Trend for Dogs, Owners." *International Business Times*. 6 Jan. 2012. Web. 19 Mar. 2012. www.ibtimes.com/dog-bark-mitzvah-revived-latest-trend-dogs-owners-photo-video-392060

Fox, Michael. "Relationships Between the Human and Non-human Animals." *Interrelations Between People and Pets*. Ed. Bruce Fogle. United States of America: Charles C. Thomas, 1981. 26. Print.

Katcher, Aaron. "Interaction Between People and Their Pets." *Interrelations Between People and Pets*. Ed. Bruce Fogle. United States of America: Charles C Thomas, 1981. 53. Print.

Perin, Constance. "Dogs as Symbols in Human Development." *Interrelations Between People and Pets*. Ed. Bruce Fogle. United States of America: Charles C Thomas, 1981. 78. Print.

Pets for Profit. Dir. Marianne Lueck. Films Media Group, 2006. *Films On Demand*. Web. 18 March 2012. http://digital.films.com.ezproxy.library.yorku.ca/PortalPlaylists.aspx?aid=13210&xtid=37077

Tuan, Yi-Fu. *Dominance and Affection*. Binghamton: Yale University Press, 1984.

EXERCISE 12 ▶ Rhetorical Analysis

Write a rhetorical analysis of "The Pet Owner's Burden" in a conversational style. If you're not sure what to say, the following questions may prompt you to think more deeply about the paper:

- Do you think the writing is economical? Explain with examples from the paper.
- Explain the paper's overall argument or thesis.
- How does Di Luca make sure the topic is accessible to the average reader?
- Di Luca divides the paper into sections based on theories she uses. List and describe those sections.
- Does the conclusion work for you? Explain why or why not.

Assignment 2a

Note: In Chapter 1 we introduced a labelling format that helps you to see your accomplishments in revisions. You should have revised the first assignment at least once. In that case, its label should be at least 1b. If you were particularly keen on revision, you might now be at 1c or 1d. Assignment 2 starts with a label of 2a.

Suggested Topics:

1) Write a story about an incident that you observed or experienced as a child.
2) Write a story about a teacher, businessperson, or politician who speaks in an elevated, wordy style.
3) Write a short research paper that looks at everyday life through an academic lens.

Here are some suggestions for your writing:

- If you choose one of the story topics, first brainstorm two or three possible incidents in your past. Choose the one you remember the best. Jot down the story's developments in a few point-form notes. Then freewrite.
- If you choose the research paper option, first brainstorm some everyday problems or observations that you'd like to explore in your writing. At this stage, these ideas will be, of course, quite general. Second, visit your library and examine the general texts on the topic to start finding a focus. You may have to investigate readings in various academic fields, as Di Luca did above. You must then read enough on the subject to have a more specific overall argument. Reread Di Luca's paper above and model your argument after hers.
- At this point, some writers may feel a need to consult more academic models for emulation before starting. If that's how you feel, then feel free to read ahead in this book—each chapter includes one academic writing peer model. As well, consider the explanation of academic discourse in Chapter 1 and the Hierarchy of Detail for academic writing in Chapter 5. The Appendix on Research and MLA/APA Documentation at the end of the book also includes information on starting academic writing projects and documenting sources.
- Use quotations wisely—they provide a short break for the reader from the rest of your text. In stories, that may mean trying to capture the way that people speak. Before writing a story, you might think for a minute about how the people in your story naturally speak—make note of any common catch phrases or stylings—they are valuable for developing character. In an academic essay, choose quotations that are unique and interesting.
- A conversational tone—language that sounds natural when you read it out loud—works best in most writing. Avoid elevated language that doesn't reflect the way you ordinarily communicate. Student writers in particular often think they need to put on an academic mask when they write. Resist this temptation and let your unique voice shine through.
- In stories, avoid an authorial voice that looks back on the past; instead, try to write "in the moment." Of course, you don't know how you "sounded" as a writer five, ten, or twenty years ago. But attempt it. Avoid commenting on or judging your old self or others. Interrupting the narrative with current commentary only distracts the reader and delays the narrative. A good basic narrative should immerse the reader in the moment until the end.
- Remember Chapter 1's lesson about locating the writing immediately at the start of your text? Both Michelangelo's and Di Luca's writing in this chapter locate the place or mention the argument early.
- After you've written your rough draft without letting The Judge into your mind, turn to revisions. Revise on both the large and small levels described in Chapter 1.
- Apply the lessons on economy to your rough draft. Remove redundancy, phoney intensifiers, thickeners, and stretchers. The more often you apply these

lessons to all of your writing, the more you'll understand and internalize them. You may even see other cases of wordiness we don't describe here. That's when you know you truly understand the lesson.

- It's not necessary to use only words of six letters or fewer, or sentences of ten words or fewer for Assignment 2a—or any other writing you do in the future. But try not to fall back into big-word/long-sentence writing.
- Word count doesn't matter in this assignment. If you want to write 10 pages, do so. But most students in our classes write between two and six double-spaced pages. Think about quality, not quantity.
- Don't revise until you've had a few days of mental rest from the writing. You'll come back refreshed to take an objective look at what you wrote. In the heat of writing we lose all objectivity.

CHAPTER SUMMARY

In this chapter, we argued that a great deal of wordy, often incomprehensible writing still exists in professional publications, and it demands excessive mental work from readers. Good writing does not challenge the reader to decipher it. Rather, it feels deceptively simple to read, even though the author may have done many revisions to reach that point.

Ultimately, economy is not the end goal of your writing. Effective communication is. But focusing on economy is one way to revise writing for effective communication. It will also help you develop precision—the ability to choose words that reflect exactly what you want to say. An economical writer is prudent, measured, and careful with words.

Time and space constraints put pressure on journalists to conserve words when they write. The Internet has eased that pressure in some ways—a website, for example, can be as long as the writer wants, although he or she must be aware that readers will skim and search for information. Applications like Twitter, which has a 140-character limit, also impose economy.

Academic writing is often wordy too. In professional writing, however, economy is now a generally accepted principle. George Orwell elevated the significance of wordiness by making it into a political problem.

Many writers are unable to see wordiness in their own writing—and it may not be as bad as the examples in this chapter. Student writers in particular may use wordiness as a tool to meet word counts. Regardless of its origin, though, wordiness creates a barrier between the author and the reader. Exercises and practice at editing wordiness out of your work will make it easier to detect as you gain experience.

We categorized wordiness into four main types: redundancy, phoney intensifiers, stretchers, and thickeners. You may discover others as you revise your work.

Further Readings

For more about economy and directness:

Strunk Jr., William and White, E.B. *The Elements of Style*. 4th ed. New York: Longman, 1999. Print.

For more about the political consequences of wordiness:

Orwell, George. *Why I Write*. New York: Penguin Classics, 2005. Print.

Strong Verbs

SENTENCES INCLUDE MANY DIFFERENT types of words that hold them together grammatically. These types act as the scaffolding of meaning. But we believe that one type of word in the grammatical sentence is more important for writers to attend to than any other word: the verb, our second enhancing factor for good writing.

Certain verbs add life to your writing by creating concrete, real images in the minds of your readers and profluence in your stories. Oppositely, choosing the wrong verb kills a sentence and turns off readers. Sometimes, great verbs get crowded out by other words. Keep the verb in mind always—verbs are, indeed, vital words in every sentence you write.

The difficulty with verbs comes in choosing the right ones. Traditional grammar books suggest that verbs are complicated. Their forms change based on time and number and other factors. Here's a list of factors that modify the form of verbs:

intransitive	indicative mood
transitive	imperative mood
past tense	subjunctive mood
present tense	active voice
future tense	passive voice
progressive tense	first person
perfect tense	second person
present perfect tense	third person
past perfect tense	singular
future perfect tense	plural

We won't define all these factors in this book, as we don't think you need to know most of them to produce good writing. Consult a grammar book if you need more clarification. Here, we prefer to simplify the topic of verbs. A few points about these important words will help you improve your writing significantly—without having to understand subjunctive mood or future perfect tense. In Chapter 1 we suggested that you write in the simple past and present tenses. That's all you need to know for now.

The verb glues parts of the sentence together. Sentences fall apart without verbs. Without verbs, sentences become **fragments**. Writers often use sentence fragments in newspaper headlines:

a)   20 dead after collision closes highway in Calgary

b)   New York's top 10 most congested intersections

c)   Boy, 5, trapped in dad's car for three days

Why are these fragments? In the first example, the sentence is missing the verb *are* after "20". The second sentence contains no verb at all (just adjectives and a noun). The third example is missing the verb *was*. (Indeed, rather than being trapped in the car, it sounds like the boy was trapping—perhaps trapping for animal pelts—in his dad's car for three days. We don't think that was the intended meaning.)

Fragments present problems. They often (but not always) do not have verbs. They lack movement and detail without those verbs. Their use may also suggest the writer doesn't understand the importance of verbs and may need instruction on how to form a simple, proper sentence. Fragments, as we saw in the trapping example above, may also create unintended meanings.

We admit that you'll notice fragments in good writing too. As with all rules, exceptions exist. But good writers know why they're using them. Fragments may create a certain effect on the reader. Consider this example:

David heard about the explosion at his children's school. He grabbed his keys, dashed out the door, and ran and ran and ran. He finally arrived at the school to find his children safe outside the front door with their teachers and the police. Relief.

In this example, the final element—*Relief*—has no verb. It's not a grammatical sentence. The writer deliberately chose to present the father's final feeling as a fragment. It works.

We have noticed, however, that many beginning writers use fragments without realizing it. They don't know that good sentences demand good verbs—not just for grammatical correctness but for other reasons we describe below. At this point in the book, we'd prefer that you master the simple grammatical sentence before you experiment with fragments for effect.

Simple grammatical sentences start with subjects and verbs. We'll deal more with the grammatical term *subject* in the next chapter. For now, though, just make sure your sentences have the best verbs—in simple present and past tenses—they need to make specific meaning.

Let's move on to the best kind of verb, the concrete verb.

Concrete Verbs

In grade school, teachers usually call the verb an action word. It's an easy way to remember the definition of a verb. Certainly, many verbs show actions. But this definition doesn't capture all the meanings of a verb.

In addition to describing action, a verb also can show "the existence of a condition or a state of being, such as an emotion" (Chicago Manual of Style, 172). The distinction between these two kinds of verbs—action versus condition/state of being—is an important one. It has consequences for writing effective stories, research papers, interview-based articles, and personal essays.

Another helpful way of describing this distinction between verbs is to use the labels "strong," or concrete, and abstract. The everyday verbs such as *run, hit, walk* are concrete. They represent real, tangible actions that readers imagine instantly as they process your sentences. Readers have no doubt about what these words mean.

When we read the sentence *The boy popped the balloon*, we instantly see in our mind's eye the everyday action of popping. The verb pops out of the sentence, becoming its focus. The boy and the balloon are important parts, too. We wouldn't have a grammatical sentence without them either, but the pop is the point. Without the verb, the sentence has two characters—a boy and a balloon—but no action. *The Boy and the Balloon* sounds like a good title for a children's book, but it doesn't *do* anything.

Readers enjoy actions. You probably know this feeling. Good movies, just like good books, see things happen. A boy journeys across the world on a boat with a tiger. A man fights back against political oppressors. A woman chases her father's murderer. These stories attract and involve us because the characters move. Even academic writing has action: *The paper surveys the issues in the field; The theorist stopped his work after the third failure; Researchers looked at multiple options for testing the hypothesis.* People like writing that uses strong verbs because these strong verbs put a hook in the audience's chest and pull them along.

> Verbs are the most important of all your tools. They push the sentence forward and give it momentum.
> —WILLIAM ZINSSER

Here is a small selection of everyday, concrete verbs:

dance	paste	score
run	turn	read
pull	twist	write
push	flip	paint
type	burn	pour
hiss	scream	see
slide	pry	show
jump	boil	cover
yell	peel	crush
cry	play	wipe
drink	greet	crunch
shout	slap	clean
climb	slip	smile

The following full-sentence examples show this movement in practice:

a)   Molly danced and danced and danced at the wedding party.

b)   Mark runs past the police and jumps the fence.

c)   He greeted his buddies at the bar and then drank until he couldn't drink anymore.

d)   Dr. Seto wrote about the viability of the project.

e)   She painted the sign before leaving for the protest.

f)   The police officer shouted at the protester.

g)   The striker scored the game-winning goal and then danced with her teammates.

h)   The study shows that the method worked.

In each of these examples, the characters do a lot of interesting, easy-to-imagine actions. Readers see these characters living their lives as people do. Every day, people dance and run and jump and greet and drink and clean and paint and shout and score and smile. Use these words to bring the reality of life into your writing.

Some concrete verbs relate specifically to the human senses. Using verbs that evoke as many senses as possible provides a richer experience for the reader. The reader sees, smells, touches, hears, and tastes what the people in your writing do. However, we live in a sight-dominated society. Images on phones and computers and TV immerse us in sight. As a result, in our writing we tend to focus on the visual and forget about the other senses. Writing that focuses only on the visual sense provides the reader with just a fraction of your experience.

Certain events and locations that you write about may have a characteristic smell or sound. For example, when you're riding on the subway, you smell the spilled coffee on the floor or the body odour. When you're at the beach, you hear the crash of the waves or the squawk of the seagulls. When you're eating at a fine restaurant, you taste the heat of the spices or the fruitiness of the red wine. As a child, you felt the warmth of your mother's hug and the pain of a scolding. These details are as important as details from the sense of sight.

Here are more examples of concrete verbs categorized by sense:

- see, look, watch, gaze, gander, view, stare
- smell, waft, stink, reek, sniff, scent, perfume
- touch, feel, press, tickle, push, pull, punch
- hear, crackle, hum, echo, scream, whisper, groan
- taste, lick, devour, eat, munch, gobble, chew

You'll probably find it hard to find verbs for smell. We struggled to come up with the smell list above (writers tend to describe smells with adjectives). But the other categories have many more examples for any purpose.

Less-than-Concrete Verbs

Some verbs may look like concrete verbs, but they aren't quite as effective as the ones above. These verbs often have –ate and –ize endings. Consider the images and actions these verbs create in your mind's eye:

anticipate	categorize
administer	customize
incorporate	formulate
utilize	localize
authorize	personalize
manipulate	revolutionize
inculcate	vocalize

Can you "see" these verbs? What images or actions spring to mind when you read *inculcate*? Or *actualize*? Or *administer*? Not many. Readers instead feel a vague sense of these actions. These actions are much more abstract than *run*, *walk*, and *hit*.

These less-than-concrete verbs do, however, have their purposes in some kinds of writing such as research papers. Academic writing often deals in abstract concepts and theories. But if we want to make reading easy for our readers, and if we want to let readers sense what we sense, these verbs won't help. *The scholar interrogates the subject in a way that will transfigure the theorization of the field* may sound academic but it doesn't help the reader see the point. This is better: *The scholar deals with the subject in a way that will change drastically the field's theories.*

Similarly, a tendency exists in business writing to use these –ate and –ize verbs. Consider these sentences:

a)   The accountant was authorized to manipulate the numbers.

b)   Utilize the manual to understand how to administer the drug.

c)   Darren formulated a plan to revolutionize the industry by anticipating next steps.

Often these types of sentences come from business writers who want to impress. They want to look smarter than they are. Other writers may simply think these verbs fit the expected discourse of business writing. But none of these examples communicates as effectively as it could. Vagueness of verbs leads to less tangible meaning. These verbs have their place, at times, but their regular use only shrouds meaning in generalities.

We all fall into these verbs without realizing it sometimes. It's a nasty habit to break. When you find yourself using these verbs, stop and consider using an everyday replacement. In revision, think of alternatives that communicate more easily, alternatives that anyone can understand. For example, alternatives for *authorize* and *manipulate* include *allow* and *alter*. An alternative to *utilize* is *used*. These are a bit better, although still not as concrete as *eat*, *gargle*, or *press* (academic and business writing may find little use for such concrete verbs). Alternatives for *formulate* include *form*, *design*, or *create*.

> Probably no other language has such a vast supply of verbs so bright with color. Don't choose one that is dull or merely serviceable.
> —WILLIAM ZINSSER

Sometimes the verbs you use may not be as awful as these –ate and –ize examples. Yet you could still revise them into more concrete verbs. Consider the following extended example. A trend today sees writers—particularly journalists—using the phrase *made . . . way* to show movement:

a)   Jeannie makes her way to work.

b)   Kunal made his way home to Edmonton.

c)   The travellers faced traffic as they made their way across the city.

Made isn't the worst verb—it's not as bad as *vocalize*. But the reader still cannot see how Jeannie, Kunal, and the travellers moved. The solution: substitute the vague verb for a concrete verb. So many concrete verbs exist to express movement. These are better:

a)   Jeannie walks to work.

b)   Kunal biked home to Edmonton.

c)   The travellers faced traffic as they drove across the city.

You can judge verbs on a scale from clear to vague. Some verbs may fall in the middle—not the best but not the worst. In revision, try alternative verbs that fall toward the clear side of the scale.

EXERCISE 13 ▶ Verb Lists

In this exercise, we want you to get a feel for concrete verbs. Write three lists of concrete verbs (do not include any of the verbs specifically listed above—that's too easy). Each list should contain 25 verbs. Write each list on a different day—you'll get more out of exercises that you do over multiple days. If you cannot think of enough verbs, look through a dictionary, or pull concrete verbs out of a piece of writing you like. Don't include any less-than-concrete verbs. Soon you'll see verbs everywhere.

EXERCISE 14 ▶ Verb Variety

As writers, we have a tendency to use the same vocabulary over and over. To get you out of that vocabulary rut, this exercise requires you to think of verb synonyms. Come up with 25 other words to express the verb *walk*. Then come up with 25 others words to express the verb *look*. Do each list quickly at first. When you're exhausted, draw a line below the incomplete list. Then consult the Internet and find the rest. This helps warm up your brain.

Killing the Classics: An Experiment in Weakening Strong Verbs

Writers of good fiction know the power of the strong verb. They understand that fiction must move along—things must happen. They know that the difference between a strong verb and a weak or dead verb means the difference between capturing and losing a reader's attention. Readers' attention increases as actions happen.

Now imagine fiction without strong verbs. Characters would just *be*. They'd exist, the way a garbage can or a shoe exists. Nothing would happen, though, just as nothing happens when you sit on the couch watching television. Stories just wouldn't be stories without strong verbs.

With this in mind, we want to perform an experiment. We want to see what great fiction looks like without the best verbs. Two classic works of fiction—John Steinbeck's *Of Mice and Men* and Toni Morrison's *Tar Baby*—use strong verbs regularly to great effect. But without strong verbs, their writing looks like Superman under the effect of Kryptonite.

continued

Of Mice and Men tells the story of two ranch workers, George and Lennie, in California during the Great Depression. In the following excerpt, we've changed the strong verbs to weak ones and added dead verbs too:

> The flame of the sunset elevated from the mountaintops and dusk was into the valley, and a half darkness was in among the willows and the sycamores. A big carp ascended to the surface of the pool, ingurgitated air and then submerged mysteriously into the dark water again, leaving widening rings on the water. Overhead the leaves were moving again and little puffs of willow cotton were falling down and coming to rest on the pool's surface.
>
> "You gonna get that wood?" George beseeched.
>
> "There's plenty right up against the back of that sycamore. Floodwater wood. Now you get it."
>
> Lennie went behind the tree and transported out a litter of dried leaves and twigs. He discharged them in a heap on the old ash pile and proceeded back for more and more. It was almost night now. A dove's wings were sounding over the water. George perambulated to the fire pile and ignited the dry leaves. The flame made lots of noise among the twigs and fell to work. George unfastened his bindle and extracted three cans of beans. He erected them about the fire, close in against the blaze, but not quite touching the flame.

Now read Steinbeck's original, with all the wonderful strong verbs:

> The flame of the sunset lifted from the mountaintops and dusk came into the valley, and a half darkness came in among the willows and the sycamores. A big carp rose to the surface of the pool, gulped air and then sank mysteriously into the dark water again, leaving widening rings on the water. Overhead the leaves whisked again and little puffs of willow cotton blew down and landed on the pool's surface.
>
> "You gonna get that wood?" George demanded.
>
> "There's plenty right up against the back of that sycamore. Floodwater wood. Now you get it."
>
> Lennie went behind the tree and brought out a litter of dried leaves and twigs. He threw them in a heap on the old ash pile and went back for more and more. It was almost night now. A dove's wings whistled over the water. George walked to the fire pile and lighted the dry leaves. The flame cracked up among the twigs and fell to work. George undid his bindle and brought out three cans of beans. He stood them about the fire, close in against the blaze, but not quite touching the flame. (Steinbeck 10)

Doesn't the original feel more natural than our version? Our version replaces strong verbs with verbs that don't quite capture the intended meaning. Our verbs sound awkward and unusual, given the context. Our weak and dead verbs don't sound as smooth as the originals. They contain less action and imagery. Our version looks like a shadow of the original, even though we kept all of the other words.

Now let's look at the opening sentences of Morrison's *Tar Baby*. The story begins with a scene of a man on a ship. Once again, we've replaced the verbs with awkward and unusual ones:

> He was standing at the railing of H.M.S. Stor Konigsgaarten and was inhaling great gulps of air, his heart pounding in sweet expectation as he looked at the harbor. Queen of France looked interesting in the lessening light and descended her lashes before his gaze. Seven girlish white cruisers oscillated in the harbor but a mile or so down current was a deserted pier. Carefully casual, he descended to the quarters he had with the others, who had gone on shore leave, and since he had no things to gather—no book of postage stamps, no razor blade or key to any door—he merely bent more tightly the blanket corners under the mattress of his bunk. He withdrew his shoes and entangled the laces of each one through the belt hoop of his pants. Then, after a leisurely surveillance, he crouched through the passageway and made it back to the top deck. He moved one leg over the railing, equivocated and tossed around the idea of diving headfirst, but, trusting what his feet could tell him more than what his hands could, altered his mind and simply went away from the ship.

Now, read the original paragraph with Morrison's strong verbs returned:

> He stood at the railing of H.M.S. Stor Konigsgaarten and sucked in great gulps of air, his heart pounding in sweet expectation as he stared at the harbor. Queen of France blushed a little in the lessening light and lowered her lashes before his gaze. Seven girlish white cruisers bobbed in the harbor but a mile or so down current was a deserted pier. Carefully casual, he went below to the quarters he shared with the others, who had gone on shore leave, and since he had no things to gather—no book of postage stamps, no razor blade or key to any door—he merely folded more tightly the blanket corners under the mattress of his bunk. He took off his shoes and knotted the laces of each one through the belt hoop of his pants. Then, after a leisurely look around, he ducked through the passageway and returned to the top deck. He swung one leg over the railing, hesitated and considered diving headfirst, but, trusting what his feet could tell him more than what his hands could, changed his mind and simply stepped away from the ship. (Morrison 3)

In Morrison's original, readers don't have to spend much time processing the verbs. She uses everyday words, unlike our *equivocate*. Our revision's phrasings seem slightly off—Morrison's are just right. Our introduction of *was* in the opening sentence doesn't expand or enhance meaning. Our revision looks like a parody of writing. Morrison's looks authentic.

These two examples show that great writing dies without strong verbs. And without strong verbs, your writing cannot ever hope to achieve precise movement and visual detail of great writing.

▌ Abstract Verbs

Abstract verbs—we call them dead verbs—creep into the writing of all writers at some point.

An abstract verb, usually expressing a condition or state of being, creates a different effect than a concrete verb does. When readers encounter an abstract verb, they don't see an image. These verbs become an interfering factor in writing.

Consider the following practical example. If someone says the word *run*, you immediately understand and see the act of running. If someone says the word *punch*, you immediately understand and see the act of punching. These actions occur in the concrete realm of everyday life, a realm every reader knows. No one fails to see an image with these words. And if we want to communicate quickly and easily with readers, we want to use words they immediately see in their mind's eye.

But if someone says the word *were* (a form of the verb *to be*) what comes to your mind? How about *is*? What images or actions do *were* and *is* create in your mind? None.

Abstract verbs like *is, are, was, were* evoke a condition or state of being but don't stand alone as meaningful. These verbs look generic. These words also need helpers—they need other words to complete the meaning. Writers unaware of their vagueness pepper them all over their writing.

The dead verb contributes to wordiness. A reader who encounters a dead verb needs more words to understand the point of the sentence. For example, consider these sentences with abstract verbs:

a)   The boy is hungry.

b)   The dog was sick.

c)   I was a risk-taker.

d)   The concept was difficult.

If these sentences ended after the dead verbs, they'd make no concrete meaning. *The boy is, The dog was, I was, The concept was* suggest mere existence: the subjects don't move anywhere and no concrete images are evoked. *The boy, The dog, I,* and *The concept* sit there dead and useless while we wait for more information. In these cases, we wait for the words *hungry, sick, risk-taker, difficult.*

We don't advise completely avoiding these types of sentences—if the boy is hungry then write that he is hungry. Yet dead verbs become crutches if taken too far. Writers can become lazy and choose dead verbs over better concrete alternatives. Let's convert the verbs in the four sentences above into concrete ones:

a)   The boy wolfed down his first meal in three days.

b)   The dog puked all over the white carpet.

c) All weekend I skydived and bungee-jumped.

d) The concept stumped students and scholars alike.

In all four revised cases, we immediately see the actions: *wolfed, puked, skydived, bungee-jumped, stumped.* We get to experience first-hand the actions of these subjects. No dead verbs clutter the sentence, doing nothing. The bonus of the revised sentences? The reader participates in the making of meaning. The writer doesn't tell the reader what's happening with adjectives after dead verbs. Instead, the writer shows through actions. As a result, the reader must be the one to assess the sentences. The reader realizes the more abstract points in the originals: these subjects are hungry, sick, a risk-taker, and difficult. Show, don't tell.

> Throw up in your typewriter every morning. Clean up every noon.
> —RAY BRADBURY

Dead verbs creep into sentences often as complements of concrete verbs, weakening the effect of concrete verbs in the way that too much water weakens the taste of a soup. For example:

My friends were running behind me.
Revised: My friends ran behind me.

In the original, the writer includes the root of a strong verb but it hides in the weeds. The dead verb *were*—also called an **auxiliary**—becomes an emphasis point in the sentence. The concrete verb deserves emphasis, not the auxiliary. After all, the verb makes the sentence go.

The grammatical construction above requires the writer to tack on an –ing ending to what is normally a strong verb *run. He ran; she ran; they ran*—those look concrete and straightforward. But the introduction of the dead verb and the –ing ending shrouds the strong verb in awkward clothing. The root verb no longer stands out among all of the other words. In the revised version of the sentence, the writer has thrown off the shackles of the verb and, as a result, it shines. Look for –ing endings—these present red flags for revision.

Some grammarians will object to the revised sentence above. They will note that the sense of time is slightly different in the revised version. This results from the change in verb tense. Less-than-careful editing of this sort could alter this sense of time. Grammar considerations, however, must take into account the resulting effect on the reader. Many perfectly correct phrasings make reading difficult. A writer who serves grammar rather than the reader won't have many readers.

We agree that the continuous action of *were running* is slightly different in meaning than the past action of *ran*. But we argue that this distinction is a small one, and the benefit of removing the –ing endings to liberate your verbs is in clarity and focus. And still, the meaning of the sentence remains essentially the same: the friends still ran behind in a continuous action. Until we write that they stopped running, they ran. If time is important, writers can suggest that without using complicated tenses. Consider this example:

> Friday, October 13, 1992: I stand with my sister at the corner of Portage and Main.

In this case, the reader receives the date of the story from the first part of the sentence, and receives the sense of immediacy—of standing there with the writer and his sister—from the strong present-tense verb in the second part.

Consider this example in academic writing:

> The idea of community was growing in the minds of writers in the 1920s.

The revised version takes out the dead verb:

> The idea of community grew in the minds of writers in the 1920s.

The revision doesn't change the meaning; the notion of continuously growing still exists in the simple past tense *grew*. Writers shackle their verbs in the worst ways when they use extended verb tense combinations like these:

a)   They had been trying to walk to the store

b)   I will have been working for six hours by the time you arrive.

c)   The man would have been driving for fifteen hours by then.

These sentences are in the **past perfect continuous, future perfect continuous,** and **conditional perfect continuous** respectively. There are occasions when these drawn-out tenses are useful. But mostly these combinations feel heavy to the reader, like lifting a 20-kilogram weight. If you find these constructions creeping regularly into your sentences, judge whether you need them. If not, find an alternative or remove them. The more complicated tenses exist for perfectly good reasons, but for most non-fiction, other options exist. Release the chains that surround strong verbs and let them carry the sentence. Choose the simple present or past tense most often.

Beyond forms of *to be*, other dead verbs clutter sentences. Some writers over-use the auxiliary verb *would* when more straightforward options exist. For example:

a)   Every evening that summer we would buy ice cream.
    Revised: Every evening that summer we bought ice cream.

b)   When he got mad, his eyeballs would pop out of his head and his veins would bulge in his neck.
    Revised: When he got mad, his eyeballs popped out of his head and his veins bulged in his neck.

In both of these cases, the revised versions make virtually the same meaning but readers now focus on the strong verbs: *buy, pop, bulge*. The *woulds* are unnecessary. With the revisions, the *woulds* no longer shackle the strong verbs. In these two examples, the revisions do not radically alter the originals. Rather, they remind us that editing works best when it improves the original content with small, focused changes. The writer will appreciate the preservation of the core elements of the sentences.

Another often unnecessary auxiliary verb is *can/could*. Consider how *could* adds nothing to the verbs in this extended example:

> I sat in the forest with my binoculars. I looked around for the rare black and white woodpecker. I could hear its distinctive pecks on a nearby tree.

In this case, the concrete verb *hear* isn't as powerful. *Could* distracts. Changing the sentence to *I heard its distinctive pecks on a nearby tree* preserves the meaning yet places the emphasis back on the verb where it belongs.

Similarly, the verb *has* and its many forms evoke no imagery in the mind of the reader. As a transitive verb, *has* needs an object to answer the question *has what?* Just like the forms of *to be*, *has* does not suggest any images or actions in the reader's mind. Consider the following examples:

a) My uncle has a dog.
Revised: My uncle owns a dog.

b) The boys had a plan.
Revised: The boys created a plan.

In the first sentence, the revised version's verb *owns* is more concrete than *has* (although not as concrete as *burp* or *juggle* or *bite*). *Owns* also suggests more precisely the relationship between the uncle and the dog. In the second sentence, *created* is more concrete than *had*. *Created* also suggests more agency on the boys' part. They did this act.

A final troubling dead verb is *come*. When writers get lazy with verbs, they turn to verbs like *came, comes, come*. Consider this example:

> The sculptor came into the class.

This generic verb doesn't show us much. We can't see what *came* looks like. Did the sculptor *run* or *stumble* or *dash* or *stroll*? Consider this rewrite:

> The sculptor stumbled into class, ricocheted across the room, and grabbed a chair for support.

This isn't a sculptor who just came into class. He came into class like a hurricane. These strong verbs also suggest, perhaps, that the sculptor may be drunk. If that's what you want to imply, these three verbs suggest that idea well. Allow the reader to make that assumption. Sometimes the strongest technique is to back off and let the details of the writing evoke opinions and judgements.

Let's now turn to an extended example of this verb problem. In the last chapter, you read Julie Michelangelo's personal narrative "My Mom and Bramalea." Below, we've added dead verbs to her introduction. Compare this with the original paragraph, which follows our "dead verb" revision:

With dead verbs

I have been living in a new house in Bramalea, in Section J where street names all begin with J. I have been standing at the end of Jeffrey Square, where I am waiting for my yellow school bus to arrive for 7:45 a.m. Old leaves from last autumn are drifting in short gusts of wind across the twenty acres of field, cleared for development and more J-named streets. The bus is squealing and is stopping in front of me. I am mounting the steps. I am seeing faces that I do not know.

Without dead verbs

I live in a new house in Bramalea, in Section J where street names all begin with J. I stand at the end of Jeffrey Square and wait for my yellow school bus to arrive for 7:45 a.m. Old leaves from last autumn drift in short gusts of wind across the twenty acres of field, cleared for development and more J-named streets. The bus squeals and stops in front of me. I mount the steps. I see faces that I do not know.

What's the effect of adding dead verbs? Our revision feels heavier. It lacks flow. It de-emphasizes actions. Notice the difference in length too: the revision is 11 words, or 13 per cent, longer, for no good reason.

Writers do need abstract verbs and auxiliaries. We couldn't have written this sentence or, indeed, this book without them. But many writers depend upon them unnecessarily and unconsciously.

EXERCISE 15 ▶ Dead Verbs in Publications

This exercise will help you recognize dead verbs in other people's writing. Find an article in a newspaper or magazine and highlight or underline all of the dead verbs you can find. Write a concrete verb above each example (the verb could be a simplification of the one the writer used or it could be a new one). Ensure that your revision is grammatically correct. To make this exercise easier, choose a lesser-quality publication such as *The National Enquirer* or *The Sun*. Higher-quality publications like *The New Yorker* or *The Globe and Mail* may not provide many instances of dead verbs.

The Greater Consequences of Dead Verbs

Some writers resist our suggestions for what looks like, at first glance, a small and insignificant edit. They say *Can editing little words like* were, was, has, *and* would *make a difference?* This is a reasonable response. These little words don't look like much.

We argue, however, that the verb is the most important word in the sentence. Everything builds off the action of the verb. Without it, the sentence becomes a mere fragment. With a concrete verb, the sentence lives. Anything that crowds out the verb, or reduces its power, or draws attention away from it becomes the enemy during revision. In this light, the importance of editing out dead verbs looks obvious. It clears a path for readers, who can then move more directly through the writing. Making life easier for readers is an important goal for writers.

And that's not all. Overuse of these tiny words signifies two greater writing problems: 1) the tendency to generalize and 2) a lack of movement in plot or exposition.

Let's look first at the tendency to generalize. Readers dislike generalizations. They love details—specific information about characters, places, actions, facts, and ideas that brings writing to life. Whether you're using a description of a person's clothes in a narrative or an explanation of a point in a research paper, your attention to detail will appeal to readers.

Consider the detail evoked by verbs in this student peer model excerpt from a childhood story, "Sesame Street," by Laurel Waterman:

> I scramble my feet out the side of the sheet and slide down from my pink canopy bed onto the shaggy green rug. I feel crumbs with my bare feet as I walk the two steps from my bed to the door. The hinges squeak as I pull the door open.
>
> The narrow hall to my Dad's room seems long and dark. I see only shapes. The wooden railing guides my trip to the end. Dad's breathing gets louder. He snorts at the end of each breath, pauses, and starts a new one. I stand in the doorway. He looks different without his glasses—like someone else's dad. (5)

These paragraphs contain no dead verbs. Rather, the writer's concrete verbs bring sensory detail to the reader's mind: *scramble, slide, feel, walk, squeak, see, guides, snorts, stand,* and *looks.* The reader experiences the moment because Waterman has given us great, precise, specific details. A world without this kind of detail is a bland place. By using these concrete verbs, Waterman also moves the story along. The character—herself—doesn't sit and exist in conditions or states of being. She moves and joins her father in the other room. Something happens, however innocent those actions look.

Dead verbs, on the other hand, allow generalizations to emerge. Take, for instance, this sentence:

> My father was angry.

The dead verb *was* requires the adjective *angry* to complete the meaning of the sentence. This sentence is not grammatically incorrect (indeed, much of what we talk about in this book is not a question of grammar but of style). But considering the requirement of detail in writing, the sentence fails. Angry can mean many things to many people.

Using the dead verb *is* allows the writer to avoid describing that anger. But the reader needs to see or feel that anger, not simply be told about it. *My father was angry* generalizes anger, an abstraction from real actions that show anger. The reader stands one step removed from the reality of that anger (as if the reader is outside the room when it happens).

Many possible ways exist to fix this problem. The most important reminds us of the "show, don't tell" mantra. Consider this detailed snippet of a story:

> My father sat at the wooden kitchen table. He picked up his cell phone and called the voicemail number to get the final message from his lawyer. My father, hard of hearing, always turned the phone volume up to the maximum.
>
> He listened. I heard the voicemail lady give him his options. He pressed the new messages button and listened. My hands shook. I sweated.
>
> My father's faced reddened as the lawyer spoke. The vein on the side of his forehead pulsed. He scrunched up his face. He looked disgusted.
>
> My father took the phone from his ear and threw it against the wall. He slammed his fist down on the table and screamed.

Now *that* is anger. No reader would misinterpret these actions as anything else. The reader gets a specific, concrete image, a story, of angry actions. He or she isn't told a thing. The revised sentence does what good non-fiction personal narrative writing does: it specifies rather than summarizes. This passage is not a summary of anger assisted by a dead verb. In your own writing, let the reader experience the emotions of the individual as if he or she is standing there. Imagine the reader as an interloper, a ghost watching the events unfold.

The second consequence of dead verbs is stopped action. Overuse of dead verbs, particularly forms of *to be*, emphasizes conditions and states of being over action. Details disappear and plots stop. The writing becomes static. Consider this example:

> Samir was happy. He had supported his wife Andrea through her health problems. Andrea had been in the hospital for two years, wondering when

she would go home. Samir was kind to her, knowing she would do the same for him. Andrea was comforted by the idea that he was there for her no matter what happened. Andrea was delighted when Samir would bring her little gifts to the hospital. Samir was glad when the doctor said she would be coming home.

The issue in this paragraph is not grammar or spelling or any other picky point: the problem is a poor style assisted by dead verbs. There is little happening in the story. The dead verbs allow the writer to summarize feelings and actions, without having to do the hard work of detailed description. We as readers feel removed from the real moments of the story. We're not quite in the room with Samir and Andrea. Rather, we're hearing what has happened after the fact, at a distance.

The revised version of this story lets us experience the story as Samir and Andrea did:

Samir sat in a chair in his wife's private room at St. Clair General Hospital. The worn-out chair cushion needed repair. The doctor stood next to Samir, looking at Andrea's chart. The doctor shook Samir's hand and left. Samir smiled and sat back. Samir looked at Andrea as she lay back sleeping in the hospital bed. Every day, Andrea counted the days: 710 in the hospital so far. Samir's memories of the long hospital stay flooded back. A month in, he brought Andrea a new wedding ring to replace the one she lost. For Mother's Day, he arranged a party in the room with her mom and her grandmother, complete with non-alcoholic beer and finger snacks. For Christmas, he hired a Santa Claus from the mall to visit Andrea's room. Andrea even sat on Santa's lap.

A number of changes make this major revision superior to the original. The strong verbs do real work. They become the focus of each sentence. Thanks to detail they provide, the reader becomes immersed in the scene, not distanced from it. The story shows, rather than tells. It moves along. Actions of all kinds happen. Finally, all of the summary points in the original version find a place in the new version in new forms: expanded parts that show rather than tell. The expanded story does everything the original does, in a much more detailed and realistic way.

Academic Writing and Strong Verbs

In academic writing with lots of dead verbs, abstractness dominates and exposition doesn't move along. The following paragraph is an edited version of an article Duncan Koerber published in the journal *Media History*, with dead verbs substituted for the original concrete verbs. After you've read it, read the original below it to see the difference.

Revised version:

. . . until the 1820s there were no widespread public means of communication and a decentralized population was not able to come together face-to-face as a mass on occasions to feel like a collective (Craig 131; Noel 24). Until that time, the newspaper business was only a sprinkling of weekly newspapers, and most of them were influenced, were owned, or were directed by government-friendly printers. Conversely, in the 1820s and 1830s people were facing fewer difficulties in starting up a newspaper, as cheaper printing technology, rising literacy and an increasing population through immigration was enabling the great growth of newspapers (Errington 90, 1; McNairn 133; Raible 50; Stabile). In 1829, one in five families had a newspaper, but by 1841, that number was up to one in two (McNairn 130). Newspapers were to become soon a major public institution.

Original version:

. . . until the 1820s no widespread public means of communication existed and a decentralized population meant people could not come together face-to-face as a mass on occasions to feel like a collective (Craig 131; Noel 24). Until that time, the newspaper business saw only a sprinkling of weekly newspapers, most of them influenced, owned, or directed by government-friendly printers. Conversely, in the 1820s and 1830s people faced fewer difficulties in starting up a newspaper, as cheaper printing technology, rising literacy and an increasing population through immigration enabled the great growth of newspapers (Errington 90, 1; McNairn 133; Raible 50; Stabile). In 1829, one in five families took a newspaper, but by 1841, that number had increased to one in two (McNairn 130). Newspapers quickly became a major public institution. (Koerber, *Early Political Parties* 129–130)

The original reads better because it includes a number of verbs stronger than *to be* verbs: *existed, come, enabled, increased, became.* The writing also uses some strong verbs common in personal narrative writing: *saw, faced, took.* With the dead verbs gone, the writing flows more freely and directly. It moves. The meaningless, dead words don't weigh down the writing or evoke a feeling of stasis.

Writing using the five senses and with movement is easy in narrative, which deals with concrete actions, but a challenge in academic writing, which deals more often with abstract ideas. In our everyday lives, we *gab* and *shake* and *munch* and *kiss* and *suck* and *dive*. Readers see these actions immediately in their mind's eye.

Academic writing, however, discusses existence and states of being more than concrete action: *The process is found in . . . Williamson considers this question . . . His argument was essential to . . .* Readers don't use their senses much at all when reading academic writing.

Academic writers who take our lesson on dead verbs seriously may feel lost without the verb *to be*. The tendency then is to give up on editing out dead verbs in academic writing and revert completely back to *was*, *were*, *is*, and *–ing* suffixes. Recognize, though, that our rule against using dead verbs is not absolute (we use these verbs in this chapter, even in this sentence). Sometimes you need to suggest continuous action or states of existence. As well, you may need dead verbs to list adjectives. However, that does not give writers a licence to ignore the point. The ratio of strong verbs to dead verbs changes in academic writing, but you should remain sceptical of dead verbs and test them at every instance, making sure no other, stronger options exist.

Strong verbs can infuse academic writing with strength and confidence. Consider these examples:

a)   The two scholars were in agreement.

b)   Marshall McLuhan was the inventor of the terms "hot" and "cold" media.

We've seen worse sentences than these. Both examples, however, could be better. In both cases, the solution is to replace the dead verbs with strong ones. Consider these revisions:

a)   The two scholars agreed.

b)   Marshall McLuhan invented the terms "hot" and "cold" media.

The revised sentences make the same points as the originals. The verbs are relatively strong. The verbs demand attention. And finally, the sentences are more concise in revision. The reader need not spend extra time processing them—if the sentences are located within a larger paragraph, the reader can move easily to the next sentence with full understanding of the key points.

With few opportunities for everyday verbs like *carry*, *gurgle*, *wind*, or *melt*, academic writers may fall back on a limited vocabulary of verbs like *argue*, *cite*, *theorize*, and so on. But many more relatively strong options exist even for the academic writer.

Dominique O'Neill of the Writing Department at York University teaches students that, to present arguments convincingly, one must choose correct attributive verbs—verbs that reference other scholars' ideas and writing. In her instructions for students, O'Neill explains that "the choice of attributive verb depends on whether the writer wishes to stress the *type of intellectual activity* that the expert engaged in, or the *strength and positive value* with which the authority expresses his viewpoint, or *the faith (or lack thereof)* that the writer has in the expert's quote" (O'Neill). Consider the variety of options for attributive verbs in academic writing from O'Neill's verb lists below.

TABLE 3.1 Attributive Verbs by Strength

FAIRLY NEUTRAL

advances	discusses	proposes
adds	evaluates	presents
analyzes	explains	puts it/puts forward
asks	focuses	relates
comments	finds	remarks
compares	illustrates	reports
concludes	indicates	responds
depicts	investigates	reveals
describes	notes	says
defines	observes	sees
develops	points out	writes

BOLDER

affirms	demonstrates	mocks
argues	denies	predicts
articulates	denigrates	questions
asserts	denounces	reasons
attacks	derides	reminds
believes	disputes	shows
confirms	emphasizes	states
counteracts	establishes	stresses
criticizes	expounds	supports
condemns	insists	urges
declares	maintains	

WEAKER

appears (to believe, to think)	implies	perceives, seems to (believe, think)
assumes	infers	speculates
claims	intimates	suggests
considers	insinuates	supposes
contends	interprets	thinks
hints	mentions	
	offers	

TABLE 3.2 Values (to describe the author's viewpoint)

POSITIVE

agrees	confirms	recommends
advocates	corroborates	reminds
attests	demonstrates	supports
champions	emphasizes	urges
celebrates	endorses	validates
condones	opts for	verifies

NEGATIVE

accuses	derides	mocks
complains	denounces	questions
condemns	disagrees	takes issue
critiques	disowns	with/warns
denigrates	disputes	
deplores	laments	

TABLE 3.3 In a debate, the scholar may either . . .

CONCEDE

acquiesce	allow	confess
admit	concede	compromise
acknowledge	defer (to someone)	recognize
agree	grant	

REFUSE TO CONCEDE

contend	dispute	refute
contradict	denounce	reject
deny	insist	respond
disagree	maintain	retort
discredit	question	take issue
disprove	refuse	

Having examined a problem, scholars often include warnings about the gravity/seriousness of the situation and recommend possible solutions, as in the following verbs.

TABLE 3.4

WARN

adjure	criticize	remind
admonish	denounce	reprimand
caution	decry	sanction
censure	fear	suspect
condemn	foresee	warn

RECOMMEND

advise	encourage	propose
advocate	endorse	recommend
champion	exhort	support
commend	favour	uphold
counsel	promote	urge

▌Final Thoughts on Strong Verbs

Now that you've got dead verbs on the brain, try to put the topic aside when you write your rough drafts. As we suggested in Chapter 1, it's best to freewrite without the burden of The Judge reminding you of wordiness, dead verbs, and so on. Revise for dead verbs only when the piece is done—that is, the major parts sit in proper order. Applied to a well-constructed story, essay, or research paper, verb revisions tighten up writing and emphasize actions that engage the senses in the reader. If you notice a lot of dead verbs during the revision process, transform them into concrete verbs as often as you can.

I'm not a very good writer, but I'm an excellent rewriter.
—JAMES MICHENER

EXERCISE 16 ▸ My Dead Verbs

Editing other people's writing for dead verbs is often easier than editing our own. To help you see your own writing objectively, this exercise requires you to find dead verbs in your previous assignments. Print a copy of the work you did for Assignment 1 or 2. Circle all the forms of the dead verb *to be*.

▌Peer Models for Emulation

The next peer model story takes place in school. Schools exist as communities, and as such they play a large part in defining our character. We share joys with classmates, and we fight with classmates. The teacher, as authority figure, either

rewards or disciplines us. Many good stories with interesting characters are based on the writer's experiences at school. Jennifer Lee's story below presents a complicated portrait of Chinese schools in Canada, a very particular sort of school community. Verbs play a key part in Lee's writing. Keep verbs and movement in mind as you read her story.

Going to Chinese School

BY JENNIFER LEE

I never got to see a complete line-up of Saturday morning cartoons. While Adrienne and Marie watched Casper, Alvin and the Chipmunks, and Spiderman, I went to Chinese school on Saturday mornings. Chinese brush painting classes kept me busy over the summer. Chinese speech contests and Chinese compositions kept me from going to birthday parties during the year. I was born in Canada and taught Canadian values and traditions. My parents always found a way of reminding me of my Chinese roots.

"You don't want to grow up not knowing how to read and write in your own language," said Mom.

She made me copy paragraphs out of ancient Chinese study books before I could ride bikes with Adrienne and Marie. Every time a Chinese holiday came up, Mom and Dad made my brother and me call my grandmother. We always had the same conversation.

"Wai-po how," I yelled into the phone.

"You eat supper yet?" she asked.

"Yes."

"You study in school?"

"Yes."

"Lots of homework?"

"Yes."

"Good. Nice girl."

Every year the same thing. Sometimes I just wanted to tape my voice and play it back over the phone, but Mom would get angry.

"No respect for your grandparents," she'd say.

When our grandparents' anniversary came up, Mom bought a card for my brother and me and made us write a long message in Chinese to our grandparents. I asked her if she could write the message on the card and we could just sign our names at the bottom. She looked shocked at first, and then slapped the card over my head and said "Tao yang," which means annoying or bothersome, and made me write an extra-long message.

My parents first took me to Chinese school when I was six years old. Because my mother was a teacher, she knew all the other teachers and often spoke to them to find out what I learned and what I needed improvement in. I always needed improvement.

My parents wanted me to have the best education possible, so they moved me from one Chinese school to another. They said the other teachers from the Chinese School Association were not doing their share of the work, something they called "inside politics." I didn't understand. Since I constantly changed Chinese schools, I never bothered to make friends. My friends were the kids I played soccer with during the week at Hawthorn Public School. Chinese school didn't matter to me.

When I enrolled in Quang Hwa Chinese School in Scarborough, things changed. I met Julia, Ellen, and Sandra. I was ten.

The drive from Mississauga to Scarborough seemed a lot shorter because I knew I would share jokes and secrets with Julia, Ellen, and Sandra once I got to class. I could almost memorize the route to Chinese school: pass Toys R Us, pass Labatt's Brewery, exit onto Kennedy and a right into Albert Campbell School, and we were there. Once I got to class I took my seat beside Julia and behind Ellen and Sandra. We passed notes and laughed at the guys.

"Look Jennifer, Tommy's falling asleep," said Julia. I looked over. Tommy's head slowly dropped to his chest, and then fell to the side and landed on the shoulder of the girl beside him. She freaked and pushed him to the other side. Tommy's head hung to the right in mid-air. His mouth dangled open. He snored. Julia and I looked at each other and giggled.

Sometimes we drew pictures of our teacher, Ms. Chao, as an old widow from mainland China. Once a month, she brought in tapes of some old folk songs and played them for us. We gagged at the high-pitched screeching sounds of the Chinese fiddle.

Julia, Ellen, and Sandra knew more Chinese than I did. My mother put me in the advanced class because she said the teacher was good. When an unfamiliar word came up, Julia, Ellen, and Sandra helped me with the pronunciation. Slowly, my grades improved. That year, my marks went from a C to an A topped off with two awards in composition and speech. I couldn't wait for Chinese school to start again in September.

For the first day of my second year at Quang Hwa Chinese School, I bought a new bag with pencils, paper, sharpeners and erasers. I had so much to tell Julia, Ellen, and Sandra. We took our usual seats near the back of the class and talked about where we went over the summer and we threw eraser bits at Tommy until the back of his ears turned red.

As we walked through the halls to my classroom, my mother told me Ms. Chao had been replaced by a younger teacher, Mrs. Chen. The students who had Mrs. Chen last year complained she was mean and unfair and didn't really know how to teach. I held my mother's hand as she brought me to my classroom. We arrived early.

My mother introduced me to Mrs. Chen. Mrs. Chen smiled at me. I did not like Mrs. Chen's smile. It wasn't real. My mother chatted with Mrs. Chen for a while. As they spoke, my mother's grip on my hand tightened. I could not understand what they were saying in Chinese, but I remember seeing my mother's calm features gradually change to a fixed smile and stare. Narrow lines formed between her eyebrows. Mom re-adjusted her hat and pulled her bag firmly over her shoulders. She clasped my hand even tighter and turned to me.

"Go wait in the car, Jennifer. We are going somewhere else," she said.

I obeyed.

As we drove home that night, my mother turned to my father and said, "That new teacher is unfit to teach. She said the only reason Jennifer got the awards last year was because I kept pressuring Ms. Chao. That's not true. Jennifer deserved those awards."

I looked out the window. It rained lightly. The streetlights reflected off the damp highway. We passed them one by one as we drove home. I used my finger to trace a raindrop that gently rolled down the window. I said good-bye to Julia, Ellen, and Sandra.

That night my parents decided to find another, better, Chinese School that I could go to. I wondered how far we would have to drive this time.

(Lee 48–51)

EXERCISE 17 ► Rhetorical Analysis

Write a rhetorical analysis of "Going to Chinese School." Write it conversationally, as you did for your previous rhetorical analyses. This may also be another opportunity to freewrite. Correctness does not matter in freewriting. Just get your ideas out onto the page. The following points may help you think more deeply about Lee's story:

- What detail does Lee use to show what people look like?
- List some of the concrete verbs in the story. How do they contribute to plot movement?
- Lee does use some *to be* verbs, against the general advice of this chapter. Do you think these instances are okay, or should she have edited them out? If you think she should have edited them out, then suggest concrete verbs to take their places.
- Do you think the story ends at the right moment? If not, should it be shorter or longer? How do you feel about the ending?
- Do you think this story has an argument or thesis, the way good academic writing does? If so, explain what that the overall or thesis argument may be.

Your ideas about this story should help you consider revisions for your own writing. You may also recognize similar incidents—ideal for story treatment—in your past.

The next piece of peer model writing, a research paper, deals with the issue of cultural appropriation. Graeme Scallion wrote this careful consideration of the topic in one of our second-year courses. As you read, think about Scallion's choice of verbs and how he weaves together historical narrative and the ideas of other scholars into a coherent whole.

Stealing Spirituality: The Non-Native Use of Native American Spirit Guides

BY GRAEME SCALLION

"This is what you're going to do. You're going to count back from one hundred, and when you get to about ninety-three, Red's going to start coming through, and at about ninety the transformation will have happened." Bill Urquhart counts backwards as he watches Crow, an acclaimed medium, enter into a deep trance. Urquhart has driven from his home in East Toronto to Mississauga Bay for an audience with Crow, or more importantly, her "Indian spirit guide," Red. Crow contributes to a long list of mediums who claim to exchange with Native American spirit guides. Jan Fridegard, a Swedish psychic, regularly contacted "an Indian guardian spirit, the ghost of a medicine man," (Hultkrantz 74) and the spiritualist preacher Leafy Anderson called upon the spirits of Black Hawk and Sitting Bull for guidance.

Indeed, Native American spirit guides thrive among mediums, and serve as a stamp of "spiritual authenticity" (Jenkins 11) for occult enthusiasts. But does this pattern indicate a respect for traditional Native American spirituality, or are these mediums exploiting Native Americans to make money and promote "their own beliefs and doctrines?" (11). Philip Jenkins argues that modern non-natives covet Native American spirituality and relish "the idea of the Native as Natural Mystic" (136). A miniscule fraction of the American population—in 1900, Native Americans accounted for under 0.3 per cent of the national population (7)—Native Americans are a touch of the exotic in our own backyard, and non-native lack of knowledge of Native cultures prompts this spiritual reverence. To the non-native, the Native American serves as a "guardian and guarantor" (11) of all things spiritual, and this seal of approval promotes the sales of "dream-catchers, crystals, medicine bags" (1), and other New Age paraphernalia. The lack of public knowledge about Native Americans allows mainstream America to project its own understandings and religious beliefs onto Native American practices, so non-natives can market Native spirituality in many ways.

The rise of Spiritualism in the mid-nineteenth century inspired worldwide interest in psychics and mediums. The spiritualist movement began in 1848 with Katherine and Margaretta Fox, teenaged sisters in New York who believed spirits created tapping noises around their home as a form of communication (Brandon 1–2). America delighted in these occurrences, and an industry developed around the desire to contact the Otherworld. Even those who knew little about Native American spirituality understood that "these people held strong beliefs about the supernatural" (Jenkins 12) and spiritualists became excited by the Native American ability to "cross the worlds between living and dead" (2). Occult enthusiasts especially glorified the spirits of "chiefs or medicine men who would have had a special link to the otherworld" (136) and mediums sought council with prominent spiritual leaders from history, such as Chief Sitting Bull. Native American spirituality became a tool with which to experience unearthly events, and while spiritualism slowly lost popularity, the mainstream infatu-ation with Native spirit guides flourished.

The spirits of medicine men garner ample admiration among spiritualist mediums, but how do traditional Native American medicine men interact with the spirit world? In 1955, Ake Hultkrantz witnessed a traditional sweat lodge ritual at an Arapaho reser-vation in Wyoming, an experience he recorded in his book, *Belief and Worship in Native North America*. An Oglala Sioux medicine man named Mark Big Road conducted the ritual in an effort to re-familiarize the Arapaho with the traditional *yuwipi* ceremony, in which the medicine man calls upon spirits to heal the sick. Big Road performed the ritual in a small dark cabin with "some sixty persons" present (Hultkrantz 67). The Arapaho filled the cabin with steam and drummed a steady beat as Big Road assem-bled an altar to Skadi, a spirit guide passed down to him by his father and grandfather. Two Arapaho tribesmen bound and covered Big Road with a blanket. All the while, Big Road chanted and sang to induce a state of ecstasy. Once Big Road announced Skadi's arrival, the Arapaho pleaded with the spirit to cure sick family members, present and absent. Big Road interpreted Skadi's messages for the Arapaho and closed the cer-emony with a promise that the sick would be cured (Hultkrantz 65–71).

Hultkrantz' account of the Arapaho ceremony indicates how spirit guides are used in traditional Plains tribe ceremonies. While non-native mediums have adapted these rituals, these practitioners differ in their use of Native American spirit guides. Mother Leafy Anderson provoked the black spiritualist movement in early twentieth-century New Orleans. Mother Anderson's churches, and other spiritual churches, deviated from traditional Catholic churches in the belief in and practice of healings, prophecies, spirit guides, and spirit possessions (Jacobs and Kaslow 149). While Anderson enter-tained many spirits, including dead family members and the Virgin Mary, her Native American spirit guide Black Hawk "has risen to pre-eminence" (136). Anderson's con-nection with Black Hawk inspired "Black Hawk services." Mother Anderson originally directed these rituals herself, but other churches adopted them after her death. Like the *yuwipi* ceremony, these rituals take place at night and to "a strong steady beat that is said to be associated with Indian spirits" (138). Also in tandem with the Sioux ceremony, the preacher erects an altar in honour of the spirit guide. Otherwise, these rituals lack much structure, but often the congregation burn incense, sing hymns, and dance (138–140).

While similarities exist between these rituals, Anderson's services and the beliefs behind them reflect an array of inconsistencies with the original Sioux ceremonies. Possessions, commonplace in these spiritualist ceremonies, seldom occur in Native American rituals (Hultkrantz 83). As in the ceremony performed by Mark Big Road, medicine men communicate with the spirits and pass messages on independently, rather than allowing their bodies to be overtaken and spoken through. Another contradiction: in Black Hawk services, the spirit may possess a number of congrega-tion members, either by the will of the spirits or at the command of the preacher (Jacobs and Kaslow 132). The medicine man, however, "attains his profession through an ecstatic experience in which the guardian spirits have appeared and delegated their power to him" (Hultkrantz 64) and only he may commune with the spirit world. Furthermore, one must note that Mother Anderson's churches worshipped Christ above all else, and Black Hawk was one of many Native American spirits incorporated "into the churches' hagiography as guides" (201) between the world of the living and the world of the Saints. This Christian re-appropriation of spirit guidance mirrors an endless pattern of non-natives "sampling and adopting ideas [about Native American culture] they find congenial" (Jenkins 5), and while Anderson paid homage to traditional Sioux ceremonies, her services ultimately reassigned these traditions to suit her own beliefs.

Modern mediums who use Native American spirit guides support themselves by charging fees for performing séances and readings. For her session with Bill Urquhart, the medium Crow charged $150, a common amount for the services she provides. But how does this align with the doings of traditional Plains medicine men? Mark Big Road told Ake Hultkrantz "that the spirits had imposed many taboos on him, amongst other things, the prohibition to make money in his work" (Hultkrantz 71). True, not all Plains tribes adhere to this belief, but a medicine man generally refuses monetary payment for his services.

Big Road did, however, request a spirit tribute before the ceremony could take place. Two women volunteered to have "thin slices of skin and flesh" (69) cut from their arms, and this sacrifice facilitated the arrival of Big Road's spirit guide and other spirits. Aside from her fee, Crow required no such sacrifice from Urquhart to prompt Red's arrival, though a form of tribute occurs in black spiritualist churches during Black Hawk services. Rather than pay a blood toll, however, a congregation member may purchase and light "a red votive candle to receive a special blessing from Black Hawk" (Jacobs and Kaslow 139). The preacher sells these candles in addition to passing a collection plate, and the money ultimately benefits the church.

Few modern mediums adopt the spirit tribute practice, but those who do demand not a symbolic procedure as in the *yuwipi* ceremony, but further monetary compensation. The "vast hunger for Native American spirituality" (Jenkins 1) has created a lucrative industry, but while the mediums profit from this "mass market" (4), they misrepresent traditional Native American values and practices in the process.

Though modern mediums capitalize on Native American spirituality, the characters that materialize in séances and readings are often caricatures of "the white man's Indian" (Jenkins 6). Rather than include traditional Native American names, mediums refer to their spirit guides by anglicised names that cater to non-native ignorance and perpetuate Native American stereotypes. "Time and time again we meet them," writes Ruth Brandon in *The Spiritualists*, "Raging Bull, White Feather, Pink Cloud" (37), names that have been influenced and dictated by European perspectives. Even Mother Anderson, who claimed to be half-Mohawk herself (Jacobs and Kaslow 137), referred to her spirit guides by English names. The same practice transpires in instances where the spirit speaks through the medium. During his session with the medium Crow, Bill Urquhart spoke directly to Crow's spirit guide, who identified himself as "Red, an elderly member on an Indian tribal council." Red embodies the "natural mystic" stereotype that Urquhart and other psychic fans pay to see, and the way the character identifies reveals the intent behind his existence, and for whose benefit he appears.

While certain "guides" identify as the souls of specific historical figures—Chief Sitting Bull frequently appears to non-native mediums—others appear to be unoriginal representations of the "noble savage" stereotype that are used and reused by mediums around the world. British Occult enthusiast Maurice Barbanell is one of many mediums to channel the spirit of Silver Birch. In Barbanell's words, Silver Birch is "one of those Red Indians frequently encountered in Spiritualism" (116), and many spiritualists have published self-help books under his guidance. Indeed, the majority of native spirit guides fall into one of two categories: a prominent historical figure, such as Sitting Bull or Black Hawk, or a character like Silver Birch with an established following in the psychic community. Ruth Brandon questions the "remarkably little initiative" (37) taken to come up with original characters, especially in contrast with the endless "crowd of spirits" (Hultkrantz 87) described in Sioux sweat lodge ceremonies. Many mediums, such as Leonora Piper in the late 1800s, discover their powers by attending readings as a client (207), so a medium's understanding of spirituality may be contingent on the understanding of previous mediums. In this way characters are passed down and popularized. Whatever the case, the prominence of certain figures among non-native mediums indicates a limited pool of knowledge of Native American culture.

Though the practices discussed reflect poorly upon non-natives who fawn over Native American spirit guides, the widespread infatuation with Native spirituality originates from admiration of, and interest in, the culture. As Philip Jenkins states, mainstream America once regarded Native religions and traditions as devilry and black magic (3), and the last century has seen a remarkable reversal of this perspective. The "natural mystic" stereotype may not represent or encompass Native religion as a whole, and mediums may be misusing spirit guide rituals, but there are elements of respect and honour behind these perceptions. Still, positive or negative, these stereotypes harm the Native community, and those who exploit Native American cultures for monetary or religious purposes do a great disservice to the people they admire so fondly.

Works Cited and Consulted

Barbanell, Maurice. *Spiritualism Today*. London: Jenkins, 1969. Print.

Brandon, Ruth. *The Spiritualists: The Passion for the Occult in the Nineteenth and Twentieth Centuries*. New York: Knopf, 1983. Print.

Hultkrantz, Ake. *Belief and Worship in Native North America*. Ed. Christopher Vecsey. Syracuse, NY: Syracuse UP, 1981. Print.

Jacobs, Claude F., and Andrew Jonathan Kaslow. *The Spiritual Churches of New Orleans: Origins, Beliefs, and Rituals of an African-American Religion*. Knoxville: University of Tennessee, 1991. Print.

Jenkins, Philip. *Dream Catchers: How Mainstream America Discovered Native Spirituality*. Oxford: Oxford UP, 2004. Print.

EXERCISE 18 ► Rhetorical Analysis

Write a rhetorical analysis of "Stealing Spirituality: The Non-Native Use of Native American Spirit Guides." Write it conversationally, as you did for your previous rhetorical analyses. The following points may help you think more deeply about Scallion's paper:

- List 10 strong verbs in the research paper. Are these verbs unique to academic writing or could you use them in personal narrative too?
- The paper includes quotations from academic sources. Do you find the quotations unique and interesting? Should any of them be paraphrased instead? Explain.
- What purpose do examples of history play in the paper?
- While not a personal narrative, this paper does include storytelling. Describe the stories Scallion tells. Do they help or hinder the argument?
- How economical is Scallion's writing? Do you see opportunities to edit it further for conciseness and clarity? List some examples.

Your ideas about this paper should help you consider revisions for your own writing. You may also recognize similar topics—ideal for research paper treatment—that interest you.

Assignment 3a

After freewriting the rough draft of this assignment, edit your writing not just for dead verbs but also for wordiness, as discussed in the previous chapter. Only through regular application of all the lessons to your earlier writing will you internalize these lessons.

Suggested Topics:

1) Write a narrative about an incident you have experienced in a classroom between classmates. You may be the central character, or you may have been on the periphery, watching the incident.
2) Write a narrative about an influential teacher you've had. Describe one scene that best exemplifies his or her influence on you.
3) Identify two competing academic theorists in a field or on a topic you study in class. Write a short explanation of the debate between them. Why do they disagree? Tell the story of their debate. Refer to Dominique O'Neill's academic verb list on page 82 and choose verbs to characterize their competing views.

Here are our suggestions for your writing:

- Keep the writing short—anywhere from one to four double-spaced pages. If you choose assignment topic one or two, the incident should not encompass four years of high school or one year of middle school but rather a short, specific scene or set of scenes. For the third topic, one or two pages will suffice.

- Establish location in a few sentences at the beginning of your story. Some questions you may consider include: Which school? What age? What town? Which theorists? What's the debate?

- If you choose to write a narrative, avoid a great deal of back story. You are not trying to write a novel here. When writing about school days in particular, some writers feel like they have to describe all the relationships and events leading up to the story's main incident. But readers don't need the history of the relationships between all the characters to enjoy the scene. If the action of the first scene begins more than one double-spaced page in, then you may have too much background. Assignment topic three doesn't require an introduction—jump right into the description of the debate.

- You can only write non-fiction personal narrative from your perspective. Forget describing what's going on in the minds of other people. You cannot know what other people feel or think—only what they've said or done. In other words, the feelings and thoughts of the other characters in your story can be expressed only by their physical actions, speech, and behaviour. In academic assignments, don't speculate or speak for the theorist you're discussing—quote and paraphrase them accurately.

- If you're not sure how to end the writing, keep going—perhaps the appropriate conclusion will come. If writing more doesn't help, you may need to backtrack: perhaps the perfect ending exists in what you've already written.

- After you've completed your draft, rest for a few days. Let the writing simmer. With a fresh mind, come back and edit the big points we discussed in Chapter 1. Once you've completed the big revisions—and this could take hours, days, weeks, or months—turn to the micro-level edits. Revise for wordiness and dead verbs.

- Many beginning writers tell us they have trouble identifying dead verbs in their writing. This is natural—all of these lessons will help to develop your "editor's eye" over time. If you're having trouble at this point, search for dead verbs (*to be*, etc.) using the find feature in your word processor (don't forget contractions: *it's* contains the dead verb *is* and *I'm* contains the dead verb *am*).

CHAPTER SUMMARY

In this chapter, we first argued that the verb is the most important word in a sentence. Strong verbs bring sentences to life and move stories along. However, grammar books make verbs complicated by providing too many options for modifying them. Those options obscure good verbs. Many factors influence the way verbs are formed, including moods and unusual tenses. We argued that most writers just need to pay attention to a few points about verbs. Simple past and present tenses and use of the first person will suffice for most good writing.

Many beginning writers write in fragments, which are sentences often without verbs. Maybe the writer is unaware of just what verbs are or simply doesn't realize their importance. We demonstrated that importance in several ways. While it's true that good writers sometimes use fragments, they probably also have a good understanding of grammatical sentences and use fragments to achieve a certain effect. We encouraged beginning writers to avoid fragments for now: master grammatical sentences before breaking the rules.

Two main types of verbs exist. Some show a condition or state of being while others show action. We call the action verbs concrete verbs. But even those verbs have different levels of concreteness. The most concrete verbs immediately evoke an image of action in the mind of the reader. They are quickly and easily understood.

Verbs can also be categorized by the senses to which they relate: sight, sound, taste, smell, and touch. Verbs that evoke the senses add detail and enhance the reader's experience. Some less concrete verbs, such as those ending in *–ate* or *–ize*, do not easily evoke images. They might evoke a sense of action, but those actions are not clear or routine or everyday actions. For example, *manipulate* or *equalize* are hard to see in the mind's eye. Verbs that refer to a condition or a state of being—we call them abstract or dead verbs—evoke no easy action images in the reader's mind. For example, we don't "see" anything when we read the verbs "are" or "is."

We suggested ways to edit out dead verbs, if possible, while retaining the meaning of the sentence. If no alternatives exist, then it's okay to keep them. An editor's job is to see alternatives, whether obvious or not, and to use ones that don't change the author's intended meaning.

The process of editing out dead verbs may seem picky, but an abundance of them may suggest greater problems in writing, the most severe being a tendency to generalize. Readers love specifics and details, not vagueness. Concrete verbs bring more detail to writing.

▌ Further Readings

For more about verbs:

Clark, Roy Peter. *Writing Tools: 50 Essential Strategies for Every Writer*. New York: Little, Brown and Company, 2006. Print.

For more about the craft of storytelling:

King, Stephen. *On Writing: A Memoir of the Craft*. 10th Anniversary Edition. New York: Scribner, 2010.

For more about grammar:

Kolln, Martha, and Robert Funk. *Understanding English Grammar*. 9th ed. Boston: Pearson, 2012. Print.

Active Voice

> We have not passed that subtle line between childhood and adulthood
> until we move from the passive voice to the active voice—that is, until
> we have stopped saying "It got lost," and say, "I lost it."
>
> —SYDNEY J. HARRIS

READERS PROCESS LANGUAGE FOREMOST on a conscious semantic level. When they read the sentence *Daniel threw the ball*, they process the meanings of the words to imagine a male named Daniel using his arm to send a round object through the air. These words look simple and straightforward.

Readers become confused when writers use complex words and phrasings. The sentence *David vacillated over John's obfuscation* may send readers running to their dictionaries. Wordiness and dead verbs—as we discussed before—bog readers down as they struggle to process sentences. As writers, we can appeal to readers by making it easy for them to understand our experiences and ideas.

Also affecting a sentence's level of difficulty is its underlying grammatical structure, even though most readers don't see it. You can make a stronger connection with your readers by making sure the grammatical structure of your sentences is clear. It may also help you clarify your thinking.

If you have read about or studied grammar, you may be confused or frustrated by textbook explanations of grammatical structure. They often present models of sentence structure—10 basic forms of sentences in the English language—that place certain categories of words in certain orders.

In the previous chapter, we argued for simple verb tenses. In this chapter, we argue for simplicity in terms of word order, too. There are two types of word order—active voice and passive voice—and if you understand these (how they are structured, and their effect on the reader) you'll improve the clarity and focus of your sentences.

We also recommend the enhancing factor of active voice over the interfering factor of passive voice—most of the time (we'll explain later on what we mean by *most of the time*).

Writers who don't understand the enhancing factor of the active voice often lapse into the passive voice, to the detriment of their writing. Mastering all of the grammar rules won't necessarily make you a better writer—although it will make you a more correct one. But mastering this one particular rule, we feel, will benefit your style and communication immensely.

Word Order

Simply put, passive-voice word order produces a difficult sentence that can appear incomplete or even evasive.

In the previous chapter, we argued that you should avoid sentence fragments (sentences usually without verbs) until you've mastered the basic grammatical sentence. Let's look again, then, at simple sentences with verbs, which serve writers well. (We'll deal with more complex sentences later in the book.) Some readers of this text may find this concept simple. For others, it may seem like an introduction to a new language. Regardless of which camp you fall into, bear with us for now as we go through this lesson on grammar.

Active Voice

A simple sentence in the active voice has two word-order patterns. The following equations name and number the required parts of each pattern. (You can think of the grammatical pattern underlying the sentence as the part of an iceberg sitting below the surface of the water.)

$$[1] \quad [2]$$
a) Subject + Verb

$$[1] \quad [2] \quad [3]$$
b) Subject + Verb + Direct Object

In equation (a), the subject is the "doer" of the verb's action. Consider the doer of action in these examples:

a) Joe talked.

b) David painted.

c) Kylie ran.

d) Travis smiles.

e) William slept.

f) Arianna sang.

g) Zenatha looks.

h) The dog eats.

i) The giraffe grunted.

j) The boy jogged.

The subjects *Joe, David, Kylie, Travis, William, Arianna, Zenatha, The dog, The giraffe,* and *The boy* act. That is, they do an action described by the verb: *talked, painted, ran, smiles, slept, sang, looks, eats, grunted, jogged.* These verbs are all concrete, the kind we argued for in Chapter 3. They evoke the senses and move writing along.

Subjects need not be human or animal either. Consider the things in the following sentences that function as actors:

a) The oven beeped.

b) The microwave dish circled.

c) Dad's car stopped.

d) Jamie's printer died.

e) Sammy's phone jingled.

f) A plane crashed.

g) The sign fell.

h) San Francisco shook.

i) Fredericton boiled.

j) The sidewalk cracked.

In these examples, an *oven,* a *microwave,* a *car,* a *printer,* a *phone,* a *plane,* a *sign, San Francisco, Fredericton,* and a *sidewalk* act too. This may sound a bit strange at first—how could these things act? But in grammatical terms, they do: they *beep* and *circle* and *stop* and *die* and *jingle* and *crash* and *fall* and *shake* and *boil* and *crack.* Humans and animals don't have a monopoly on action.

In both sets of examples above, the sentences are all grammatically correct: they don't require any words after the verb. That is because the verbs in these examples are, to use a term from the grammar books, **intransitive verbs.**

Now let's turn to the second equation for a simple sentence in the active voice. In this equation, the writer must add what's called an object. The object in the active voice comes after the verb.

In the following examples, the actor doesn't just act: he or she (or it) also acts upon someone or something. That something is the object—the receiver of the subject's action.

a) The awards committee named the winner.

b) The dog broke the door.

c) Carey straddled the fence.

d) Simon punched the intruder.

e) The computer sends the message.

f) Clouds blanket the sky.

g) The organization chose the CEO.

h) He grabs the suitcases.

i) William bit the dog.

j) Cyclists circled the track.

In grammar terms, the verbs in these sentences are called **transitive verbs**. They affect an object—a person, place, or thing. Some transitive verbs can function as intransitive verbs. Others work only with objects. For example, it would be ungrammatical—not to mention nonsensical—to write *The awards committee named*. Named what? Transitive verbs demand more to complete their meaning.

The second type of active voice sentence (with an object) is as effective and easy to understand as the first type (without an object). You'll find that both types, in either the simple present or past tense, will serve you well for most of your writing. Keep these two variations in mind later on as we tackle the passive voice.

The active voice places the agent of the action—the "doer"—at the start of the sentence. In narrative writing, the agent will often be a character in the story. In academic writing, the agent may be a theorist or yourself, the researcher. In either case, the agent drives the action, making the active voice a dynamic grammatical pattern.

▌ Passive Voice

In contrast to active voice, the underlying structure of passive voice is more complex. The following equation describes the required parts and the word order:

[1]		[2]		[3]		[4]		[5]
Direct Object	+	*To Be* Verb Form	+	Participle Form of a Verb	+	Optional Preposition	+	Optional Subject

Let's explain the elements in the equation:

- **Direct Object:** Instead of an actor (the subject) acting upon something, we have the receiver of the action (the object) coming first in the sentence. Think about that logic for a second: before we even know what the action is and before we even know who did the action, we meet the receiver of the action. (As we explained before, the object here is not necessarily a thing. It could be a person or an animal. *Object* is the grammatical term.)

- ***To Be* Verb Form**: Chapter 2 described *to be* verbs as dead verbs that come in forms such as *was, were, is, are, am.*
- **Participle Form of a Verb**: Participle verb forms can look like regular verb forms or they can look irregular. An irregular verb form doesn't fit the usual conjugation pattern (regular verbs are conjugated with *–s, –ed,* and *–ing* endings). Some examples of participles and their irregular forms include: *broken, worn, stolen, thrown, beaten.* (Compare those to regular verb forms like *drink, drinks, drinked, drinking*). A simple test that puts the verbs in an active voice sentence shows that they don't function the same way regular verbs do: *I broken the toy. He stolen the car. Alex thrown the ball. Sandra beaten the eggs.* These sentences remind us of how children sometimes speak before they have learned the correct tenses of verbs.
- **Optional Preposition**: We'll talk more about prepositions in the next chapter. For now, think of prepositions as linking words between parts of a sentence. Why are they optional? We'll get to that in a moment.
- **Optional Subject**: The subject acts out the verb. We'll explain why it's optional in the next section. Unlike in the active voice, the doer of the action in the full passive voice equation moves to the end of the sentence.

This all may seem complicated at first. But these elements will help you to understand the difference between active and passive voice, to see why the active voice works better in writing, and to find passive verb structures and remove them from your writing.

Now let's compare the two basic active voice equations on page 96 with the passive voice equation. A complete passive voice equation requires three more words just to complete a grammatical sentence. This adds wordiness and dead verbs, both interfering factors to good writing.

We can convert most—but not all—sentences from one voice to the other. Intransitive verb sentences affect something. That means they have a direct object, the essential first element in a passive voice sentence. Transitive active voice sentences, on the other hand, don't have objects, so you can't convert them to passive. A sentence like *The wall was white* has no object. It looks like *white* is the object, as it comes after the verb, but it's actually an adjective (not everything that comes after a verb is an object, and adjectives sometimes come after *to be* verbs—not just before nouns). In this case, the verb doesn't affect the colour.

> The active voice is usually more direct and vigorous than the passive. . . . The habitual use of the active voice . . . makes for forcible writing. This is true not only in narrative principally concerned with action, but in writing of any kind.
>
> —WILLIAM STRUNK AND E.B. WHITE

One point to remember: the passive voice equation includes *to be* verbs but the presence of *to be* verbs does not necessarily indicate passive voice. Voice does not equal tense. Passive voice requires many more grammatical elements than just a dead verb.

The following sentence, for example, is in active voice despite the existence of a *to be* verb: *The war was over.* It's active voice because the subject *The war*—the doer of the action— comes before the verb *was*.

Conversion is a technique for editing passive voice out of your writing while preserving the meaning of the sentence. The active voice transitive examples on page 98 look like these when converted to passive voice:

a) The winner was named by the awards committee.

b) The door was broken by the dog.

c) The fence was straddled by Carey.

d) The intruder was punched by Simon.

e) The message is sent by the computer.

f) The sky is blanketed by clouds.

g) The CEO was chosen by the organization.

h) The suitcases are grabbed by him.

i) The dog was bitten by William.

j) The track was circled by cyclists.

Compare these passives with their active originals. Which version do you like better? Let's pick apart these sentences to find the essential elements:

- **Objects**: *winner, door, fence, intruder, message, sky*
- **To Be Verbs**: *was, were, is, are*
- **Participles**: *named, broken, straddled, punched, sent, blanketed, chosen, grabbed, bitten, circled*
- **Optional Preposition**: *by*
- **Optional Subjects**: *awards committee, dog, Carey, Simon, computer, clouds, organization, him, William, cyclists*

What's interesting is that, in both versions, the sentences make the same essential meanings. The difference is that passive voice sentences make that meaning indirectly. In other words, if we choose active voice, we can say exactly the same thing as in passive voice but with fewer words. This is economy.

Looking at the equations, it appears at first glance that the difference between active and passive word orders is a simple reversal (just flip all parts of the active voice sentence). But that's not the case. We know that the verb will have to change to its participle. We know that we'll have to introduce an awful dead verb. What actually happens in conversion, however, is more complex than just a reversal of words, as we see in the example below.

> Active: Laura invited Nancy to a party this Saturday night.

> Incorrect: To a party this Saturday night Laura invited Nancy.

> Passive: Nancy was invited by Laura to a party this Saturday night.

The incorrect attempt at conversion just moves a phrase to the start of the sentence. It uses no *to be* verbs or participles. In this original, the subject + verb + object portion that matters to us is *Laura invited Nancy*. Only that part can be converted to passive—if we even wanted to do such an awful thing. When converting between active and passive, the elements not found in the equations usually remain in their original locations.

> The difference between an active-verb style and a passive-verb style—in clarity and vigor—is the difference between life and death for a writer.
> —WILLIAM ZINSSER

More Examples

Removing passive voice during the revision stage requires recognition: you need to be able to see the passive voice structure to remove it. All of the lessons in this book will help you develop your editor's eye; with practice, soon you'll see passives everywhere.

Here are more examples of active and passive sentences to help you see them more clearly. A simple action takes place in the following sentences:

a)   The diamonds were pilfered by the thief.

b)   The citizens were infected by the virus.

c)   A dog was poisoned by the man.

d)   The theory was developed by the theorist.

e)   The business plan was approved by the committee.

f)   John's shoes were stolen.

In these examples, the passive is less effective than the active. Passive adds two additional words to each sentence—the dead *to be* verb and the preposition *by*—violating the enhancing factor of economy.

The active voice sentence, on the other hand, places the subject first, as in these active voice versions of the passive structures listed above:

a)   The thief pilfered the diamonds.

b)   The virus infected the citizens.

c)   The man poisoned a dog.

d)   The theorist developed the theory.

e)   The committee approved the business plan.

f)   Sally stole John's shoes.

Active voice has a logic that readers easily follow: A to B to C—the doer, the action, and, optionally, the receiver of the action.

Besides contributing to wordiness, passive voice is troubling because it renders some elements—the preposition and subject, in the case of the last passive voice sentence—optional. Only thanks to the active voice did we learn that Sally stole the shoes. The removal of the optional words hides the doers of the actions—despicable actions now occur without actors. Who stole John's shoes? Imagine if we didn't have the information about who pilfered the diamonds, what infected the citizens, who poisoned the dog, who developed the theory, and who approved the business plan. Readers surely want to know.

> The best writers make the best choices between active and passive.
> —ROY PETER CLARK

In the following examples, identify which sentences are active and which are passive, and convert each sentence to its opposite before checking the answers below. In some cases you'll have to make up subjects, but do not add any new words beyond those the equations require as this may change the sentences' meanings.

a)   The money was taken.

b)   I threw the ball.

c)   Furballs are hated by cats.

d)   The light bulb was invented by Thomas Edison.

e)   This book was translated into six different languages.

f)   Huge amounts of earthworms are eaten every spring by robins.

g)   We were cheered by the news that the board meeting was cancelled by the winter storm.

h)   A mistake was made by the lawyer, and a mistrial was declared by the judge.

i)   The professor was mad because the term paper was handed in late.

Compare these converted sentences:

a)   He took the money.

b)   The ball was thrown by me.

c)   Cats hate furballs.

d)   Thomas Edison invented the light bulb.

e) The editor translated this book into six different languages.

f) Every spring robins eat huge amounts of earthworms.

g) The news that the winter storm cancelled the board meeting cheered us.

h) The lawyer made a mistake and the judge declared a mistrial.

i) The professor was mad because the student handed in the term paper late.

Despite having the same meaning as the active voice versions, the passive voice sentences create a different feeling. In the passive form, readers encounter the action before they find out who did it. They must wait, as they would for the punch line of a joke or the solution to a mystery novel, and wade through more words than needed to achieve the same understanding as the active voice versions. Delaying meaning has a place in writing but few beginning writers do it deliberately.

A full passive voice sentence makes the same meaning as its active voice version, but does it indirectly, includes dead verbs, and makes reading difficult and inefficient. Why use more words than you have to to make your point?

The active voice is used in a structure known as a **right-branching sentence**. In this form, word order is straightforward and logical, making the subject matter easy to follow. Right-branching sentences have focus, and are emphatic in their simplicity. If you want to draw your reader's attention to your point, use an active voice sentence that says one point. No reasonably educated English reader will skip over or misunderstand that kind of sentence.

Much writing contains sentences that start not with a subject but with a modifying phrase. Consider these sentences:

a) When I went to class, I showed up on time.

b) Considering the lack of theory and the few research studies, this paper creates a new map of the field.

c) Actively promoting the new brand, we will send associates out to our customers.

Here subject and verbs do not begin the sentences; they sit buried in the middles. The modifying phrases at the start of each sentence force the reader to wait to the get to the key point. The reader must essentially hold the modifier in working memory and then apply it to the clause that follows it. That's unnecessary brain work—always make it easy on the reader through the ordering of words. A better option is to start the sentences with the subject and verb, as shown in the examples below:

a) I showed up on time when I went to class.

b) The field has a lack of theory and few research studies so this paper creates a new map of the field.

c)   We will send associates out to our customers to actively promote the new brand.

> Never use the passive where you can use the active.
> —George Orwell

Why do writers avoid starting sentences with subjects and verbs? When subject and verb are at the head of the sentence, meaning is bare and clear, open for criticism. Writers feel naked and exposed. We start with modifying phrases to hide ourselves, to avoid judgement, just as we do with wordiness. The problem is that this introduces a sense of hesitancy into our writing, a heaviness that weighs down the beginnings of sentences. However, the front part of the sentence works better when you foreground the doer of the action. The most valuable real estate in the sentence is the start—don't waste it.

Occasionally writers complain about active voice sentences: *The sentences are too simple. I'll sound like a kid when I write!* This is a natural response. When we were kids, we spoke simply and communicated clearly. As we got older, we felt pressured to write more complex constructions to meet our assumptions about academic or business discourses. Increasingly, however, people realize that even those discourses can be simple and straightforward. Indeed, readers enjoy academic and business writing that communicates clearly. Complex constructions are fine but when they dominate the writing and weigh it down, edit them.

At this point in your writing, you should simplify and clarify, moving away from complex sentences that require full, constant concentration for readers to follow. With active voice sentences, we're arguing for a move toward simplicity as an initial step in writing. Once you've tried out these simple sentences in your stories, you can bring back complexity and still project clarity. We'll talk more about that in Chapters 7 and 8.

EXERCISE 19 ▸ Active/Passive Conversion

It's one thing to read these lessons and quite another to put them into practice. This exercise will help you to add practice to theory.

Write 10 sentences in active voice. Then beneath each sentence, write its passive version. Next, write 10 completely new passive voice sentences. Then beneath each sentence, write its passive version. Write several of your sentences so that the passive form evades something unsavoury or uncomfortable. If you're having trouble converting a sentence or if the conversion seems overly awkward, determine whether it has an object. You cannot convert active voice sentences that don't have objects: they are essential for the passive voice. Do not add any words or roots of words that do not exist in the original.

The Morality of Passive Voice

The previous example of Sally and John's shoes seems relatively innocent. Why does it matter if it's written in passive or active voice if it means the same thing either way?

We've already given a technical justification for eliminating the passive voice: it adds more words to a sentence. A greater issue, however, exists in many cases: the morality of passive voice when the sentence doesn't include two elements, the optional preposition and doer of the action. Removing the two elements serves more serious purposes, as shown in the next example. Imagine a writer stating the following:

> The village was bombed and seven children were killed.

In this case, the objects of the verbs—the village and the children—take centre stage while the perpetrator of these murderous actions remain obscured. Who bombed the village and killed the children? The government? Terrorists? The reader wants to know. The absence of actors raises questions in the minds of readers and can make them mistrust you. In other words, use of the passive voice arouses readers' suspicions. The honest, direct, active voice version of this sentence would be this:

> Here's a life tool: always apologize in the active voice.
> —ROY PETER CLARK

> Government planes bombed the village and killed seven children.

People often use the passive when they want to evade responsibility. Consider the following examples of a boss giving a termination notice to an employee:

> Dear Sean Partridge,
>
> Please note that your position in the company has been eliminated. No other position for you has been found. Details about severance packages will be sent to your home address.
>
> Sincerely,
> William Thompson

The passive creates more questions than it answers. The boss does not say who eliminated Sean's position, who tried to find another position for him, or who will mail out the severance package. This last detail is particularly important: if Sean doesn't receive the package, he'll need to track down the sender. Who will send it? Passive voice allows all of these doers of serious actions to disappear.

The next letter shows a tax official using passives to deny a person's request:

> Dear Kristy Bolan,
>
> Thank you for your request for leniency regarding the payment of your 2012 taxes. The request was reviewed and denied on the grounds that

the deadline for application was missed. The tax payable will have to be submitted immediately. If you fail to submit your taxes within seven days, your wages will be garnisheed.

Yours Truly,
Matilda Eve Baker

What questions remain for Kristy thanks to the official's use of passive voice? Ms. Baker doesn't say who reviewed and denied the request. Was it her or someone above her? Without details of the doer of the action, Kristy can't assume it was Baker. The letter also doesn't state who will approve the garnisheeing of Kristy's wages. The effect of passive here is to diffuse authority. Sometimes this kind of diffusion serves a purpose—business writing textbooks, for example, favour passive over active for relaying bad news; it can help soften the impact of unpleasant news, particularly news that isn't a result of the writer's own decision. However, deliberately employing the passive voice to downplay responsibility in decision-making can be unethical.

Revealing the doer of action (i.e., use of the active voice) allows the reader to confront the writer; using the passive voice without the optional subject makes this difficult. Even young children know how to use the passive voice to escape this confrontation—for example, "The cookie jar was broken, Mommy." The honest, direct approach for the child is to speak in the active voice: "I broke the cookie jar, Mommy." This certainly won't help the child avoid responsibility, but the mother will respect the child's candour. Most people using passive voice, however, aren't dealing with childish mistakes. With power—in business or politics—comes the obligation to take responsibility for actions that affect others.

The Permanence of Passive in Various Fields

Passive voice still finds a home in science, academic, and journalistic writing. Let's look at some common examples. A scientist deliberately writes the following in a lab report:

A limited sample was taken and tentative conclusions were drawn.

The scientist removes the optional preposition and subject to appear objective—as if no human subjectivity affected the taking of the sample and the drawing of conclusions. Of course, we know science is not perfect and the human element never disappears. Similarly, the passive voice in academic writing may take this form:

The subject was roundly criticized.

In this case, the reader naturally wants to know who did the criticizing, but the author hasn't provided that information. A citation would help the reader track down the sources that lead to this statement. In the next example, a historian writes

> The document was found in the archives of the university.

Here the writer does not want to suggest that he or she found the document—that wouldn't be "objective." We believe, however, that saying in active voice *I found the document in the archives of the university* does not tarnish the image of the academic as objective.

Next, a journalist writes

> Citizens were asked about their thoughts on the budget.

This construction hides the fact that the journalist asked the citizens about their thoughts while appealing to the norm of objectivity in journalism. However, journalism scholars have thoroughly critiqued objectivity as an impossible goal— can a subjective human reporter ever cover an issue from a completely objective position? Can a single newspaper article contain all the points of view and information required to satisfy the demands of objectivity? On the other hand, writing *I asked the citizens their thoughts on the budget* places the subjectivity of the writer in the foreground and admits that the questions themselves are subjective. This approach is honest.

Should the human element in the writing about these fields disappear? We believe that admitting human subjectivity is one step towards ethical writing— writing that reveals all the elements that factor into its development.

EXERCISE 20 ▸ Passive in Publications

To further develop your eye for passives, this exercise requires you to find a newspaper article that includes a great deal of passive voice. Skim through the article, highlight all the passive sentences, and identify their subjects. Can you identify them all or must you guess at them? How much information about doers is lost? Do you think the writer used the passives on purpose, or did he or she simply not know who did the actions?

EXERCISE 21 ▸ Buried Subjects and Verbs

Find a patch of writing that buries its subjects and verbs in the middle of sentences. Textbooks or academic journal articles usually do this. Find five of these kinds of sentences and revise them to push the subjects and verbs to the heads of the sentences.

Openness and Honesty in Active Voice

In 2008, many people across Canada became sick after eating tainted meat. Agencies traced the problem back to meat sold by Maple Leaf Foods, a major Canadian company. Of the 57 cases of illness after eating the tainted meat, 22 consumers died. The problem was listeriosis, a bacterial infection. The company's machines had become contaminated with listeria bacteria. Soon after being notified of the source, Maple Leaf Foods recalled products from grocery stores and shut down its plant in Toronto.

With the problem contained, the company set out to control the crisis and limit potential damage to its image and share price. CEO Michael McCain became the spokesperson for a wide-ranging media campaign that public relations professionals consider one of the best responses to crisis in Canadian history.

Part of the response included television commercials where McCain made an authentic—but surely carefully written—statement to the public about the listeria crisis and the company's work to solve it.

Let's take a look at the role of active voice in McCain's speech to Canadians. McCain's delivery of the script was natural. He looked like he cared. As well, we believe a factor in the success of the commercial was the way he and his public relations advisors wrote it. Keep an eye on the subjects and verbs in this speech:

> As you may know, listeria was found in some of our products. Even though listeria is a bacteria commonly found in many foods and in the environment, we worked diligently to eliminate it. When listeria was discovered in the product, we launched immediate recalls to get it off the shelf, and then we shut the plant down. Tragically, our products have been linked to illnesses and loss of life. To Canadians who are ill and to the families who have lost love ones, I offer my deepest sympathies. Words cannot begin to express our sadness for your pain. Maple Leaf Foods is 23,000 people who live in a culture of food safety. We have an unwavering commitment to keeping your food safe with standards well beyond regulatory requirements. But this week our best efforts failed and we are deeply sorry. This is the toughest situation we've faced in a hundred years as a company. We know this has shaken your confidence in us. I commit to you that our actions are guided by putting your interests first. (McCain)

Here are some of the active voice subject + verb constructions in the speech:

We worked ... We launched ... We shut ... I offer ... Our best efforts failed ... We are deeply sorry ... We know ... I commit ...

As a food producer, Maple Leaf Foods has a particularly important obligation to its customers. The crisis showed that food contamination costs lives. Maple Leaf isn't selling shoes here. McCain had a much more important duty. By using these active voice sentences, McCain does not shirk his duty to his customers. Rather, he stands openly in front of his customers, both in the writing style and in his videotaped speech. He admits failure, apologizes, and asks for forgiveness. The use of the subject *we* implies the team works with him. He's not alone. The use of the subject *I* shows that he takes responsibility as the leader of the company. He does not place blame on employees or the contaminated machinery used to process the meat. He also covers a great deal of ground in the economical style demanded by a short commercial: He explains what listeria is, he mentions the recalls, he recognizes the loss of life, he acknowledges the damage done, he promises to keep food safe, he offers an apology, and he commits to improvements. He couldn't have spoken any more directly or comprehensively.

You probably noticed that McCain's script is not completely in the active voice. McCain uses passive voice in these sentences too:

a) Listeria was found in some of our products
b) When listeria was discovered in the product
c) Our products have been linked to illnesses and loss of life

What possible active alternatives exist to these passives?

a) Inspectors found listeria in some of our products
b) When inspectors discovered listeria in the product
c) Tests have linked our products to illnesses and loss of life

These active voice alternatives are excellent because they're direct and clear. However, the passives work fine too, in this context, since they don't seem intended to hide information. In these cases, the damage, the bacteria, and the fouled products still remain prominent. The discoverer of the listeria bacteria is not as important as the listeria bacteria itself. McCain's use of the passive voice creates no ethical problem here.

EXERCISE 22 ▸ Passive Conversion

Imagine if McCain had instead used the passive always and spoken indirectly to his audience. In this exercise, we want you to do exactly that: take McCain's original text and convert each active voice element into passive voice. Remember that some active voice constructions lack objects and you will not be able to simply convert them to passive. But try to convert as many instances as possible. When you've finished, read the two versions out loud and consider the effect of passive voice in speaking to victimized audiences.

▌ Is It Ever Okay to Use Passive?

Earlier in the chapter, we said you should use active voice most of the time. Some exceptions do exist. Don't robotically convert every passive into active. In the revision stage, you need to judge each case's unique circumstances because in some situations, the passive actually works better than the active. For example, a writer may choose to emphasize the object of a sentence in this way:

> The Confederation Bridge was opened in 1997.

This passive does not include the optional preposition *by* and the optional subject, raising the question of who opened the bridge. But such information is unimportant here. No one person opened the bridge—it was a group effort. The active voice version could be

> Dignitaries opened the Confederation Bridge in 1997.

But this de-emphasizes the bridge—its opening is no longer the key point of the sentence. Instead, the emphasis is on the dignitaries, which clouds the picture. Keep the passive word order to focus on the bridge.

Just as the bridge itself was the focus of the example above, discussions about inventions often take place in the passive voice to focus on the invention rather than the inventor. Consider this example of a recent technology:

> The Segway, a personal vehicle, was introduced in 2001.

The passive construction begs the question: who introduced the Segway? Well, Dean Kamen, the inventor, did. If we're more interested in Dean Kamen himself, we can write the sentence using active voice:

> Dean Kamen introduced the Segway, a personal vehicle, in 2001.

But if he's not that important to our writing, then the passive construction works well to keep the focus on the Segway.

Writers may choose to employ passive because they honestly don't know who the doer of the action is. The following well-known example reflects this case.

> American President John F. Kennedy was assassinated today in Dallas.

On that day in 1963, nobody knew the identity of the shooter (and to this day, debate continues about who did it, despite the conviction of Lee Harvey Oswald) so journalists naturally used the passive voice to place emphasis on the assassination itself. Today, a historian may deliberately choose to use the passive to emphasize the president and the action of the killer:

> American President John F. Kennedy was assassinated by Lee Harvey Oswald in 1963.

The passive word order is, we hope, chosen carefully. The writer should first consider the active and use the passive only for emphasis. Imagine a book or TV show not about presidents but about political assassinations in history. A writer may want to emphasize the assassins. With the shooter's identity clear, the writer could say the following:

Lee Harvey Oswald shot John F. Kennedy in 1963.

A clear reason sits behind the writer's choice of active voice. Another example shows a passive that we've come to accept as the norm:

Sandra was born in 1983.

Who's the doer of the action here? Well, of course it's Sandra's mother Helen. Sandra is the object of the action of giving birth. While we generally prefer active voice, it would be absurd to convert this passive into active voice just for the sake of rules:

Helen bore Sandra in 1983.

How do we know not to apply the conversion here? Because our ears tell us. Nobody describes births using the verb *bore*. It's awkward. People who want to emphasize the doer usually say, in the active voice, *She gave birth to twins*. This is not the same as *She bore twins* but it sounds more natural to us. Use your ears to tell you when phrasings are correct.

> An essential element for good
> writing is a good ear:
> One must listen to the sound
> of one's own prose.
> —BARBARA TUCHMAN

Now that you've seen these examples of exceptions, keep them in mind when you're editing. You may also come across other types of passive that we haven't discussed here. That's good—it means you understand the underlying grammatical structure of sentences. It also means you're editing consciously, not robotically, testing each case as you go along. The various types of passive voice may work perfectly well depending on the context. But maybe they'd work even better in the active voice.

Academic Writing and Active Voice

Active voice remains just as useful for academic writing as for any other mode of writing. Yet many academic writers fall into a bad habit of passive voice. For example, students who don't find out the doers of actions use passive voice as a tactic to avoid more research. Passive voice hides the missing information. Often the solution is to do more research and answer the question *Who did what*? For example, consider this general statement common in academia:

The critical philosophy movement was recognized as important by the 1930s.

Some academics caution against such statements because they generalize too much and hide important information. The active voice revision reinstates that important information:

> Williamson, Davidson, and the wider scholarly community recognized the critical philosophy movement as important by the 1930s.

The revised sentence proves that the writer knows exactly who did the recognizing—it's detailed and specific. It also places emphasis on the verb, the main point of the sentence: recognition.

Passives also surface in academic writing because of the bias against using the pronoun *I*. Pseudo-objectivity reigns, and using *I* becomes a sort of academic sin. However, despite what you may have heard, scholars disagree on the issue. Some academic journals—which take submissions of articles from researchers—publish articles that use *I*.

The ban on *I* typically causes students to create awkward passive voice phrases, like this one:

> It will be shown by this paper that the Germans wrongly assumed the debt.

In avoiding the personal pronoun, the writer must employ an antecedent-less pronoun (we explain antecedents and pronouns in the next chapter) at the start of the sentence and the passive word order. The result is a needlessly long sentence that sounds unnatural—you wouldn't speak this way in regular conversation, would you? Two options exist for a revision, one that uses *I* and one that does not:

> I will show that the Germans wrongly assumed the debt.

This option is concise and straightforward and does not hide behind pseudo-objectivity. If your instructor bristles at the pronoun, we have another option that works just as well: just change the doer of the action of showing.

> This paper will show that the Germans wrongly assumed the debt.

Here the sentence emphasizes the paper, not its author. Whichever option you choose in the final copy, we believe you should still draft academic papers using *I*. This approach allows writers to focus on straightforward, clear, active voice sentences. Cultural historian Robert Darnton felt comfortable using the first person in his famous chapter about the history of reading. He speaks of his research process:

> I ran across a solidly middle-class reader in my own research on eighteenth-century France. He was a merchant from La Rochelle named Jean Ranson and an impassioned Rousseauist. (4)

If Darnton is allowed to use *I*, we all should be. Using the first person pronoun also reminds writers of their personal conviction about—and interest in—the subject. Even though it's an academic paper, it is still a personal project to you. Phrases like *I think* and *I believe* make the writer take a personal stake in the content because they foreground one's subjectivity. You cannot be disengaged from the subject when you use *I*.

If a teacher or an editor refuses to accept the personal pronoun, just edit it out when your paper is complete:

> Original: I argue that the United Nations acts weakly towards countries that violate its rules.

> Revised: The United Nations acts weakly towards countries that violate its rules.

In the revised sentence, the *I* is implied—we know from your name on the title page of the paper that these opinions come from you.

> I almost always urge people to write in the first person. . . . Writing is an act of ego and you might as well admit it.
> —WILLIAM ZINSSER

Final Thoughts on Active and Passive

Even though rare exceptions exist to our rules, it's still important to remove passive voice as often as possible. Most of the time writers unknowingly and excessively employ passive voice when a better active voice option exists. This is not a small matter. Author William Zinsser said a succession of passive voice sentences "will sap the reader's energy" (67). As you follow through the lessons in this book, it's easy to use the exceptions as an excuse to fall back to old ways. Don't fall back to using passive voice out of laziness.

Finally, we believe the benefit of active voice goes beyond just the important goal of improving communication for readers. Many of our students report that this lesson on the underlying structure of sentences and word order helps them think and speak more clearly. They think in active voice. They speak to friends in the active voice. Clarity of mind develops. When applied regularly, an attention to active voice improves your writing, thinking, and speaking.

Peer Models for Emulation

The next peer model story, on family life, takes place on a trip. Many of us travel to new places, places that present different cultures and languages. If you have travelled, consider writing about an incident that happened in one of the places you visited. Nabila Rizvi's "Jafar Uncle's Chocolates" combines a unique location with detailed story about one of her relatives. With this chapter's lesson in mind, you may want to look out for how Rizvi uses active voice to move the story along and create clarity.

Jafar Uncle's Chocolates

BY NABILA RIZVI

I cross the quiet courtyard of our village house and follow the pathway of the clothes-line that hangs above me. I count the black birds perched along the white rope. I swiftly move past the henna leaf tree and the rusty hand-pump. Drips of water fall to the ground from the spout. I step onto the veranda, see sleepy relatives under the whir of ceiling fans, and decide where to go next.

Indian heat peaks in the afternoon, so everyone sleeps for an hour after lunch. But I prefer not to surrender, and instead I wander around the house.

I hope no one catches sight of me as I tiptoe into the nearest room. The white and royal blue curtains fall back into place in the doorway, and I look around. My grandmother furnished her room simply with a rickety bed, a bookshelf decorated with aged scratches, and an off-white wooden wardrobe.

The wardrobe, with its hidden treasures. I walk towards it, and just as I gently slide open the door to reach for the cardboard box of chocolates, Jafar Uncle laughs from behind me, "Nabila, *choripakargayee*—I caught you!"

Jafar Uncle reaches over my head to the stash of goodies and takes some out of the box. He holds out a handful to me. Neatly encased in purple wrapping with "Dairymilk" printed across it, the gold foil that peeks out from the edges begs me to open it. In our simple village, the shiny purple wrapping looks extraordinary.

"*Chocolate chaahiye?*" he asks with a smile. Our soft laughter mingles with the chirps of birds from the courtyard.

Like an older brother, Jafar Uncle watches out for me and lets the little kid from Canada tag along everywhere he goes. Jafar Uncle: the hard worker who goes out of his way to comfort everyone, the efficient thinker who can solve any problem, the well-mannered guy who easily makes everyone smile, and the unique person who gets along with everyone—children, adults, and the elderly—no matter what their background.

Although we live on opposite sides of the world and meet after years, he still manages to show his care when he jokes, plays games, and surprises me. Whenever he greets us at the airport, he always slips a Dairymilk bar into my hand. Over time, this phrase became exclusively ours: "*Chocolate chaahiye?*"

* * *

The next time I step out of Indira Gandhi Airport my happiness takes over just like the last time. I breathe in the familiar smell of polluted air, see poor people snoring on the side streets under the dark early morning sky, and hear the cacophony of voices as rickshaw drivers and chai vendors shout out to potential customers.

I spot him—Jafar Uncle eagerly moves forward to greet us. One by one he meets my parents and my siblings. When he reaches me, he smiles, "*Chocolate chaahiye?*"

Sure, a 16-year-old may not jump excitedly at a chocolate bar—but I still feel touched as ever by his thoughtfulness.

* * *

I land in India again, a year later. Jafar Uncle does not pick my family up from the airport. We pile into a car for the long drive to our village. I want the road to go on forever so that I do not have to step into our house of mourning.

The road ends too soon. The cries of Jafar Uncle's two-year-old daughter—Hania—reach our ears outside the house. The sound distracts from my thoughts of his last car ride and of the moments before his car flipped over three times and crashed. I cannot think of that right now—I need to comfort his daughter.

All our relatives crowd together in the courtyard as they try to console one another. In the centre, Jafar Uncle's wife sits with a blank expression, and tears roll down her cheeks. My grandmother sits beside her, her hand over her mouth in an effort to control her sobs.

Hours later, exhausted from grief, my youngest uncle shows us to our room. No one knows what to say, or whether to say anything at all. My uncle hesitates, then looks at me and says, "*Choc*—." His voice breaks. He does not continue, but places the new box on the window ledge and leaves.

I never want to eat them again, but I find myself in front of the window ledge. My mind floods with memories of Jafar Uncle. I take a chocolate bar and look for Hania. I find her seated on a rope-weave cot. She turns her tear-stained face up to me. I take a deep breath and put on a little smile for her.

"Hania—*chocolate chaahiye*?"

EXERCISE 23 ▶ Rhetorical Analysis

Write a rhetorical analysis of "Jafar Uncle's Chocolates." Keep your writing conversational, as always. If you find you're writing the same ideas as you did in previous rhetorical analyses, you may have to think more deeply about the story. Sometimes writers get into a rut. That's natural. Thinking about how you would have written the story yourself may help you break out of it. The following questions and points may also help you:

- The phrase *chocolate chaahiye* is an important detail in the story—explain why.
- Rizvi includes three scenes. Do you think they are all necessary to the greater story? Which scene is most important?
- Find five examples of active voice sentences and convert them to passive voice. What effect does the passive voice create?
- Rizvi wrote this story when she was an adult. How does Rizvi's story still evoke a child's perspective?
- Pick out three details that show rather than tell.

Now let's look at a research paper written by a student, Sara Menuck, who went through a course based on the strategies described in this book. How has Menuck applied the lessons of this chapter?

A Flourishing of Humans

BY SARA MENUCK

In his 1996 essay "Global Hunger: Moral Dilemmas," Nigel Dower makes a compelling case for why alleviating hunger, as a crucial component to human well-being and flourishing, is the moral obligation of those with the ability to take action. He states that "there is at present more than enough food in the world for no one to be hungry" (6). This statement echoes poignantly in light of the current food crisis locally, nationally, and globally. In 2004, 10.7 per cent of Toronto households reported being food insecure ("The State of Toronto's Food" 7). A 2007 Health Canada survey showed that food insecurity affects nearly one in ten Canadian households (Novek and Nichols 10). Over one billion people in the world are desperately hungry (Holt-Gimenez 593). Dower argues that not being hungry is a critical condition for flourishing of human life, and except for outstanding situations, it can be readily avoided in most communities that have enough food to feed all community members—if only those able to provide it are made aware of the situation and are willing to take action (Dower 9). The question, then, evolves into not simply whether we will allow hunger to persist, but what tangible steps can be taken to stop it? In this paper, I argue that fostering food sovereignty in the form of urban gardening is a necessary and crucial step in addressing the global food crisis, pragmatically, economically and socially.

Food sovereignty was first defined in 1996 by La Via Campesina, an international peasant federation, as "people's right to healthy and culturally appropriate food produced through ecologically sound and sustainable methods, and their right to define their own food and agriculture systems" (Holt-Gimenez 595). Neva Hassanein develops the closely related concept of "food democracy," or the idea that "people can and should be actively participating in shaping the food system . . . having the power to determine agro-food policies and practices locally, regionally, nationally, and globally" (464). Food sovereignty relates strongly to food security, the concept that every individual has a right to affordable, nutritious, and culturally appropriate food, but it takes a step further to advocate the individual's role in the food system. The individual is not merely a consumer but an active and powerful participant. Thus, food is not only a human right but also a human responsibility.

As food has become increasingly a commodity, however, this responsibility has been lifted from the hands of the public to rest "increasingly in fewer hands . . . In the middle [of food producers and food consumers] is a bottleneck representing a small number of companies that control the flow of goods" ("The State of Toronto's Food" 7–8). The average consumer has become alienated from the source and process that brought the food to their table. It's not that they no longer care about where their food came from; where their food comes from doesn't even enter into the equation anymore. In a study of small, sustainable farms in rural Canada and the UK, Larch Maxey noted that actively struggling to maintain the farm's success "helped reaffirm participants' conscious, shared commitment to run the farms sustainably in many respects" (50). Consumers who have no real stake or say in their food are at a definite loss: when we don't have to work for our food, we become apathetic. In this situation, as Dower's argument in the opening of this essay suggests, we choose not to take the moral action on issues such as hunger.

A second major concern about the current climate of the food system is urbanization. The United Nations estimated that in 2007 "the world became more urban than rural for the first time in history" (Gross 72). In the past, many discussions surrounding food systems and sustainability revolved around farms in a rural setting. I argue that this is no longer a relevant discussion. Toronto Public Health's report "The State of Toronto's Food" cites a Waterloo Region Public Health survey that found that "of 58 commonly eaten foods, all of which could be grown or raised locally, the average food travelled 4,497 km to reach stores in their region" (14). This despite that Toronto sits on some of the best agricultural land in Ontario (3), and that Toronto offers considerable agricultural potential, with green space making up to 18 per cent of Toronto's land area and 5,000 hectares of rooftop space being available across the city that could be utilized for rooftop gardening (10). But despite its potential resources for food production and food supply, Toronto has, on average, only enough fresh food available to last three days, should we experience a food supply crisis (13).

To quote such a statistic, however, overlooks that we are in a food crisis *now*: a crisis of hunger in a society in which food is already abundant, and in which food is abundantly wasted. The 2009 report released by the Value Chain Management Centre showed that people waste 1.3 billion tons of food produced for human consumption each year, which amounts to 122 kg of waste per person at the consumer and retail level—the largest portion coming from households (Tucker 2012). Much of this food is still edible, leading to the rise of such movements as "freeganism," a concentrated collective of individuals who actively reject consumer culture and subsist solely on the waste of society primarily through the practice of "dumpster diving" (searching through dumpsters for edible, nutritious food that has simply been wasted) (Gross 79).

Much of the problem is that increasingly urbanized consumer populations find themselves increasingly alienated from their food supply, a food supply largely imported from somewhere else. No connection exists between the consumer and the products on retail or kitchen shelves. Cities such as Toronto enjoy an abundance of food, but they are entirely food dependent as well: they have no means of supporting themselves, nor do consumers have any connection to their food. Hundreds of thousands of people, despite all this abundance of food, go hungry. We find ourselves in a culture of excess: excessive hunger, excessive food, and exorbitantly excessive waste. Much has been said on the subject of food and food crises, from eloquent inquiries such as Dower's into the moral duty to the hard facts outlined by the Toronto Public Health Department. However, not a lot has been said on concrete, viable steps that can be taken to begin to correct the situation.

I submit the following proposition: instead of focusing on the continued effort to alleviate hunger through food aid, which, in Dower's words, only continues to "create dependency, undermining development/self-reliance in the long run and distorting local markets" (Dower 6), instead of continuing to import billions of tons of food from foreign or far-away food producers, instead of passively allowing food production and supply to become further and further removed from consumers, we need to focus on creating a thriving, flourishing urban initiative to create food self-sufficiency through food sovereignty. Simply handing food to the poor and the hungry is not a solution. Giving them money to buy more food is not a solution, either. Nor is the problem that we need more food. The problem is where we get food from, who supplies it, and the apathy and ignorance fostered by a consumer culture in which we have no connection with our food. La Via Campesina emphasized that "solutions to the food crisis [must] be completely independent of the institutions responsible for creating the crisis in the first place [namely large corporations] ... there is an urgent need to increase ... adoption of locally appropriate and democratically controlled agroecological methods of production, relying on local expertise, local germplasm and farmer-managed, local seed systems" (Holt-Gimenez 597). One tangible way of doing this is to focus efforts on food-sovereign urban and community gardens in particular.

Community gardens are defined as "plots of urban land on which community members can grow flowers or foodstuffs for personal or collective benefit ... Though often facilitated by nonprofit organizations, apartment complexes, or grassroots associations, community gardens nevertheless *tend to remain under the control of the gardeners themselves*" (Novek and Nichols 31). The latter half of the definition identifies a key factor. Placing food supply back in the hands of consumers fosters a recursive relationship between consumer and producer in which both sides are one and the same, effectively eliminating the "bottleneck effect" identified by the State of Toronto's Food report. Recall Maxey's findings that involvement with farming even, or perhaps particularly in times of struggle, reaffirmed participants' commitment to their efforts (Maxey 50). This draws upon the Actor-Network Theory concept of translation, or the "process by which actors come together to create and maintain a forum or central network"—in this case, the central network is sustainable, healthy, local food networks (43).

Dower succinctly identifies the problem of food as the following: "The reason why the hungry are hungry is that they do not have access to food, because they do not grow it, do not have the economic power to acquire it, or are not given it or the money to buy it" (Dower 6). Essentially, hunger persists because the hungry are helpless against a system dominated by large corporations ("The State of Toronto's Food" 8) and distances from their food source.

Community gardens emerge as an obvious first step to alleviate this situation. They directly address issues of food accessibility and affordability faced by low-income and food-insecure households. Gardens are relatively low-maintenance but incredibly abundant. Fresh produce is often cited as too expensive for most low-income households to consider a worthwhile purchase; however, much produce will flourish with little effort, saving households considerable money. As an urban initiative, urban community gardens also address the problem of increasing food miles and dependency on outside food sources and suppliers. As cited by the "State of Toronto's Food" report, Toronto already has considerable resources, agriculturally and spatially, to accommodate an increased focus on urban gardening. A network of community and backyard gardens becomes the first step to reducing food dependency and creates a thriving, self-sufficient local food system. Putting food production back in the hands of food consumers naturally resolves at least part of the problem of waste. The investment participants make in their gardens, both physically and emotionally, would inherently lead to less waste: as both consumer and producer, the gardener would be reluctant to waste the literal fruits of his or her labour.

Community gardens literally lay the groundwork for a more connected community, both to its food supply and to itself. As Laura Lawson notes in her case study of a community garden in Los Angeles, California, community gardens provide "food, nutrition, household income savings, recreation, social interaction, and a place to carry on agricultural traditions" (Lawson 90). Community gardens take advantage of existing urban space, revitalizing the concept of "local" food in a dynamic way. Creating sustainable, local food systems centred on self-sufficient, food-sovereign consumers answers the initial question of Dower's about how to motivate a population to address moral crises such as hunger. Bridging the gap between consumer and producer, eliminating the consumer's dependence on external, often far-removed food sources and fostering food sovereignty re-invests the consumer in the food system and encourages a more sustainable attitude towards food, in its production and consumption. Facing millions of people who go hungry in a society abundant with food, community gardens offer a viable solution—and one that we should not neglect.

Works Cited

Dower, Nigel. "Global hunger: moral dilemmas." *Food Ethics*. Ed. Ben Mepham. London, UK: Routledge, 1996. 1–17. Print.

Maxey, Larch. "Can We Sustain Sustainable Agriculture? Learning from Small-scale Produce-Suppliers in Canada and the UK." *Taking Food Public*. Ed. Psyche Williams-Forson and Carole Counihan. New York: Routledge, 2012. 41–58. Print.

Gross, Joan. "Capitalism and Its Discontents: Back-to-the-Lander and Freegan Foodways in Rural Oregon." *Taking Food Public*. Ed. Psyche Williams-Forson and Carole Counihan. New York: Routledge, 2012. 71–87. Print.

Lawson, Laura. "Cultural Geographies in Practice. The South Central Farm Dilemmas in Practicing the Public." *Taking Food Public*. Ed. Psyche Williams-Forson and Carole Counihan. New York: Routledge, 2012. 88–93. Print.

Hasanein, Neva. "Practicing Food Democracy: A Pragmatic Politics of Transformation." *Taking Food Public*. Ed. Psyche Williams-Forson and Carole Counihan. New York: Routledge, 2012. 461–74. Print.

Holt-Gimenez, Eric. "From Food Crisis to Food Sovereignty: The Challenge of Social Movements." *Taking Food Public*. Ed. Psyche Williams-Forson and Carole Counihan. New York: Routledge, 2012. 592–602. Print.

Toronto Public Health. *The State of Toronto's Food: Discussion Paper for a Toronto Food Strategy*. Toronto, ON: City of Toronto, 2008. Print.

Novek, Joel and Nichols, Carol. *Eat Where You Live: Building a Social Economy of Local Food in Western Canada*. Saskatoon, SK: Centre for the Study of Co-operatives, 2010. Print.

Tucker, Erika. "By the numbers: Food waste." *Global News*. Shaw Media, 3 Oct. 2011. Web. 21 Mar. 2013. http://globalnews.ca/news/293299/by-the-numbers-food-waste/

EXERCISE 24 ▸ Rhetorical Analysis

Write a rhetorical analysis of "A Flourishing of Humans." Write it in the same personal, informal style as you used in other rhetorical analyses. This exercise is not an essay or an academic paper. Do not worry about structure. Just write. You might consider freewriting again for this exercise. There's no correct answer here, just your unique analysis. You may consider these points, if you like:

- Explain the paper's overall argument.
- The paper uses all of the enhancing factors described in this book so far. List a few examples of each enhancing factor: economy, strong verbs, active voice.
- Does Menuck's evidence defend her point well? Why or why not?
- How does the paper encourage the reader to care about the subject of food scarcity?
- How does the paper respond to opposing views?

Keep your insights in mind during revisions of your own writing. All writers borrow approaches and techniques from writers they admire.

Assignment 4a

You've written three assignments so far in this book. You should feel more comfortable with the enhancing factors now. Make sure you've revised your three assignments to remove wordiness, dead verbs, and now passive voice. The peer models above, or the work of other writers, may provide ideas or models for this assignment. If you learn techniques or approaches from the peer models, go back and reassess and rewrite previous assignments with those models in mind. This way your work comes into "conversation" with other writing.

Suggested Topics:

1) Write a narrative about an incident you have experienced with your family.
2) Write an explanation of your family history, a family tree of sorts.
3) Write a description of how you might study the family from an academic perspective.

Here are suggestions for writing:

- In narratives, resist the urge to openly judge your family members. Rather, show them acting as they normally act. If those actions express disgust, wonder, hatred, love, or any other emotion, that's fine. Let the reader come to those conclusions. You shouldn't say *My brother was annoying*. You should say *My brother spit his beer in my face*. Any reasonably aware reader would judge his action as *annoying* or worse.

- Some students find detailed writing challenging. They say *Nothing interesting ever happened to me* or *I forget the details* or *I don't know how much research to include in the paper*. If you can relate to one of these scenarios, don't fret. Upon deep reflection, we can all jog our memories and find something to write about. Academic writers in particular need to read widely and think deeply about their topic before they can write detailed prose.

- Don't forget to locate the story. Readers need to know where they are when the story starts. Stories in this book locate in obvious and in subtle ways. Similarly, explanations and descriptions must explain the point of the passage immediately.

- Beginning writers have a tendency to generalize, whether in stories or academic papers. Sometimes the problem is the scope of the piece. If you choose to write about a large chunk of your life in just 500 words, you'll never write in a specific way. Academic papers that attempt to prove big arguments face the same problem. Cut broad topics down to a manageable size.

- Don't think about the enhancing factor of active voice and the interfering factor of passive voice as you write the rough draft. You'll paralyze yourself thinking about subjects and verbs and objects and participles. Instead, write freely and apply the lesson of active voice only in the revision stage. By then, you'll have performed Exercise 19—the conversion exercise—so you'll know how to convert any nagging passives back to active voice.

- Get a trusted friend to read your draft. You may even want to form a writing group—friends or colleagues who meet every once in a while to read each other's writing. When reading someone else's work, be positive and talk about the strengths first. Then suggest edits. In this way, you will inspire each other to keep writing. You'll also be able to use their comments to do another revision.

- Avoid thinking about a word count. No writer has ever said *My paper will be great when I finally get to 10,000 words*. No reader counts the words the way an accountant counts dollars. Focus instead on expressing yourself in as detailed a way as you can. End your piece when the story or argument is done.

CHAPTER SUMMARY

We began this chapter with an idea: that most readers process sentences on a surface level, consciously absorbing just the meaning of the words rather than the grammatical structure. But wordiness and dead verbs get in the way of meaning. This chapter added another obstacle to the process of making meaning: the problem of word order.

Although most readers aren't aware of word order, per se, that doesn't mean it's insignificant. The word order of a sentence can greatly influence its meaning and "feel," and one word order in particular that makes reading difficult is called passive voice. Its opposite, active voice, is much easier to follow, although you can make the same surface meaning using either word order. We showed that active voice makes meaning in fewer words and does it logically.

The chapter then showed three equations that describe the underlying grammatical structure of a few basic types of sentences. Other types of sentence structures exist, but these three equations should satisfy most writing situations. The first two, which are intransitive and transitive active voice structures, are essential to good writing.

With these active voice sentences explained, we contrasted them with passive voice. The passive voice equation looks more complicated than the active voice equation and shows why readers often don't like it: it introduces dead verbs and unusual forms of the main verb, the participle. We then showed examples of active and passive voice and asked you to try a technique we call conversion. Understanding conversion helps you to remove passives during the editing process by converting them back to active voice.

More than just a stylistic barrier to communication, passive voice raises a moral issue: writers can use it to avoid taking responsibility for unsavoury actions. The actors can effectively disappear, thanks to the optional nature of the subject in the passive equation. Additionally, the responsibility for serious actions disappears without the subject/actor. In the business world, writers use the passive regularly, avoiding responsibility for firing an employee or rejecting the request of a taxpayer. Active voice alternatives present a direct and honest approach to human relationships.

Passive voice is also a problem in science, academia, and journalism, where writers often feel the need to remove themselves from the writing to create a perception of objectivity.

This is better described as pseudo-objectivity, because all writing is subjective. At every step, writing involves humans making choices, emphasizing one thing over another, and one piece of writing cannot ever include all points of view and become objective; writing is always partial. We encouraged writers to celebrate their subjectivity and write in the first person—in active voice sentences. Writing with *I* forces writers to use phrasing like *I think . . . I believe . . . I ran . . . I walk . . . I choose . . .*

In the first half of the chapter, we took an uncompromising approach towards passive voice. However, we were less rigid later on in the chapter. Yes, we acknowledge that some situations exist when the passive is acceptable. But these situations are few. When you want to deliberately foreground the receiver of action—the object—then use the passive. When you feel the active sounds unusual, use the passive. This is not an excuse to fall back to the passive side, however—always regard passives with suspicion.

The main point is to recognize passive voice and remove it from your writing by converting to active in most cases. Readers will appreciate the directness of active voice, the presence rather than the absence of the subject, and the logical flow of the active voice sentence—A + B + C. You may also find yourself thinking more clearly in the active voice.

 ## Further Readings

For more about writing groups:

Lamott, Anne. *Bird by Bird: Some Instructions on Writing and Life.* Anchor Books, 1995.

For more about how to write about your own life:

Zinsser, William. *Writing about Your Life: A Journey into the Past.* New York: Marlowe and Company, 2004.

CHAPTER
5

Strong Nouns

Never use abstract nouns when concrete ones will do.
If you mean "More people died" don't say "Mortality rose."

—C.S. LEWIS

WE ARGUED IN CHAPTER 3 that the verb is the most important word in a sentence. Strong verbs cause things to happen and create images of actions in readers' minds. Those actions touch on all five human senses. Dead verbs such as *is*, *was*, and *were* create no movement; nor do they evoke any images. Dead verbs require additional words just to help them make concrete meaning.

After verbs, the second most important word in a sentence—and our next enhancing factor for good writing—is the **noun**. Verbs are the muscle of writing, while nouns are the bones. Just like verbs, nouns can create detailed images in readers' minds. And just like verbs, some nouns are strong and some are weak, so choosing the strongest nouns will help your readers see the scenes, objects, people, and places in your writing.

Consider the images created in the reader's mind by these nouns:

City   Dog   Car

All three weak nouns—*city*, *dog*, and *car*—create vague images in the same way that dead verbs do. We all have in our minds a general image of a city, a dog, or a car. Now consider the images evoked by these strong nouns:

Winnipeg   **Collie**   **Ferrari**

These specific nouns produce much more specific images in the reader's mind—there is no confusion or doubt or vagueness. A strong noun works like a photograph, pinning such images to a reader's mental corkboard. Think of writing as though you panned a camera back and forth to different people or objects—as a visual process. Make pictures with your writing. **Strong nouns** do important work for writers in adding detail to sentences.

Let's look at personal narrative writing that evokes imagery through specific nouns. Identify the strong nouns in this peer model excerpt from Emily Davidson's story "Put a Hole in It, Won't You?"

The oven clock blinks 8:13 a.m. We have to leave by 8:30.

"Have you guys eaten yet?" Mom yells from upstairs over the blow of her hairdryer.

"We're doing it right now!" I screech from the kitchen.

Mom feels guilty leaving early because she got a job teaching problem kids at Edenrose Public School. She stomps down the stairs to approve Eric's breakfast choice—Shreddies cereal with sliced bananas and Oatmeal Crunch. She rolls her eyes at my mine—Lucky Charms with a four-to-one marshmallow-to-cereal ratio. Mom buys Lucky Charms because she likes them too.

Mom combs through the kitchen and family room and pulls rollers from her hair. She leaves them around the house.

"Have you guys seen my keys? Where are my car keys?"

Mom barks at us in the move voice, and we transform into car-key-searchers, because failure to move immediately results in the certain death of any TV privileges. The keys reveal themselves a long ten minutes later—on the hook where they belong. Mom pulls on a brown jacket. She leaves us with explicit instructions: be at least civil with each other. Yeah, right.

I sit next to Eric at the breakfast bar and spoon the last flock of floating purple horseshoe marshmallows into my mouth. (24)

Davidson includes many strong nouns in just 211 words. Some of those nouns are: *clock, Mom, hairdryer, kitchen, Edenrose Public School, Eric, Shreddies, Oatmeal Crunch, Lucky Charms, ratio, rollers, hair, keys, voice, car-key-searchers, hook, jacket, instructions, bar, marshmallows, mouth.* Even taken out of context, these strong nouns still evoke clear images in our minds. We can even get a sense of a story from that long list of words.

Names are particularly important nouns in writing. Names have meaning, and readers latch on to them, using them as a reminder of who speaks and acts. As a story unfolds, names develop character. Think of some famous names in fiction: Jay Gatsby, Romeo and Juliet, Pippi Longstocking, Captain Ahab, Harry Potter, Gollum, Big Brother, Lemuel Gulliver, Huck Finn. These unique names stand out, reminding us of specific stories and the feelings we have for them. Readers may even remember their own mental images of these characters long after they've finished reading. That's the power of names.

> Get the name of the dog.
> —ROY PETER CLARK

A peer model personal narrative by Laurie Kallis, "Willie Lavigne," emphasizes a boy's name. Think about the effect of name repetition in this excerpt from the beginning of her story:

> Willie Lavigne appeared midway through grade five.
>
> Willie Lavigne rode a ten-speed bike.
>
> Willie Lavigne had long, dirty blonde hair.
>
> I did not fit in well at Warren Park Public School, especially with the girls. I fared better with the boys though, as long as I stayed at the edges of their activities. That's why Willie Lavigne found me behind the cage of the baseball diamond. I came early every morning, before school began. With my face pressed against the cool chain link fence, I watched the guys practise their game. Nobody bothered me. The guys silently accepted me there, where the limestone screening met the grass, where I first met Willie Lavigne. (56)

This story depicts the childhood obsession of a girl for a boy. The repetition of Willie Lavigne's name hammers home Kallis's obsession: Willie Lavigne stays in her thoughts—and ours. Had she used only the pronoun *he*, the effect would not be so strong. Likewise, if you've got a good name in your own story, don't be afraid to repeat it.

Names are also important in academic writing, as you will see in this excerpt from an article by Duncan Koerber on Canadian newspaper publishing history:

> Five *Advocate* agents also were caught up in some of Mackenzie's most tumultuous events: the 1826 Types Riot and the 1837 rebellion. The Types Riot saw young Conservative men ransack and destroy Mackenzie's printing office, prompting a trial that ended with Mackenzie receiving significant damages to rebuild his shop. Paul Romney (1987) describes the Types Riot

as one of many Conservative abuses that Reformers saw against the rule of law, abuses that would spark the rebellion. One of the 12 jury members was Joseph Tomlinson of Markham (Lindsey 1862, 2: 97). Tomlinson later served as an agent for the *Advocate*. (*The Role of the Agent* 144)

The paragraph names two players in the Types Riot, a major event: *William Lyon Mackenzie* and *Joseph Tomlinson*. Other people, objects, places, and events include *Advocate, Types Riot, rebellion, office, trial, damages, shop, Paul Romney, law, abuses, Markham, agent*. If you find your academic writing lacks strong nouns, add more detail from your research that answers the classic journalistic questions: who, what, when, where, why, and how.

In the last chapter, we showed how verbs appeal to the five human senses. Strong nouns do the same. Here are some examples of strong nouns categorized by sense (some of these words even cross into other categories):

- sight: shine, lustre, glow, gleam, flash, view
- smell: stink, stench, odour, fart, aroma, fragrance
- touch: punch, hit, slap, wallop, tap, pressure
- hearing: snap, crack, pop, knock, squeal, burp, bang
- taste: zest, flavour, palate, salt, sugar, nibble

Many of these nouns also function as verbs. Indeed, many words in English move between grammatical categories. The following five sentences include a number of nouns; can you identify all of them?

a)   The moon's glow helped the hikers follow the path.

b)   He entered the wastewater treatment plant, and the awful smell hit him.

c)   Denzil's knock on the door woke David.

d)   Willy's tap on John's shoulder startled John.

e)   The lake view relaxed my father.

In the first sentence, the word *glow* can be both a verb and a noun, but here it functions as the latter—the sentence's subject; it acts to help the hikers. Likewise, *smell* can be either a verb or a noun. Here, though, *smell* acts out—it hits the man. Next, Denzil doesn't wake up David. The *knock*—behaving as a noun in this case, and the sentence's subject—does the waking. In sentence (d), *tap* does duty as a noun and startles John. Finally, in the last sentence, the *view* (another word that can be both noun and verb) acts on the *father* and relaxes him.

Now, let's change the functions of those nouns so that they act grammatically as verbs. Have a look at the examples below. Which versions do you like better?

a)   The moon glowed, helping the hikers follow the path.

b)   He entered the wastewater treatment plant and smelled the awful smell.

    c)   Denzil knocked on the door, waking up David.

    d)   Willy tapped on John's shoulder, startling John.

    e)   My father viewed the lake and it relaxed him.

Both sets of sentences have virtually the same meaning, and both are grammatically correct, but note their different effects and emphases. Each pair of sentences does similar work, but one version may sound better than the other to you—more "natural" or more elegant or more interesting. Read your work out loud to hear these differences.

One final point about nouns: writers today—particularly in business and academic writing—often turn perfectly good verbs into lifeless nouns by adding –*tion* suffixes. In the same way that verbs become bulky and less powerful with –*ate* and –*ize* endings, –*tion* endings "neuter" nouns. Usually these words are verbs converted to nouns, but sometimes the root form is a strong noun extended with the –*tion* ending.

Some examples of –*tion* nouns include:

formulation	penetration
hesitation	publication
indentation	recitation
argumentation	separation
installation	confrontation
mediation	allocation
observation	adaptation
operation	

These words have perfectly good uses—in moderation. Too many of them, however, weigh down sentences and paragraphs. Sometimes writers use them even when better options clearly exist (if they just knew where to look). Consider these six examples of sentences with –tion nouns:

    a)   Arthur's recitation of the speech was wonderful.

    b)   The boy had a confrontation with his parents that evening.

    c)   Alice created the indentation in the wall.

    d)   The lawyers were successful at mediation between the two parties.

    e)   The couple's separation occurred at the end of the year.

    f)   The CEO had an observation of falling share prices.

In all six cases, the actions seem distant. We can't see them happening right now. Yet as we've been learning, readers love to experience actions that seem to happen in the moment, as if they are standing right there with the writer as events unfold. But here we see that once the actions (recite, confront, etc.) become –tion nouns, the actions are over. Instead, let your readers see the *recitation* or the *confrontation*. To show you what we mean, we've converted those long, awkward –*tion* nouns back to their verbs to emphasize those actions:

a)   Arthur recited the speech wonderfully.

b)   The boy confronted his parents that evening.

c)   Alice indented the wall.

d)   The lawyers successfully mediated the two parties.

e)   The couple separated at the end of the year.

f)   The CEO observed the falling share prices.

These sentences work better. They let us directly experience the actions once clouded by the –*tion* endings, and they avoid wordiness and dead verbs. During your own revision, if you're seeing a lot of –*tion* nouns in your writing, circle them. Consider whether you truly need them. If not, try revising the sentences like we did above. Your readers will appreciate being more directly involved in the actions you're describing.

EXERCISE 25 ▶ Noun Clusters

Write a paragraph of 100 words or fewer where you describe all the names and key terms associated with something you're interested in. For example, if you're a fan of the NHL, you might write about the names of the important players in the league. You might name the trophies, plays, and arenas. This exercise helps you understand the importance of names and other strong nouns in writing.

EXERCISE 26 ▶ Hierarchy of Detail

The most important nouns in your writing are people. But writing well about people requires great detail. Readers need to see and hear the people you know.

This exercise requires you to choose one person in your life who you know well. With that person in mind, write what we call a **Hierarchy of Detail**. A Hierarchy of Detail is a simple point-form list of facts about a person that will help you gather details that you can use when writing.

The sections are ranked from most valuable to least valuable. Well-rounded, effective writing includes details about characters from at least the first two categories. For

continued

this exercise, list at least four details about the person you chose in each of the four categories below:

1. **Action:** List the person's regular actions. People's actions take precedence over all other details in defining their characters. Behaviour says a lot about someone.

   Examples: If you're writing a story about your parents, you may write that they travel regularly or that they clean the house every single day. If you're writing a story about a good friend, you may write that he constantly checks his smartphone or wears revealing clothing. These actions tell us something. We cannot deny that these people do these acts.

2. **Evidence of Action:** List evidence of people's past actions. People leave "evidence" around their homes, cars, and schools that says a lot about them (for example, posters on walls, clothes on the floor, documents all over the desk).

   Examples: If you're writing a story about your brother, you may write down that he owns a super-modified Honda Civic with rear spoilers and a big rumbling tailpipe. If you're writing a story about your grandmother, you may describe the stuffed taxidermy animals that hang on her living room walls. In the story, we won't have to see the characters modify the Honda or hang dead animals on walls. But the evidence exists for the reader to interpret, and it is a good indicator of your subject's character.

3. **Speech:** List the catchphrases or unique ways in which the person speaks. Stories demand **dialogue**. Readers love to hear people talk. But dialogue should sound natural. Every person speaks somewhat differently. Try to reproduce this accurately.

   Examples: If you're writing about your sister, you may write down that she always says *like* or *oh my god*. If you're writing about your uncle, you may write down that he always says *you only live once* when his siblings say they're worried about his skydiving and bungee-jumping. If the person speaks in these ways all the time, it's a fairly good indicator of character. Just like in real life, however, characters' actions in your stories will speak louder than their words: in other words, your characters may lie or exaggerate.

4. **Reputation:** List what other people say about the person. This is the lowest category in the Hierarchy of Detail because it offers the weakest, least reliable evidence. If there is a difference between what a person says he or she is and the reputation, then show it.

> When writing a novel a writer should create living people; people not characters. A *character* is a caricature.
>
> —ERNEST HEMINGWAY

A well-crafted Hierarchy of Detail will help you give the people in your writing the respect they deserve: a fulsome characterization.

You will learn about the Hierarchy of Detail for academic writing later in this chapter.

The Problem of Pronouns

So far we've made an argument about the importance of nouns: they are a resource that helps the reader to make sense of your writing. Strong nouns add vital details about characters, places, objects, and events. Without strong nouns, the reader has fewer resources to work with; as a result, they may not see the full picture you're trying to describe. Nouns that influence readers the most are ones that readers recognize immediately—everyday nouns in their everyday forms. If the reader can readily picture what you're describing, meaning-making and understanding are instantaneous.

Too many instances of the same noun, however, will annoy your readers. And that's where pronouns come in handy. As the name suggests, a **pronoun** is a substitute for a noun you've already mentioned. When used properly, they allow you to make elegant, subtle phrasings and avoid repetition. Numerous pronouns exist in English—consult a dictionary for a complete list. Here's a shortlist of some of the more common ones:

I	it
you	itself
he	me
she	my
they	myself
their	him
them	his
themselves	her
we	one
our	himself
us	herself

Below are some examples of pronouns used in sentences. You'll notice that in each case the pronoun has a tight relationship with the noun:

a)   The **team** traded **its** greatest player.

b)   **John** grabbed **his** wallet and left.

c)   The quantitative **study** had **its** own faults.

d)   The **cyclists** rode **their** bikes to the race.

e)   **Rufus the Yorkshire Terrier** ate **his** lunch.

f)   The **President** reserved **his** question for later.

In all of these sentences, the pronouns—*its, his, their*—arrive just one word after the nouns *team, John, study, cyclists, Rufus the Yorkshire Terrier, President.* That's tight. With only a small gap between noun and pronoun, the relationship between the pronoun and the noun is easy to follow. These are also straight-forward active voice sentences, the kind we praised in Chapter 4.

If we look beyond the level of individual sentences, the pronoun–noun relationship in a larger body of writing extends further until a new noun arrives to end the mental connection; in other words, we hold the original noun in our minds and relate subsequent pronouns to it. Let's look at the paragraph below, which describes an incident involving a woman named Marian:

> Marian crashed her car. She was not hurt in the crash. The ambulance took her to the hospital. Her daughter Kylie rushed over.

The first sentence presents no confusion. *Her* means Marian. In the second sentence, we still understand *she* to mean Maria. *Her* in the next sentence is also unambiguous. In the last sentence, we remember that *her* refers back to Marian, even though we now have a new person in the story: Kylie. Since Kylie only arrives after the last pronoun, the relationships between all of these pronouns and the original noun are clear. In straightforward examples like this, you can clearly see the connections between the pronouns and the nouns they replace.

Examples of Unclear Pronouns

Strong nouns, however, face an enemy, an interfering factor that reduces the noun's effect: **unclear pronouns**. With unclear pronouns, the relationship between the nouns and the pronouns is not obvious. Unclear pronouns lead to ambiguous prose that confuses readers. Consider the following examples. The first sentence has two nouns:

> Sally and Mary spent the night at her house.

In this sentence, what is the **antecedent**—that which comes before—of the pronoun *her*? We must guess. The antecedent could be either Sally or Mary. To remove the ambiguity, we replace the pronoun with a noun:

> Sally and Mary spend the night at Sally's house.

In the next sentence, identify the pronoun and then work backwards to find the noun. Most readers assume that the closest prior noun—taking gender into account—completes that mental relationship we discussed earlier:

> Napoleon sat on the horse Napoleon Junior just after losing the war and wondered how much Josephine loved him.

This writer inspires a laugh, but we can assume that's not what the writer wants. Any warm-blooded reader pictures Napoleon worrying about his horse being the rival for Josephine's affection. This sort of absurdity abounds in scholarly papers, especially in long sentences, where most prose breakdowns occur. Here's an edit that removes the unintended comedy:

> Napoleon sat on the horse Napoleon Junior just after losing the war. Napoleon wondered how much Josephine loved him.

Another pronoun–antecedent problem sometimes occurs when writers use the generalized *they*. In informal conversation, speakers often use *they* to talk about both one person or several people (singular and plural). For example, your friend may say *The club is opening tomorrow but they say it's not for all ages*. In this case, the identity and number of *they* is not particularly important to the listener. But in writing, this habit may confuse readers. Preserving the distinction between singular and **plural** will help you develop a greater precision. Two simple examples express the point:

> Never use a pronoun when it could refer to either of two words before it. . . . Uncertainty is confusing and intolerable.
>
> —DONALD HALL AND SVEN BIRKERTS

a)   In Newfoundland they used to have a lot of fish.

b)   When someone breaks a bone, they have to have a cast put on.

Can you identify the antecedents of each *they*? One might assume the prior nouns or pronouns—Newfoundland and someone—are the antecedents. But each is singular—there's only one Newfoundland and only one someone.

Of course we understand the writer's use of *they* to mean some generalized sense of a group of people in Newfoundland, and we know the second example refers to a generalized case, not a specific person or group of people. A vast gulf exists between speech and writing, and different standards apply in different situations. In speech, where things go by fast, the antecedent-less *they* or an incorrect number doesn't bother us much. In writing, however, such usage looks sloppy.

These short examples look simple—what confusion could exist? Why does this matter? Yet sentences and paragraphs with pronoun–noun relationship problems diminish the reader's faith in the writer. Why? Antecedent-less pronouns are like rattles in a car—the car still runs, but you can hear something loose. That takes away from your sense of the car's solidity and reliability—the rattle unsettles the mind. Indeed, all of the interfering factors we describe in this book diminish the reader's faith in your writing.

The relationship between words in a sentence is not trivial. When you are precise in your choice of words, your readers will gain a more precise understanding of your work.

Let's look at some examples of sentences with pronoun problems. As you'll see, sentences that start with *it* and *there* can be particularly troublesome:

a)   It was an unparalleled boxing match at the arena tonight.

b)   There were many fans of the singer.

c)   It is an awful night for a wedding proposal.

d) There are 28 days in February of a leap year.

e) It is often thought that media affects children negatively.

In all of these sentences, the initial words *it* and *there* are followed immediately by dead verbs (*were*, *is*, *was*). In each case, the result is a statement that is either vague or uninteresting, or both. Now let's look at the same sentences, revised using some of the tools we've taught you so far:

a) The boxing match at the arena tonight was unparalleled.

b) The singer had many fans.

c) The night is awful for a wedding proposal.

d) February has 28 days in a leap year.

e) Many media effects theorists think the media affects children negatively.

In each case, we've moved the doers of the action—*the boxing match*, *the singer*, *the night*, *February*, and *media effects theorists*—to the start of the sentences, eliminating the need for limp pronouns like *it* and *there*. Some dead verbs remain, but the focus is now on the stronger subjects, and meaning is clearer as a result.

We have shown both in Chapter 3 and this chapter how dead verbs and weak nouns don't evoke as much visual meaning as strong verbs and concrete nouns. Likewise, pronouns can also present problems for the writer intent on creating images, since they don't make much meaning on their own. Instead, they're contextual, meaning that they make sense only when they have a clear connection to another word (i.e., a name, an object, a place, etc.) behind or in front of them. For instance, without a precise noun, the words *it* or *he* or *she* suggest only a vague sense of existence or gender. If your friend says *It's so beautiful* or *It's cherry red*, you'll wonder what she's talking about—a car? a bike? If a colleague suddenly blurts out *He stole my wallet!* you know he's talking about a male, but nothing more. In both cases, there is confusion because the pronouns don't relate clearly to any prior nouns. They require other words to make sense.

The same holds true for your own writing: if you use vague pronouns such as *it*, *she*, or *he* with no context, your readers will have to track back to the last concrete noun you used to try to guess who or what you're talking about. Use strong nouns and names and link them carefully with their pronouns to eliminate confusion as to who's talking or acting.

▍ Pronouns and Repetition

Pronouns are often used so much to avoid the repetition of nouns. But repetition can be a good thing to engineer a certain effect. Look, for example, at music lyrics, TV commercials, memorable speeches like Martin Luther King's "I Have a Dream" speech. King repeated the phrase *I have a dream* eight times in quick succession.

Writing without Strong Nouns

Strong nouns, not pronouns, play a vital role in sentences, but writers sometimes forget how richly visual they can be. One of the finest American writers, David Remnick, has spent a career showing the deep characters of people. The editor of *The New Yorker* magazine, Remnick regularly uses strong nouns in his writing to paint vivid scenes in readers' minds. We know the old cliché: *a picture is worth a thousand words*. In Remnick's writing, strong nouns show a detailed picture.

One of Remnick's finest personality profiles tells the story of African-American writer Ralph Ellison. The novel—*The Invisible Man*—made Ellison famous. That Ellison never wrote another novel for the rest of his life intrigued Remnick. Through interviews and research, Remnick produced a long-form narrative profile of Ellison that showed the depth and subtlety of Ellison's character.

Remnick opens the article with this strong-noun–rich scene:

> In a modest apartment overlooking the Hudson, at the weld of the north Harlem and south Washington Heights, Ralph Ellison confronts his "work in progress." He has been at this nearly forty years, and rare is the day that he does not doubt his progress. He wakes early, goes out to buy a paper on Broadway, returns, and when he has exhausted the possibilities of the *Times* and the *Today Show*, when the coffee and toast are gone, he flicks on the computer in his study and reads the passage he finished the day before. (238)

The strong nouns of the story evoke many images in the reader's mind: *apartment, Hudson, weld, Harlem, Washington Heights, Ralph Ellison, work, years, day, progress, paper, Broadway, Times, show, coffee, toast, computer, study, passage*. The strong nouns do two things: they show Ellison's character and they show the character of New York City. We get a taste of New York while we learn about Ellison and his typical day.

However, what if Remnick hadn't paid attention to strong nouns? What would his writing look like with weak nouns or pronouns? As an experiment, we've edited the passage:

> In a modest apartment overlooking the river, he confronts his "work in progress." He has been at this a long time, and he rarely doesn't doubt himself. He wakes early, goes out to buy a paper, returns, and when he has exhausted the possibilities of the paper and a morning TV show, when the food and drink are gone, he flicks on the computer and reads what he finished the day before.

In this revision, the essential meaning stays the same. The verbs stay the same. But it lacks the vitality of the original. We can't quite see the place. We can't quite see Ellison's morning routine. We can't quite see what Ellison has for breakfast. Specific meaning is lost.

continued

Here's another, longer passage where Remnick carefully describes Ellison's thoughts on race and young people in America. As you read, take particular note of the strong nouns:

In Ellison's view, America is not made up of separate, free-floating cultures but, rather of a constant interplay and exchange. In the essays, he described slaves on a southern plantation watching white people dance and then transforming those European steps into something that is American; he speaks of what Ella Fitzgerald has done with the songs of Rodgers and Hart, what white rock bands did the with blues; he watched the black kids in Harlem in their baggy hip-hop gear walking down Broadway, and on the same day he sees white suburban kids on television affecting the same style. What Ellison has called the "interchange, appropriation, and integration" of American culture is evident in the music we hear, the games we play, the books we read, the clothes we wear, the food we eat. For him, integration is not merely an aspiration but a given, a fact of cultural and political life. Without pity or excessive pride, Ellison also sketches the facts of his own life—especially his self-discovery, first through music, then literature—to describe the American phenomenon. *Invisible Man* itself looks not only to the experience of Ralph Ellison at Tuskegee Institute or in Harlem but to Ralph Ellison in the library, the young reader that Albert Murray remembers as "always looking to the top shelf." When Ellison finally came to New York, Richard Wright and Langston Hughes became literary mentors and friends, but their influence was secondary, following a youthful tear through Eliot, Pound, Faulkner, Hemingway, Stein, and Dostoevsky. Out of many, one. (243–244)

Remnick's poetic paragraph—a paragraph about ideas—contains many visuals in the nouns. We see the characters of the piece: *singers* and *writers* and *kids*. We recognize tangible, everyday things like *games*, *books*, *clothes*, and *food*. Readers revel in this immersive detail.

A less aware, less detailed writer may produce a paragraph like the one below. Once again, we've edited Remnick's writing to remove the strong nouns:

In his view, this country is not made up of separate, free-floating cultures but, rather of a constant dialog. In the essays, he described slaves watching white people dance and then transforming those European steps into something else; he speaks of what singers did with songs, what white rock groups did the with blues; he watched the black children in their baggy clothes walking down the street, and on the same day he sees white suburban children acting the same way. What he has called the "interchange, appropriation, and integration" of our culture is evident in every cultural practice. For him, integration is not merely an aspiration but a given, a fact of culture and politics. He also sketches his life—especially his own self-discovery—to describe this. His book looks not only to his experience at school or in his neighborhood but to his experience in the library, the young reader that is remembered as "always looking to the top shelf." When he finally came to the city, a number of writers became friends, but their influence was secondary, following a youthful tear through many other great writers. Out of many, one.

Again, the revised version isn't particularly poor. It's grammatically correct. It says most of the things Remnick said. But without strong nouns, it's weak and vague, a paragraph of generalities, not specifics. Notice how the lack of names—particularly Ellison's—makes the "characters" in the writing almost disappear; they seem like ghosts. Notice as well how the sense of place is lost without nouns like *Harlem* and *America* and *Broadway*.

Without strong nouns, writing loses a part of its soul. It no longer captivates. That's the power of strong nouns.

We'll talk more about this valuable repetitive effect in Chapter 7. All these forms of communication employ extensive and obvious repetition to hook the listener or reader. Your writing need not be different.

Understanding pronoun reference and repeating nouns can also make writing clearer for readers even when there's no grammatical reference error. Let's look at an extended example:

> Kwai told John she wanted to take him to Vancouver because, aside from Edmonton and Calgary, it was her favourite city.

In this example, the meaning is still fairly clear. But the writing has loosened due to one pronoun *it*. Vancouver is Kwai's favourite city, but in between *Vancouver* and *it*, the writer introduces two other cities, *Edmonton* and *Calgary*. It's not a difficult sentence, but the reader still has to process Edmonton and Calgary while holding Vancouver in memory. The antecedent relationship is somewhat distant. An easy solution is to reintroduce the noun:

> Kwai told John she wanted to take him to Vancouver because, aside from Edmonton and Calgary, Vancouver was her favourite city.

Repeating Vancouver serves two purposes. The repetition reduces the relational distance from the original noun. Second, the repetition reinforces the key idea of the sentence: how much she loves Vancouver. Make reading easy in this way for your readers. The difference in revision looks tiny, but writers deal in accumulations of tiny effects to produce solid writing.

To identify pronoun problems in your own writing, look for passages where you don't have many strong nouns. If you have a lot of *he* and *she* and *it* and *they* instead, maybe you're not giving nouns a chance. A simple edit replaces pronouns with nouns to solve antecedent problems.

We recommend these five steps in considering nouns and pronouns in your writing:

- don't fear repeating nouns, particularly if you are trying to achieve a certain effect
- seek out and use strong nouns if you can find them
- choose strong nouns more often than pronouns
- use pronouns when the repetition of the noun sounds unusual
- ensure that any pronouns you use refer back clearly to a noun

By using the guidelines above, you'll find yourself creating more visual and vivid writing that readers can see in their minds.

EXERCISE 27 ▶ Pronoun Revision

This exercise helps you to identify and replace unclear pronouns. In each of the following sentences, replace the pronoun with a noun and/or make the pronoun–antecedent reference clear. You may keep the sentence and just change a few words or you may completely rewrite the sentence; your choice will depend on the severity of the pronoun problem. Keep in mind, though, that rewriting whole sentences often drastically changes the author's meaning, and that is not your intent here. If you're not sure if a word is a pronoun, check in a dictionary. In addition, make sure any pronouns you add refer back to the correct noun; likewise, replace pronouns with specific nouns whenever you can.

a) A strange car followed us closely, and he blinked his lights at us.
b) It says in today's paper that the newest shipment of cars includes the Yaris.
c) At the job placement office, they told me to stop wearing ripped jeans to my interviews.
d) Any graduate student, if they are interested, may attend the lecture.
e) In the Prime Minister's address to parliament, he promised no more taxes.
f) Erindale College wants to increase parking spaces but they don't have the room.
g) Each of the astronaut candidates sent their photograph with their application.
h) Everyone wants to get their tickets before they go on sale to the public.

▌ The Morality of Unclear Pronouns

Chapter 4 showed how sentences in the passive voice allow people to avoid responsibility for their actions: the doer of the action doesn't appear until the end of the sentence—or at all. Unclear pronouns have a similar effect and also contribute to wordiness. Consider this sentence from a piece of business communication:

> It has been decided that the position presently occupied by you will be restructured and downsized as part of the company's efforts to increase productivity and value for shareholders.

Here, in just one sentence, we have four passive voice verbs and lots of corporate jargon such as *restructured, downsized,* and *productivity.* The sentence also begins with the pronoun *it* but has no antecedent, as though nobody in particular had decided to eliminate the reader's position. Passive voice and antecedent-less pronouns often travel together in the prose of shame. The writer here tries to hide from the responsibility for firing someone.

In a perfect world, we would rewrite the sentence using a noun, a personal take over and start new paragraph pronoun, and the active voice:

> My boss told me to eliminate one position from this department. I have chosen to eliminate yours.

This is not good news, but its delivery is honest and responsible. The revised sentence shows more respect for the fired employee's feelings than the evasive language of the original. The point is that readers associate loose pronouns, passives, clichés, and wordiness with dishonesty. Writers who use them are, in a sense, refusing to look their readers in the eye.

> I hate and mistrust pronouns, every one of them as slippery as a fly-by-night personal-injury lawyer.
>
> —STEPHEN KING

Inclusive Pronouns

A further issue with pronouns is that gendered pronouns (*he, she*) may cause controversy if not used wisely. Not that long ago, a writer could get away with using the universal *he* to refer to all people, all of "mankind." More than 60 years ago, in his classic article about writing history, noted historian E.H. Carr wrote:

> No document can tell us more than what the author of the document thought—what he thought had happened, what he thought ought to happen or would happen, or perhaps only what he wanted others to think he thought, or even only what he himself thought he thought. (16)

Criticizing Carr's seemingly chauvinistic language is easy now—few twenty-first century writers would dream of using "he" as a stand-in for all of humanity. But this was commonplace and indeed acceptable up to the mid-twentieth century, when women and men alike began to push for more inclusive language.

Today, to imply that all historical documents are produced by men (the implication in Carr's use of the generalized *he* pronoun) would be laughable. Inclusive (and more precise) language is the norm now, and *he* and *she* are used to refer only to individual males and females, not whole groups of people. Consider the following examples:

a)   When a student's line of inquiry is unclear, he must investigate further.

b)   If the newborn is well-fed, he will sleep for two to three hours.

c)   The best teacher rarely comes to her classes unprepared.

These sentences are unnecessarily exclusive. Inclusivity is easy, as in these revisions:

a)   When a line of inquiry is unclear, the student must investigate further.

b)   If newborns are well-fed, they will sleep for two to three hours.

c)   The best teacher rarely comes to class unprepared.

Sometimes, however, we can go a step too far in our eagerness to avoid sexist language, with unintentionally amusing results—for example, substituting *personhole* for *manhole*. In general, however, our ears (and brains) do adapt to new usages. Many of us can remember a time when using *chairperson* or *chair* instead of *chairman* (to describe the head of a committee) sounded forced and unnatural. Likewise, substituting *flight attendant* and *fire fighter* for *stewardess* and *fireman* seemed strange at first but sounds natural now.

> Words such as *he* and *man* are supposed to mean both men and women, but they really don't. If they did, then a sentence like *Anyone in Oklahoma can ask for an abortion if he wants one* would make good sense.
>
> —HARRIET OTTENHEIMER

As a society's views on gender, sexuality, and so forth shift and evolve, so too does the language that expresses those views. The initial awkwardness of new and unfamiliar language reflects the magnitude of the social shift that brought it about. Over time, however, we become accustomed to new ways of expressing ourselves and the once-new language becomes an accepted part of our linguistic landscape, indeed of our reality. But that reality is hardly settled yet—and neither is the language: rather, language is always changing, reflecting new currents of thought. While dictionaries try to pin down and cement the meanings of words, social life has different plans.

Subject–Verb Agreement

We noted in Chapter 4 that writers and readers tend to process sentences on a semantic level—that is, they process the surface meaning, the meaning of the words themselves. In that chapter we also showed how sentences have a deep structure that good writers harness for directness and clarity. In this chapter we've introduced another way of looking at words: the grammatical relationships among them. We showed above that pronouns need a strong relationship with a noun, an antecedent. Understanding this grammatical relationship helps writers see their writing objectively. This in turn helps writers ensure that the meaning they intend is the meaning actually on the page, and it helps reduce misunderstandings and confusion.

The relational concept of the antecedent is not only helpful in thinking about pronouns and nouns, but also helpful in another way. A common problem in bad writing is a lack of consistency between nouns as subjects, pronouns as subjects, and their related verbs.

As we saw in Chapter 3, verbs have many different forms and those forms are determined in part by whether the agent of the verb, the grammatical subject in the active voice, is singular or plural or in the past, present, or future.

The relationship between actors and verbs sounds simple, but often these words stand so far apart from each other that the relationship disappears in our minds, causing a breakdown in **subject–verb agreement**.

Some subjects have a clear number. For example, a strong noun such as *John* is clearly singular, so we know the plural form of a verb in the present tense is wrong, such as in the sentence *John run in the park every morning*. Here, the subject obviously doesn't agree with the verb in number.

This relationship becomes more complex, and less visible, when pronouns, either singular or plural, sit in the active voice subject position. Have a look at the pronouns listed below and indicate whether each is singular or plural by placing and S or a P beside each. You may need to consult a dictionary.

anyone	many
each	most
either	neither
every	no one
everyone	none
everything	one
both	someone
few	neither

Pronouns, like the nouns they replace, must follow the rules of subject–verb agreement. The following sentences have errors in agreement in both nouns and pronouns. In each example, first identify the verb, then draw an arrow back to the corresponding noun or pronoun.

a) Neither of the two traffic lights are working.

b) Either are fine with me.

c) The effects of violent media on children is a major concern of researchers.

d) At the university, the number of students are continuing to climb.

In each sentence, we find dead verbs—*are*, *is*, and *are*—in a relationship with the subjects *Neither*, *either*, *effects*, and *number*. In all four sentences, the subject and verb do not agree in number. They are grammatically incorrect.

Let's look at each sentence in turn.

In the first sentence, the pronoun *Neither* is the subject. It is singular (i.e., "neither one"), yet the verb is the plural *are*. Writers and speakers alike often mistakenly use *are* with *neither* because a plural (here, *traffic lights*) precedes the verb. Properly edited, the sentence becomes:

Neither of the two traffic lights is working.

Likewise, in example (b), *either* is a singular pronoun (i.e., *either one*). So the correct sentence is actually:

Either is fine with me.

Similarly, the relationship between subject and verb fails in the third sentence because *effects*—the subject of the sentence—is plural but the verb *is* is, of course, singular. *Children* does not affect the verb form. The sentence should read:

The effects of violent media on children are a major concern of researchers.

Finally, in sentence (d), *university* is not the subject. The subject is actually *the number*, a singular noun. To ensure subject–verb agreement then, the verb should be the singular *is*:

At Capilano, the number of students is continuing to climb.

An easy test for subject–verb agreement in cases like this, then, is to remove the *of* phrase and make sure that the verb agrees with the subject.

▌ Adjective–Pronoun Agreement

Another agreement problem with pronouns deals with the pronoun-as-adjective (remember, words can change grammatical type) in front of a noun in the subject position of an active voice sentence. One particular pronoun-as-adjective that can create problems is the word *each*, as seen in the following sentence:

Each student should hand in their assignment before the end of class.

Here, *each student* (singular) is the subject, but *their* is a plural pronoun. In everyday speech, this example would probably be fine, but readers (and editors!) are more discriminating than people having a casual conversation. Pairing *each* and *their* is like wearing white socks with a black suit—not the worst of sins, but it makes us look unsophisticated or uneducated in the eyes of others, such as editors, readers, and teachers.

Thankfully, there are a number of possible solutions for the problem of *each* and its antecedent. Let's take a look at each one:

> Each student should hand in her or his assignment before the end of class.

This revision, using singular pronouns, is considerate and gender inclusive, although some readers and writers may feel that it emphasizes gender more than it needs to. It also violates our rule about economy, so in that sense we're going the wrong way. The next sentence is more economical:

> Each student should hand in her/his assignment before the end of class.

Although this version is more economical, it sounds like "techno talk" or jargon. A variant of this, seen occasionally in documents related to social sciences and business and legal writing, is *s/he*. Although it may be passable (barely) in written documents, it begs the question of how to pronounce *s/he*. Here, the best solution involves removing the troublesome *each* altogether and changing the subject slightly:

> Students should hand in their assignments before the end of class.

Not only is this construction elegant, but the plural (*students*) is also gender neutral and agrees in number with *their*.

Academic Writing, Strong Nouns, and Unclear Pronouns

Strong nouns matter a great deal in academic writing. They bring specific details to what is often quite abstract writing. Strong nouns are analogous to facts, numbers, and other evidence. Robert Darnton's history of early reading practices includes a great deal of strong nouns. Consider this detailed passage:

> In the University of Leyden there hangs a print of the university library, dated 1610. It shows the books, heavy folio volumes, chained on high shelves jutting out from the walls in a sequence determined by the rubrics of classical bibliography: Jurisconsulti, Medici, Historici, and so on. Students are scattered about the room, reading the books on counters built at shoulder level below the shelves. They read standing up, protected against the cold by thick cloaks and hats, one foot perched on a rail to ease the pressure on their bodies. Reading cannot have been comfortable in the age of classic humanism. (8)

The strong nouns include *University of Leyden, print, library, books, volumes, shelves, walls, students, counters, cloaks, hats, foot, rail, pressure.* Not surprisingly, many strong nouns are found in good narrative. We can see the reading room in our mind's eye—it isn't an abstraction but rather something alive with people, things, temperatures, and textures.

Can you pick out all the strong nouns in the following excerpt from Isabelle Lehuu's book on early print culture in America?

> When historians of book publishing have emphasized the breakdown of the traditional world of print and described the shift from cohesion to fragmentation, they have often pointed at technological change as the cause. Yet even historians of technology have begun to challenge this technological determinism. Their conclusions suggest that the popularization of reading stimulated as much as it resulted from technological innovations. The technology of papermaking and printing improved tremendously during the second quarter of the nineteenth century; steam power and rotary presses made it possible to print more reading matter at a lower price. But machinery alone could not create the demand. (24)

This passage contains *historians, publishing, breakdown, world, print, shift, change, cause, technology, papermaking, printing, quarter, century, power, presses, price, machinery, demand.* These words are concrete and tangible—few readers wouldn't understand them. Lehuu's bigger theoretical idea of technological determinism, while abstract, comes down to our level thanks to the strong nouns, which help us relate the difficult idea to the everyday.

Unclear pronouns, however, can spoil the effect of strong nouns in academic writing. Two common offenders are *It has been shown that* and *There are many factors that affect.* In both examples, the pronouns *it* and *there*, respectively, have no antecedents. The first phrase is a passive: we wonder who, exactly, has *shown.* In the second phrase, the writer wants to make a point about *many factors* but does it indirectly, almost shyly. Even if the author doesn't want to say *I think many factors affect*, he or she could write *Many factors affect.* If you find yourself starting sentences with pronouns, reconsider and introduce a clear noun.

Earlier in this chapter, in Exercise 26, we listed a Hierarchy of Detail for narrative writing. We can also define a Hierarchy of Detail for academic writing, which emphasizes five categories of information—nouns themselves—that readers expect in good papers:

1. **Facts, Figures, Statistics:** Use primary evidence from reputable sources. Facts, figures and statistics reign supreme in modern public discourse— even if they can be used to mislead. The academic project is to find truth, so these details help back up arguments.

2. **Arguments:** Bring in specific arguments from proven, unbiased, reputable sources. Academic writers routinely "stand on the shoulders of giants," to quote the old cliché, distilling the work of others down into straightforward statements that they then build upon in their own work.

3. **Quotations:** Quote directly from proven, unbiased, reputable sources—let us hear other voices directly; they function in a way similar to dialogue in personal narrative. And as in personal narrative, quotations in academic writing need to be interesting and unique. Scholarly writers must be cautious, however, not to overquote. Overquoting can lead to cut-and-paste "pinball essays," where the writer becomes only a moderator at a debate, leaving theorists speaking in long quotations page after page.

4. **Paraphrases:** Restate in your own words, without condensing, relevant ideas or arguments from your sources. When you paraphrase, you provide a 1:1 restatement of someone else's words in your own unique way. Be wary, however, of plagiarizing, as discussed in Chapter 1.

5. **Summaries:** Condense longer passages of the work of proven, unbiased reputable sources into significantly shorter passages completely in your own words. As with paraphrasing, be careful not to plagiarize.

Including all of these elements in your academic writing will satisfy readers who demand both evidence of your own ideas and assertions and connections with previous literature on the topic. Refer to Chapter 1 and to the Research and Documentation Appendix for a more detailed explanation of these and other elements in academic writing.

Final Thoughts on Nouns and Pronouns

The point in this chapter is not to revel in the seemingly small relationships between verbs and subjects and pronouns and subjects. We're not grammarians trying to uphold the finer rules of English.

Rather, we are stylists who believe that when writers look at pronouns and nouns more closely, they develop a greater precision in their use of language. Writers who attend to such small details see sentences as a whole more clearly and can more readily spot potential landmines.

Peer Models for Emulation

The next peer model story deals with work. Anyone who has ever held a job, whether part- or full-time knows that jobs have a character of their own and typical nouns—co-workers—within them (for example, the hospital has the nurse and doctor, the courtroom has the lawyer and the judge). As you read this story, observe how the nouns and pronouns the writer uses create vivid pictures of people, objects, and places in your mind's eye.

Two Weeks at Notre Dame Hospital

BY ERIC RAMADI

The warm sun shone through the window down the hall. The emergency wing smelled like bleach. Nurses dressed in white ran up and down the hall, carrying clipboards and papers.

I stood with my back to the wall, took a deep breath, and closed my eyes. All the work they'd asked me to do had drained me. I had volunteered to help out at the Notre Dame Hospital two weeks ago and hoped it would give my university application some edge.

That day, I had restocked the needles in the second floor supplies cabinet after carrying fifteen boxes from the truck in the basement, helped clean out rooms one through six in the emergency wing, and helped sort at least fifty patients' files.

"Just three more weeks. Just three more weeks," I said to myself. I had developed that mantra after my first two days of working here. I took a week off the five week total at the beginning of each week.

The white clock on the wall in front of me said it was noon. A picture of the Virgin Mary hung below the clock. Only two hours were left before I could get out of this dump.

Dr. Elias rushed by.

"Glad he didn't see me here," I thought.

I sighed and walked slowly away, in the opposite direction.

"Eric, could you go help out Nurse Yazbek in room 28C?" Dr. Elias said. I cringed and turned around.

I nodded and tried to keep a blank face. Dr. Elias turned away and dashed down the hall. I dragged myself to 28C.

Nurse Yazbek had earned a reputation for being a merciless bitch over her twenty years at the hospital.

"I think her job is to make interns and volunteers cry," John, an intern at the hospital, had once told me.

She stood by the window with an enormous needle in her hand. I peered at her and held my breath. Her hook-like nose seemed to stare back at me.

"I need you to hold Michael's arm out for me while I give him his shot. Someone's been a naughty boy, playing with stray dogs."

The high-pitched noise emanated from her tiny, pursed lips. A tiny woman in her mid-fifties, with long black hair that looked like she'd chopped it off at its end with an axe, leaving it pointy and uneven—it didn't take much to imagine her as a witch—the emergency room witch—as John called her.

Michael's eyes watered at the sight of the needle, a big needle. He sat quietly on the white hospital bed and stared at Nurse Yazbek.

"It's okay. It's not really going to hurt," I lied.

I held his arm out as Nurse Yazbek disinfected it. She lifted the needle and drew it close to Michael's arm.

Michael shrieked, wiggled his arm free from my hand, and darted out of the room.

"You idiot," Nurse Yazbek snapped. "All I asked you to do was hold the kid still."

"Go look for him or you're not coming back tomorrow!"

I sprinted out of the room without a word, hoping that the hospital didn't send detailed recommendations—and more importantly, that Nurse Yazbek had no hand in writing them.

I spent the next hour looking for Michael. He hid under an empty bed in 35A. I escorted him back to 28C. Nurse Yazbek gave him his shot and eyed me the whole time. Her gaze made me feel cold.

I decided not to come back the next day.

(Ramadi 211–213)

EXERCISE 28 ▶ Rhetorical Analysis

Write a rhetorical analysis of "Two Weeks at Notre Dame Hospital." Continue with the conversational style you've used before. If freewriting is working for you, keep it up. If not, revise your work only after you've got all your ideas on the page. We propose the following questions and points to help you think about what to write. You need not answer them all, but maybe one or two will set you on the right path.

- Identify the strong nouns in the story. Are there opportunities to use strong nouns more often or are the pronouns used properly?
- Create a Hierarchy of Detail for this story. In each category, write down the details Ramadi includes to flesh out Nurse Yazbek's character.
- Describe the tone of Ramadi's writing.
- List the concrete verbs Ramadi uses. What role do they play in the plot?
- What's your feeling about Nurse Yazbek after reading this story?

The next peer model writing is a research paper about health care. Elizabeth Dancey examines a lesser-known cancer caused by smoking cigarettes. As you read the paper, note the nouns Dancey uses to provide both detail and evidence.

Tobacco Cigarettes as a Cause of Urinary Bladder Cancer

BY ELIZABETH DANCEY

The cigarette butt burns as it hits the ground and a feeling of satisfaction takes over. Urgency and frequency set in. Trips to the restroom become routine and a visit to the doctor answers why there is pain and blood. Described here are the symptoms of urinary bladder cancer, the fourth most common type of cancer in the United States, accounting for roughly five per cent of all diagnosed cancers (Sengupta, Siddiqui, and Mumtaz 228). The most common type of cancer associated with smoking cigarettes is lung cancer, but recent scientific evidence gives current and former smokers another type of cancer to fear. Smoking tobacco cigarettes causes urinary bladder cancer in both men and women, leaves former smokers at a high risk for bladder cancer and even when treated, bladder cancer has a low survival rate once tumors have developed.

Urinary bladder cancer is any kind of cancerous growth in the urinary bladder. Normal cells become exposed to carcinogens as they pass through the bladder, allowing them to mutate and transform into malignant cells. Malignant cell growth becomes rapid and uncontrollable (Tidy). Carcinoma, one of the main four types of cancer, is the cancer of the skin tissue or the lining of the internal organs, present in bladder cancer (American Cancer Society). Roughly half of all cell carcinomas of the bladder are connected to cigarette smoking because of the high number of carcinogens present in cigarettes (Sengupta, Siddiqui, and Mumtaz 228).

A cigarette smoker's risk of developing bladder cancer is four times higher than the risk of a non-smoker, a risk that directly relates to the number of cigarettes smoked as well as the extent of smoking. Those who smoke more than twenty cigarettes a day have a substantially higher risk of developing cancer than those who smoke fewer than twenty cigarettes a day. Furthermore, studies have shown that those who smoke for more than twenty years will develop cancer at a rate two to three times faster than those who have smoked fewer than twenty years (Zeegers et al. 635). Cigarette smoking is responsible for bladder cancer in both men and women, but roughly seventy-five per cent of patients with urinary bladder cancer are male, with no current evidence as to why (Sengupta, Siddiqui, and Mumtaz 228).

The increased frequency and urgency normally associated with urinary tract infections become two of the first symptoms of urinary bladder cancer experienced by both men and women. These symptoms are then accompanied by dysuria (pain upon urinating) and possibly hematuria (passage of blood in urine). Cystoscopy, a procedure in which an instrument is inserted into the urethra for examining the bladder, is the main method used in diagnosing bladder cancer (Sengupta, Siddiqui, and Mumtaz 228). A cystoscopy is partnered with anesthetic, while other investigations into hematuria may include a urine sample or an x-ray that will detect cancers in the kidney and ureter (a tube that carries urine from the kidney to the bladder).

Studies on different kinds of tobacco cigarettes and different ways of smoking cigarettes produce interesting results about male and female development of urinary bladder cancer. Black (air-cured) cigarettes pose a higher risk than blond (flue-cured) cigarettes in the development of bladder cancer in both genders. Cigarette smokers of both genders who inhale tobacco smoke possess a higher risk of urinary bladder cancer when compared to smokers who do not inhale. Tobacco chewing and smokeless tobacco products do not produce evidence of an increase in risk of bladder cancer in either gender. Former cigarette smokers of both sexes still have a high risk for bladder cancer; however, the risk is lower than for current smokers. Involuntary exposure to tobacco smoke by males and females does not show any evidence of an increased bladder cancer risk (Boffetta 49–52).

The universally accepted method of classification of bladder tumors is the TNM (Tumor Nodes Metastases) System used for both men and women. Scientists categorize bladder tumors based on how far the tumor has penetrated into the bladder wall. Categorization also depends on the existence of lymph nodes and spreading of the cancer into other areas of the body. Small tumors that are flat are classified as Tis. Tumors that are papillary (larger) are classified as pTa. Tumors that penetrate the bladder walls are categorized as pT1, and Stage T2 and above are tumors that have penetrated the muscle layer and pose a high risk of spreading to the lungs, liver and bones (Sengupta, Siddiqui, and Mumtaz 228–229). Determining the classification of tumors uses the same method for both men and women suffering from urinary bladder cancer.

The treatment of tumors is different for the different kinds of tumors. Surgeons can remove Tis and pTa tumors with a procedure called endoscopic transurethral resection. The rate of recurrence, however, is between fifty and seventy per cent within the first two years. If a recurrence happens, men and women are treated with medicine that is directly inserted into the bladder (Sengupta, Siddiqui, and Mumtaz 228–229). Check ups are necessary every three months for one year, twice a year in the second year after the procedure, and then annually for an extended period of time. Tumors that have penetrated the muscle (pT1 or Stage T2 and higher) cannot be removed the same way as the smaller tumors. Men and women diagnosed with urinary bladder cancer and possessing tumors that have penetrated the muscle have less than a five per cent chance of survival when the tumors are left untreated, and they usually do not live longer than another three years. The only other option for these patients is cystectomy (removal of the bladder) or radical radiotherapy, which only yields a fifty per cent response rate (Sengupta, Siddiqui, and Mumtaz 228–229).

The survival rate of men and women with urinary bladder cancer varies with the stage of cancer they have. Patients with Stage T2 bladder cancer have an 82 per cent survival rate. Patients with Stage T3 bladder cancer have a 55 per cent survival rate. Finally, patients with Stage T4 bladder cancer have less than a 25 per cent survival rate (Sengupta, Siddiqui, and Mumtaz 228–229). In short, the larger the tumor size, the smaller the chances of survival stand for men and women with urinary bladder cancer.

The carcinogens found in tobacco cigarettes are the direct cause of urinary bladder cancer in both men and women, put former cigarette smokers at an elevated risk for developing bladder cancer, and are responsible for the low survival rate after tumor development. Although quitting the cigarette habit lowers the risk of developing urinary bladder cancer, the amount of carcinogens that has already passed through the body is irreversible and permanent.

Works Cited

Boffetta, Paolo. "Tobacco Smoking and Risk Of Bladder Cancer." *Scandinavian Journal of Urology and Nephrology* 42 (2008): 45–54.

Sengupta, N., E. Siddiqui, and F.H. Mumtaz. "Cancers of the Bladder." *Perspectives in Public Health* 124.5 (2004): 228–9.

Tidy, Colin. "Bladder Cancer." *Patient.co.uk*. N.p., 24 Jan. 2012. Retrieved from www.patient.co.uk/health/bladder-cancer-leaflet, 29 Oct. 2013.

"What is Bladder Cancer?" *What is Bladder Cancer?* American Cancer Society, 17 Jan. 2013. Retrieved from www.cancer.org/cancer/bladdercancer/detailedguide/bladder-cancer-what-is-bladder-cancer, 29 Oct. 2013.

Zeegers, Maurice P.A., Frans E.S. Tan, Elisabeth Dorant, and Piet A. van den Brandt. "The Impact of Characteristics of Cigarette Smoking on Urinary Tract Cancer Risk." *Cancer* 89.3 (2000): 630–639.

EXERCISE 29 ► Rhetorical Analysis

Write a rhetorical analysis of "Tobacco Cigarettes as a Cause of Urinary Bladder Cancer." Use the natural style you've developed in other exercises and assignments. Continue freewriting if you like. If you've chosen to stop freewriting, make sure you don't judge your work until after you've exhausted all of your ideas. The following points may spark ideas for this exercise.

- Dancey explains difficult terms for her audience. List some examples of those terms and Dancey's explanations.
- What role do statistics and evidence play in this paper? Explain with examples.
- The balance between strong verbs and dead verbs is different here compared to Ramadi's narrative. Do you see opportunities for introducing additional strong verbs in Dancey's paper or are her choices the best ones?
- Do you think the paper requires any additional elements like narrative?
- Notice that the paper doesn't include any direct quotations. Do you think this is a problem or a positive here?

We hope these questions and points help you to think more deeply and critically about the paper. This reflection should make you a better writer and a more careful editor on your next assignment.

Assignment 5a

Before you tackle this assignment, go back and revise your previous four assignments with economy, strong verbs, active voice, and strong nouns in mind. By now, you should be up to revision level *d* or *e* on the previous assignments.

Suggested Topics:

1) Write a narrative about an experience you've had in a job.
2) Using the details you gathered about a person from Exercise 26, write a narrative about that person.
3) Write a short description of a health topic you'd like to investigate. Consider how you'd examine the topic in a scholarly way and also in a personal way.

Here are suggestions for writing your assignment:

- Write up a Hierarchy of Detail before you begin your work to help you decide which details to include.
- Balance is the key to drawing portraits of people. People are complex. If you write about someone you admire, avoid idealizing them. Likewise, if you write about someone you don't like (an easier task), don't paint the person as a villain. In other words, avoid telling your reader what to think about the person, whether good or bad. Let the details, including dialogue, do the work.
- In research papers, it can be difficult to keep your topic relevant and interesting to your readers. One solution is to use storytelling in your exposition of facts and details.
- Avoid overusing quotations. Beginning writers often produce underdeveloped stories that read like movie and TV scripts: just people speaking and little in between, so that readers hear the characters but do not "see" them. If you find that your rough draft looks like a movie script, spend some time adding actions or visual descriptions between snippets of dialogue. Describe how the characters look as they speak. Show their actions. Tell your reader how others (or you) react while another character talks: *I looked away and gazed over at the painting on the wall*. Similarly, in academic papers, flesh out quotations with your own thoughts and ideas; otherwise the reader simply "pinballs" among quotations from theorists with little guidance from the author.

CHAPTER SUMMARY

We began this chapter with a reminder that the verb is the most important word in a sentence. The noun finishes closely behind. Strong nouns in particular evoke images in reader's minds. These images help readers see the people, things, places, and ideas in your writing. Some nouns are stronger than others, though. The noun *Winnipeg* provides stronger imagery than *city*, for example.

One type of strong noun is the name. Some of the names in classic fiction are famous and instantly evocative—mention Ebenezer Scrooge, for example, and a whole book, an entire cast of characters and events, springs instantly to mind long after we have finished reading the story. Names matter in academic writing as well, providing detail and bolstering the writer's argument. We encouraged you to seek out and use interesting names and not fear repeating interesting ones.

Nouns evoke the five senses in the same way verbs do. In addition, many nouns (*glow, hike*) do double duty as verbs. Sometimes it's better to get sensory meaning into our writing through nouns; at other times, verbs work better. Let your ear be the guide.

Be wary of nouns that end in –tion. These words (*recitation, hesitation*) make the original actions (*recite, hesitate*) seem distant and add unnecessary "bulk" to your writing. We showed how converting –tion nouns to their verb forms helped to create stronger sentences and let readers experience the action firsthand.

We then provided a way to think about characterization through an exercise called the Hierarchy of Detail. In personal writing, four categories of detail are required to flesh out a character: action, evidence of action, speech, and reputation. In academic writing, there are five categories: facts, figures, and statistics; arguments; quotations; paraphrases; and summaries. Good writers in both genres include as much detail from the relevant sets of categories as they can.

After the defence of strong nouns, the chapter presented the next interfering factor to good writing: unclear pronouns. Pronouns are little words like *he*, *she*, and *they* that take the place of nouns, creating a mental relationship for the reader between themselves and previous nouns. Pronouns ease problems of noun repetition; each should refer back clearly to the noun it replaces.

Handy as they are, however, pronouns can present two problems. First, they evoke little imagery and in some cases they evoke only a vague sense of gender. Second, and more importantly, sometimes these poor little pronouns forget whom they replaced. They get amnesia. This is called a breakdown in the pronoun–antecedent relationship. Luckily, this breakdown can be remedied fairly simply, often just by reinserting the original noun in the orphaned pronoun's place. Now your readers can once again follow your meaning without wondering *Who is "he"? Who is "she"?*

Like passive voice in Chapter 4, unclear pronouns, especially sentences that start with pronouns like *It is* . . . or *There are* . . . are not only unnecessarily wordy but they also allow writers to hide their actions behind a veil of seeming impartiality. This is particularly common in business correspondence, as we showed.

Writers sometimes overuse vague pronouns like *it* and *they* in an attempt to avoid repeating nouns. But as we demonstrated, sometimes repetition can be a good thing, particularly if the nouns in question are interesting (e.g., an unusual name or item that you want to stick in the reader's memory). Let your ear and your intent tell you if repetition sounds right.

Pronouns also present gender issues. Until recently, writers routinely referred to the whole human race with the pronoun *he*. Over time, however, people challenged this usage because it excluded women. Language is constantly evolving; be aware of both current and outdated usage.

The idea of relations between words came up in this chapter: a pronoun must relate clearly to a noun. This relates to another writing problem: subject–verb agreement. Subjects must agree with verbs in number. Often subjects are pronouns and it can be unclear whether a given pronoun (say, *each* or *every*) is singular or plural. We showed some simple examples of subject–verb agreement problems, and then some quite difficult ones where pronouns were subjects.

The point of this sermon on pronouns was not to be picky and avoid the big picture, but to help you see your sentences carefully. Being aware of the issues covered in this chapter will help you revise your work to create more detailed, clearer communication with readers.

▌ Further Readings

For more about the debates over pronouns and gender:

Livia, Anna. *Pronoun Envy: Literary Uses of Linguistic Gender.* New York: Oxford University Press, 2001.

For more about academic writing:

Henderson, Eric. *The Active Writer: Strategies for Academic Reading and Writing.* 2nd ed. Oxford University Press, 2011.

6

Original Language

> Make it new.
>
> —EZRA POUND

FACED WITH THE CHALLENGE of understanding and applying all the lessons we've presented so far, you may be wondering whether it's possible to write originally—to express new, fresh ideas in a voice that is uniquely yours.

You may expect new writers to write originally—they see the world in ways veteran writers perhaps don't see. But many new writers bend under the weight of literary or cultural influence. They overtly emulate the styles of other writers. They copy exact phrasings. They draw on old sayings passed down from grandparents. They copy ideas.

Contrary to what you might think, original language is not language that's *never* been written or spoken. We share a language and a culture. We must use common linguistic resources to make meaning. Without such common linguistic resources, we wouldn't be able to communicate. Writing just cannot be a completely individual task without influence. The writer whose writing is unaffected by his or her culture doesn't exist.

Instead, we see originality as the way each of us puts the common linguistic resources together to make a point or express an experience. The way you, as a writer, put your language together can be original—within limits, of course. Unoriginal or borrowed language won't sound like yours—the literary or cultural influences will be too obvious.

Another way to consider originality in writing is to think about frequency. Words that circulate frequently are too familiar to feel fresh or original. Infrequently used language, on the other hand, looks and sounds interesting. Your readers won't have seen it before, or at least often. The idea of frequent versus infrequent, then, should guide you as a writer because readers, particularly teachers and editors, delight in our fifth enhancing factor for good writing: original language.

You instinctively know the feeling of original language at the level of the word and phrase. When you hear someone say something in a way you haven't heard before, you enjoy it and then use it in turn in your own conversation. Language is social—it changes and adapts. Language we accept as the norm today is often language that was new decades ago.

The words and phrases *Totally awesome*, *bling*, *dude*, and *an apple a day keeps the doctor away* excited people when they were first used. Each seemed unusual and original; none was common.

Like a viral video on YouTube, these words and phrases have passed from person to person, year after year, until they've become widely known and a part of our linguistic and cultural heritage. The media plays a major role in this process, circulating words and phrases quickly to wide audiences. Not surprisingly then, writers draw upon these words and phrases to varying degrees when they sit down to write. It becomes easy—perhaps too easy—to use them as resources for putting together sentences.

But all trends eventually become old—it's in their nature. People no longer want to wear flared-bottom jeans or cut their hair in a bob. Neither do they want to say *I've got bling* or *Hey, dude* or *My boyfriend is a diamond in the rough* (although some people continue to do so in spite of a trend's death).

At some point, popular words and phrases come to sound stale, worn out, and overused. You might choose to use them only when joking around. They no longer represent a product of the current time. Instead, they sound the way an old song sounds: like an amusing relic of the distant past. We don't want our writing to be a historical curiosity, though.

And this brings us to our fifth interfering factor to good writing: the **cliché**. In writing, a cliché is a word or phrase that has become unoriginal through overuse. Clichés usually, but not always, fall into the category of **figurative** language, the realm of **metaphors** and **similes**.

The word is the past participle of the French *clicher*, to **stereotype**. In early publishing, printers would stereotype—that is, they would create a metal plate mould from individual letters of type. Once they engraved the metal plate with words and rolled on the ink, printers could reprint pages over and over again without have to reset the type. Duplication reigned thanks to the printing press.

Cliché has since escaped its printing press origins. Writers and editors are more aware of clichés and avoid or eliminate them where possible, opting instead to use original, fresh language. However, in the school system, some teachers still reward students for stringing together clichés.

The recognition of hot and cold language is an important skill. If you recognize clichés, you're aware of the currents of writing today. Usually writers develop this awareness by reading the latest and best writing in their fields. If you recognize clichés, you can remove them from your writing and get on the path to original language.

Let's have some new clichés.
—SAMUEL GOLDWYN

Examples of Clichés

Most clichés seem innovative and exciting when they're first coined. But over time, as they become part of our everyday language, they begin to seem worn out and, frankly, annoying. Faced with clichés in personal or academic texts, readers will often simply tune out.

Many clichés are passed down from generation to generation. Over time, they lose their history. Those clichés were created far in the past, in such a different culture from our own.

For example, when we ask our students the origins of the old saying *Once in a blue moon*, almost everyone has no idea. If they read the sentence *He cleans his room once in a blue a moon*, they intuitively know this means he cleans his room infrequently. But what's a blue moon?

We had to look up the definition. A blue moon exists when two full moons occur in the same month (and it doesn't look blue). This cosmic rarity happens only about every 28 to 30 months.

What culture would have produced this metaphor? Not our Digital Age, but an age rooted in the natural world, where farmers took keen interest in the changes in the environment, the sun, and the moon. Our day-to-day lives don't depend on the phases of the moon.

To help you recognize clichés, we provide a selection of examples below. We're sure you can fill in most of the blanks without much thought:

a) It's raining cats and _____.

b) Don't bite the hand that _____.

c) She's as free as a _____.

d) He's a pain in the _____.

e) Last but not _____.

f) The Princess lived happily _____.

g) His daughter was the apple of _____.

h) Still waters run _____.

i) You should walk a mile in my _____.

j) His back was against the _____.

Next, we present a series of double- or even triple-whammies: See if you can identify all the clichés in the sentences. If you're unsure about any of them, check the Internet or your library. Cliché websites, databases, and books abound.

a) We are sick and tired of the tried and true approach to office management and are seeking a breath of fresh air from the new plan.

b)   It was raining cats and dogs, but we slept like logs through the storm.

c)   She stopped dead in her tracks. Lying on the floor was her son, crying his eyes out.

d)   I get a kick out of seeing you have a whale of a good time.

e)   The naked truth is that he's the ace in the hole for the company.

f)   She was barking up the wrong tree when she asked George for a helping hand.

g)   The squeaky wheel always gets the grease so I gave him a piece of my mind.

h)   The show must go on if we're going to succeed in the long run.

i)   Timothy needed to grab the bull by the horns if he was going to keep up with the Joneses.

j)   Jada was up in arms after the boss let David off the hook for his indiscretions.

Finally, have a look at the list of clichés and buzzwords below and see if you can figure out which decade each expression comes from. Some may be familiar to you from your own childhood, and you may recognize others from books or movies.

Swag	Far out
Not!	Get down
Playa	Bummer
Amped up	What up, Dog?
Boy toy	Burn out
Buggin'	Catch my drift?
Cowabunga	I dig it
Eat my shorts	What a drag
Radical	Foxy
Get real	Groovy
Head banger	Crunk
Noob	Joshin'
My posse	Gnarly
Righteous	Peace out
My bad	Shag
That's sick	Talkin' jive
Sweet	Go bananas
Psyche	Totally awesome
Hey shorty	Wicked

As we said above, these words and phrases point to specific historical periods. Expressions like "talkin' jive" and "groovy" point to the 1960s and 1970s. "Totally awesome" suggests the 1980s, and "my bad" reminds us of the 1990s. You may have stopped using some of these (or never have used them at all). As a speaker you may use them to get a laugh out of your friends; in writing, they can be useful, when used judiciously, to evoke the dialogue or customs of a specific era.

Whether a cliché is a positive or a negative depends on the context. For example, in the 1960s throwback movie *Austin Powers*, actor Mike Myers takes all that era's clichés of fashion and speech (his striped bell-bottoms and "Yeaaah, baby!") and uses them to huge comedic advantage. Deploying the same fashion and speech clichés in, say, a business meeting or a university seminar, however, would be grossly inappropriate.

The point we're trying to make here is that intent matters: accidental use of clichés or stereotyped phrases and behaviour can make your writing seem outdated and tired. Wisely and artfully deployed, however, those same clichés can instantly evoke a time period, a look, or a whole set of values for your readers.

EXERCISE 30 ▶ List of Clichés

We've listed some clichés so far. Now it's your turn. Make a list of cliché words or phrases you hear or see over the next five days. Try to collect at least 20 per day (100 or more in total). Gather them from radio and television, the conversation of your family and friends, your teachers' lectures, the newspaper—any place. Identify your sources. This assignment may sound difficult, but you should be able to collect 20 clichés in a matter of minutes. By the end of this exercise you should be able to *spot a cliché a mile away*.

Figurative Writing by Three Canadian Columnists

While it's important to avoid clichés, you should not ignore figurative language completely. Fresh figurative language can help readers understand your meaning more deeply and completely. The problem is that many professional writers use stale figurative language, avoiding the hard work of creating new similes and metaphors.

Professional writers' use of figurative language varies, from stale and obvious to fresh and subtle. In some cases, professional writers use figurative language as overtly as *a man yells fire in a crowded theatre*. Other times, it's more discreet and hard to notice, like *an undercover police officer sitting in an unmarked cruiser*. It helps to look at how professional writers—in this case Canadian newspaper columnists—use figurative language in different ways, on a spectrum from original to unoriginal.

In an article in the *Toronto Sun*, columnist Michael Harris writes about Prime Minister Paul Martin:

> As every source-sucking sluggo in Ottawa knows, Mr. Martin is about to ascend to the leadership of the Liberal Party. Ergo, there is much to be gained by tugging one's forelock before speaking to the great man, and nothing from kicking him in the shins when his arrogance, lack of liberalism, or misplaced fiscal conservatism shine through. In the current dust-up over what to do about the recommendations of the House of Commons subcommittee on sport, all three deficiencies have shown up like zits on a beauty queen.

Let's assess the origins and effectiveness of each instance of figurative language:

- **source-sucking sluggo:** This phrase is used as a pejorative for a journalist, who sucks information out of sources (people who provide information). This phrase is original and hasn't reached the level of a cliché—in other words, we don't hear it used much. It requires, however, a certain level of journalism knowledge to understand it.
- **ascend:** This word remains fresh. Martin won't literally ascend—to some throne, for example—but he will become the top person in the party.
- **tug one's forelock:** This is an old British cliché meaning to show respect to a superior.
- **Great Man:** Historians of the eighteenth century tended to write histories about Great Men, not regular people. In scholarship today, historians use this cliché regularly to describe that historical focus. But it also reflects sexist language.
- **kicking him in the shins:** Of course, no one will literally kick Martin in the shins. The author's cliché suggests petulance by subordinates.
- **shine:** This fresh, strong verb evokes enlightenment. It relates to the cliché *see the light*. To shine light on something is to expose it to the public.
- **dust-up:** This cliché from the late 1800s means a quarrel. *Dust-up* provides an image of the dust kicked up during a fight on a dirt road.
- **zits on a beauty queen:** This phrase clearly suggests imperfection. The reader needs little extra knowledge to understand it.

The scorecard on Harris's figurative language is mixed: some originality, some cliché. The first instance attempts originality but may not resonate with all readers. Perhaps it tries too hard to be original. *Ascend* and *shine* remain effective, original words. But the others need reconsideration.

As we saw in Chapter 5, writers often use figurative language to capture someone's essence in the fewest words possible. Here is an excerpt from a column by *Globe and Mail* writer Christie Blatchford in which she uses metaphor and clichés to describe Mississauga mayor Hazel McCallion.

continued

She is spunky, even cute. Why, she still drives! At 89! She's as sharp as a tack, as even her critics admit, albeit usually in order to plead that she should leave the building now, while she's on top of her game—for her own good, they always say, by which they usually mean for theirs.

The thing is, as anyone who knows her or has even seen her in action recognizes, a reason Ms. McCallion would have all her marbles—another favourite of the wet-behind-the-ears set—is so she is well-armed to rocket some at your head.

Let's look at the origins and effectiveness of the figurative language Blatchford employs:

- **sharp as a tack:** This cliché suggests intelligence. Someone who is smart is often called sharp. Tacks are pins with a sharp end.
- **leave the building:** This plays on a cliché common to public address announcers: *Elvis has left the building* (originally used to get Elvis fans to leave a concert hall).
- **on top of her game:** This sports cliché refers to a top-notch professional athlete. McCallion is not a top-notch professional athlete, but the comparison suggests she's just as effective in politics.
- **for her own good:** This phrasing plays on the cliché *She's too smart for her own good.*
- **all her marbles:** The origin of this cliché is difficult to find, but some suggest it refers to a child losing his or her toy marbles. Many readers know what this means—losing one's mind.
- **wet-behind-the-ears:** We know this classic cliché to mean someone who's inexperienced and naïve. What's the source? In the early twentieth century, the phrase came about to mean a baby still wet after birth. No one could be more inexperienced than a newborn.
- **well-armed to rocket:** An uncommon phrase, this figure of speech invokes a military metaphor common to political writing.

Blatchford's paragraphs use a great deal of clichés in a short patch of writing. Given her experience as a journalist, this choice was likely intentional.

A final example comes from *National Post* columnist Andrew Coyne, who is known for his fresh, precise, to-the-point language. In this excerpt from his article about Barack Obama's inauguration speech, Coyne's figurative language appeals to the physical senses:

Inaugural addresses are often embarrassing. Lacking the historic moment to support their oratory, presidents reach for the lyrical, and end up grasping at air.

Speechwriters take note: fine writing is always to be avoided, but never more so than when you risk making the world's fool of your boss.

This was not one of those occasions. After a bruising first term, Barack Obama was not in the mood to be lyrical. Instead, it was brisk, businesslike and brutal—not by any means the shortest inaugural, but surely among the punchiest. Where some inaugurals seek to lift up, this one threw down; where some extend a hand, this drew a line. It was focused, blunt and unequivocal, the most full-throated defence of liberalism in an inaugural since FDR's second, to which it bears some resemblance: the same hymns to the power of the collective, the same us-and-them taunting of the wealthy, and quite a bit more scolding of the opposition.

Let's consider how Coyne goes beyond the literal:

- **reach for the lyrical:** This uncommon phrase makes us imagine Obama extending his hand to grab words. A Google search of this exact phrase found just 10 uses on the Internet—that's certainly original.
- **end up grasping at air:** This more common (but perhaps not yet cliché) phrase fits with the previous one—to *reach* and to *grasp* reflect the sense of touch. It also plays on the line *gasping for air*.
- **world's fool:** This original phrase suggests a Shakespearean fool designed to be clever, like a jester.
- **bruising; punchiest:** At this point in the paragraph, Coyne moves into a sort of extended boxing metaphor. It's subtle—these references perhaps don't rise to the level of cliché. But he clearly suggests that Obama has had a difficult time, difficult enough to leave bruises. Calling Obama's speech "punchy" reminds us of George Lakoff and Mark Johnson's (2003) assertion that writers often describe politics in terms of fighting. Perhaps that language itself is cliché.
- **lift up—threw down; extend a hand—drew a line:** These two pairs of clichés set up a contrast between helping actions and harming actions. This parallelism—we discuss parallelism in Chapter 7—is easy to follow. No one is literally being lifted up or thrown down by Obama's speech, but the stark contrast of each action, and the images they call to mind, resonate with readers.

These authors use figurative language in different ways. The success of the usage depends upon the intended audience, the subject matter, and the style of the writers. Some writers may use clichés to appeal to an indiscriminate **populist** audience—the clichés make quick, easy meaning. Other writers may use clichés for amusement. Finally, some writers may employ fresh figurative language to mark themselves as originators.

> **EXERCISE 31** ▸ Cliché Article
>
> Clichés lurk all over—even in the writing of well-known professional writers. For this exercise, copy a page of a newspaper or magazine and circle the clichés you find. If you want to make it easy on yourself, pick a fashion or sports page. Can you think of alternatives to the clichés?

▌ Why Would Any Writer Use Clichés?

We've noted that some writers, particularly seasoned journalists, sometimes use clichés to make a point. But how do they slip into other people's writing? One reason is a lack of awareness. Awareness of clichés requires regular reading—newspapers, websites, blogs, books. If you're not reading the works of others in whatever area you enjoy, you won't know what's now reached the status of a cliché.

> [Ready-made phrases] will construct your sentences for you—even think your thoughts for you, to a certain extent—and at need they will perform the important service of partially concealing your meaning even from yourself.
>
> —GEORGE ORWELL

It also requires a larger awareness of the culture in which you're living and writing. Clichés are cultural, born out of specific times and places—all cultures and languages have them. They are passed down from parents and grandparents, from children's stories, and so on. If you grew up in a non-English/non-Western country or culture, you may not recognize that some phrases you hear (or use) in your adopted home are clichés. You may need to do some extra work (by using online resources, for example) and become familiar with them.

Sometimes a writer's use of clichés may simply be a response to the difficult work of writing. Clichés make writing easy: you just string together a bunch of clichés passed on to you by your grandparents, parents, friends, and culture, and your work is done. It's not you writing, it's your genealogy.

Some journalists, particularly in populist newspapers, feel their audiences don't care about the use of clichés. They believe that readers respond favourably to clichés because they seem so familiar. It's a tool for an easy connection between the writer and the reader. This is a minority position on clichés, however. If done right, original language is not more difficult to understand than clichés. We show some examples below.

The one thing a newspaper columnist cannot do is fail to write an article. We never open the newspaper and see a blank space with a notice: *This columnist had nothing original to say today.* Dead air will get a radio announcer fired. Media workers labour under powerful pressure to fill spaces with words—whether the words say anything or not. So they do the easy thing: they reach into their stock of prefabricated phrases and fill the spaces they are paid to fill.

Finally, we believe some writers use clichés because they believe it's stylish. They become the Egotistical Stylist, emphasizing the style of their communication over the substance. Now, we talk a lot about style in this book. But we're not being hypocrites. Egotistical Stylists employ certain styles not to communicate better but to show off a perceived facility with language, like Michael Harris did above in the case study.

Look back at your writing assignments from earlier chapters and see if you've used clichés. If you have, you may worry that you won't have anything left once you edit them out. It may seem difficult to give them up, like giving up your favourite food. Making original meaning is a hard, hard thing to do.

> If a man writes clearly enough anyone can see if he fakes.
>
> —ERNEST HEMINGWAY

EXERCISE 32 ► Cliché Paragraph

Now it's time to try writing clichés—just this once. Write a paragraph of about 100 words on any topic, using as many clichés as possible. Use at least one cliché per sentence. Your objective is to make no original meaning whatsoever. Love and business make good topics. When you concentrate the clichés in a paragraph, you become a comic writer.

Is It Ever Okay to Use a Cliché?

Clichés do have a place—a small place—in writing. They fulfill three purposes: 1) for dialogue, 2) for creating a sense of historical time, and 3) for play.

Let's begin with dialogue. In stories, clichés help to create realistic dialogue because we all talk in clichés occasionally. Perhaps your grandmother says *A bird in the hand is worth two in the bush*. In a story about your grandmother, you wouldn't edit this sentence out because that's the way she typically speaks. She perhaps encountered the phrase as a child, when it seemed original.

Clichés are also valuable for creating atmosphere that belongs to a particular time or era. If you want to establish the atmosphere of a high school cafeteria in the 1980s, then you bring in the clichés that belong to that era. If you want to establish the atmosphere of a factory assembly line, then there are clichés that belong to that scene that will help you do the job. If you want to show life in a hairdressing salon, a children's sandbox, a university chemistry class, or an athletic locker room, then appropriate clichés can serve a good purpose. Similarly, a scholar writing an academic paper may choose to describe the clichés of thought once found in his or her field of study. For example, early scholars of communication believed in a "hypodermic needle" effect of media—that is, they believed that media messages, like propaganda, directly caused people to do actions against

> A bird in the hand was worth two in the bush, he told her, to which she retorted that a proverb was the last refuge of the mentally destitute.
>
> —W. Somerset Maugham

their will. This theoretical position is cliché today—the place of media in people's lives is believed to be much more nuanced.

Finally, writers play with clichés. You can wink at the reader with full knowledge that you're using an inverted or distorted cliché. For example: *cool as a carrot*, *a bull in a pastry shop*, *a babe in the desert*.

Advertising and comedians often mock clichés with a twist to get a laugh and make a point. A good example of this came in a set of National Hockey League TV commercials that poked fun at sports clichés—athletes and coaches are well known for spouting clichés in locker-room interviews. In one commercial, a hockey coach dressed in a suit and fedora stands in front of his players in the locker room. He gives them a pep talk before the match:

> Alright, listen up. Today I want to talk about giving 110 per cent. Giving 100 per cent means giving everything you've got. Giving 110 per cent means giving 10 per cent more than is humanly possible. If we're going to win as a team, we need 100 per cent of you guys giving 110 per cent 100 per cent of the time. If only 50 per cent of you guys give 110 per cent, and 50 per cent of you give 100 per cent, I guarantee you 100 per cent we'd only win 50 per cent of our games. Suppose 75 per cent of 110 per cent gave only 50 per cent, and 50 per cent of 100 per cent gave 25 per cent, and 75 per cent of 100 per cent were not feeling 100 per cent, then we'd be in a heap of trouble. That's why we need 100 per cent of you guys giving 110 per cent, 100 per cent of the time. Okay. Let's go out and play some hockey!
>
> Source: NHL Network. www.youtube.com/watch?v=Pz3KpY5lrRc&list=PLADD38D7C97C79203

This commercial plays on a common sports cliché: *I'm going to give 110 per cent.* It shows the absurdity of the cliché—how is effort measured? Why is effort 110 per cent and not 150 per cent or 200 per cent? How would you give that extra 10 per cent anyway? Under scrutiny, the cliché falls apart. We laugh.

In the second commercial, the same coach gives a post-mortem to reporters after his team's loss. The coach riffs on another common sports cliché:

> Why'd we lose? Well, I thought we shot the lights out in the first two periods. In the third period we just couldn't put the biscuit in the basket. We just couldn't put the stuffing in the turkey, or we couldn't even put the turkey in the oven. We couldn't put the car in the garage. We couldn't put the train in the station. We couldn't put the rod in the water, the lightning in a bottle, the cat in the hat. I mean that's really why we lost tonight: we couldn't put the cat in the hat.
>
> Source: NHL Network. www.youtube.com/watch?v=IjkUMbrT5SU

The coach plays on the common *biscuit in the basket* metaphor (the biscuit being the puck and the basket being the net) to the point of absurdity: it echoes the title of Dr Seuss's children's book *The Cat in the Hat*. We laugh at the clichés the coach plays with here, but both commercials are rooted in a social truth: many people speak in clichés without realizing it. They become unintentional comedians.

Here is the crucial point: clichés chosen consciously by the writer form part of that writer's observations of the world. Clichés used unconsciously, however, are destructive to the writer's goal of making writing original. Most readers instinctively suspect those formulaic expressions. Writers who rely on clichés sacrifice their readers' trust.

▌ Original Phrasing

Turning to clichés to make meaning is like turning to a dealer for drugs. Kick the habit *cold turkey*. To recap, some simple steps should make this intervention easier:

- Develop your sensibility for clichés through reading current (not Victorian Age) writing in publications you enjoy.
- Remove clichés as often as you can during the revision process.
- Use effective detail to describe situations.
- Use fresh figurative language only when you're comfortable with it.

In the next three examples, we show how the third point—using effective detail—helps writers avoid clichés. It's not just a strategy—it's also an attitude. The act of describing your experiences and ideas precisely and vividly produces wonderful, fresh language. But consider this cliché-filled paragraph in a story:

> Milo Thomas stood on the green, green grass of home—finally. He'd been in the city for what seemed like forever. Many people enjoy the bright lights and the big city, but there was no place like home on the farm for him. He stood and stared at the mountains in the distance, which looked as pretty as a picture. He wanted to drive up to the summit and have a bird's eye view of his farm, but his pickup truck was on its last legs. Instead, he decided to stick around for the day at his farmhouse, which looked as old as dirt.

Green, green grass of home . . . bright lights and the big city . . . no place like home . . . All English speakers know these clichés. The writer has *taken the easy way out* and reverted to familiarity, not originality. The writer wants to suggest a whole lot of meanings about the farm and the landscape, but it comes across as mindless meaning-making—writing as simply stringing phrases together.

> Originality does not consist in saying what no one has ever said before, but in saying exactly what you think yourself.
> —JAMES STEPHENS

Now, let's look at three writers who describe places with fresh, vivid details. A passage from a peer model story by Vaia Barkas shows a journey of two women through Alberta.

> We had passed through Assiniboia when the clouds still lagged behind us, an hour north of the Alberta-Montana border where the wide prairie rolls with low relief. Low grass hills rolled back, rolling in smaller and smaller waves as they approached the horizon, and the road rolled and dipped through the hills. Between the hills, in flat wide fields, grey barns sagged and listed against an invisible wind. We banked around small patches of snow, leftover from a late April cold snap, crusting in the gullies beside the road. Clouds coasted through the sky, flat-bottomed prairie clouds, trailing behind us and piling in drifts and we drove, dazzled, into the sun. Two dusty pick-up trucks rattled past us and the drivers waved. Andrea and I waved back. (162)

Barkas writes in a way that emphasizes effective communication: economy, active voice, strong verbs. Beyond that, Barkas does the difficult work of trying to put into original words what she saw on the drive. Her good details provide our minds with images of hills and roads and barns and snow. These words are not new to us, but the collective effect engages us as readers. The passage sounds poetic.

One of the finest academic writers was James W. Carey, a communication theorist who wrote about concepts in an easy, sometimes even poetic style. One of his most famous articles, on the theory of communication, used original language to classify communication into two types:

> The transmission view of communication is the commonest in our culture—perhaps in all industrial cultures—and dominates contemporary dictionary entries under the term. It is defined by terms such as "imparting," "sending," "transmitting," or "giving information to others." It is formed from a metaphor of geography or transportation. . . .
>
> The ritual view of communication, though a minor thread in our national thought, is by far the older of those views—old enough in fact for dictionaries to list it under "Archaic." In a ritual definition, communication is linked to terms such as "sharing," "participation," "association," "fellowship," and "the possession of a common faith." This definition exploits the ancient identity and common roots of the terms "commonness," "communion," "community," and "communication." A ritual view of communication is directed not toward the extension of messages in space but toward the maintenance of society in time; not the act of imparting information but the representation of shared beliefs. (12–15)

Carey doesn't lazily fall back upon clichés. Instead, he comes up with his own original language, including the metaphors of transmission and ritual. Carey's originality made this description of communication's nature so popular that most communication studies teachers include this article on course reading lists.

Finally, another writer—the former Member of Parliament for the federal riding of Trinity Spadina in Toronto—uses great detail to show her city as she runs through it on the way to an important site. Olivia Chow's memoir, *My Journey*, begins with this scene:

> ... I start running east, along College Street. In black shorts and T-shirt, I jog by university students with backpacks heading to their classes, nurses and doctors in their whites entering the hospitals, cyclists in the bike lanes. My iPod is playing Jesse Cook, Latin guitar music I used to listen to with Jack Layton, my late husband, while we watched sunsets and danced on our back porch. Soon I cross Jarvis Street, not far from the high school I attended when I came to Canada. Farther along, I run by Allan Gardens, a park with a Victorian greenhouse I used to visit as a teenager. ... I run north on Parliament Street, then east again on Winchester Street, past elegant front yards full of hostas, cheerful black-eyed Susans and feathery reed grasses yielding to the breeze. I am almost at Jack's final resting place, the Necropolis cemetery in Cabbagetown. (Chow, Prologue)

We see no clichés here. Instead, Chow carefully relates the moment as she remembers it. Notice Chow's use of strong verbs (*jog, watched, danced, cross, run, visit*) and strong nouns (*College Street, shorts, T-shirt, students, backpacks, nurses, doctors, hospitals, cyclists, lanes, iPod, Jesse Cook, music, Jack Layton, sunsets, porch, Jarvis Street, high school, Canada, Allan Gardens, park, greenhouse, teenager, Parliament Street, Winchester Street, yards, hostas, black-eyed Susans, grasses, breeze, Necropolis cemetery, Cabbagetown*) to bring in details that arouse the human senses. Chow also uses the active voice to make a complex paragraph run smoothly (*I jog, I cross, I run*). Chow doesn't try too hard to impress with style: the writing includes no overdone or awkward metaphors or similes. She simply leads us along, as if we were running with her through the streets. Only through this great detail can we feel like we're there, too. Readers who have visited the city will feel a sense of familiarity and authenticity; readers who haven't visited the city will now feel like they've been there. Chow's writing also includes attention to parallelism and sentence rhythm and sound, which we'll look at later in this book.

EXERCISE 33 ▸ Original Language

Now that you know what a cliché is, and you've read some original writing, it's time for *you* to create original language. The following exercise is designed to help you develop your observational skills and produce original writing. Translating your observations into writing develops your sense of detail.

Sit in a public place (bus, library, coffee shop, a gym etc.) and write three short paragraphs:

Paragraph 1: describe the actions of a person or people in that place
Paragraph 2: describe how the place looks
Paragraph 3: describe the sounds you hear in that place

continued

Notice everything. Bring the place to life. Of course, do not use any clichés. Two additional restrictions: 1) do not use any forms of the verb *to be* (*am, is, are, was, were, been, being,* including contractions such as *it's* for *it is* or *I'm* for *I am*), and 2) write only in the active voice (no passives). These restrictions make writing difficult, but in the process you'll discover the level of detail required for good writing.

Fresh Figurative Language

We believe you can survive without using clichés and without worrying a great deal about creating new metaphors and similes. Describe well what you've experienced and you'll entertain readers. Many of the stories in this book do just that—and the authors find ways to show real life in new ways.

> Detail makes the difference between boring and terrific writing. It's the difference between a pencil sketch and a lush oil painting. As a writer, words are your paint. Use all the colors.
>
> —RHYS ALEXANDER

When you finally feel comfortable with straightforward, detailed writing like the kind we showed above, you may want to create fresh figurative language. This meaning-making isn't easy. It's difficult to get it right. But used sparingly, figurative language helps readers better understand your new ideas and experiences.

Metaphors and Similes

Metaphors and similes are two types of figurative language. A metaphor compares two different, unrelated realms of experience. When a television commentator compares a political debate to a war, the commentator takes one realm of experience (politics) and compares it to another unrelated realm of experience (military battle).

George Lakoff and Mark Johnson believe these comparisons directly affect how we see and judge these actions. They think people would act differently in a political debate if the dominant metaphor for it was not battle but dance (4–6):

> In the debate, the two candidates danced to an agreement on economic policy directions.

Of course, that never happens. Instead, we get this in political writing:

> In the debate, the two candidates fought tooth and nail over economy policy directions.

Indeed, political candidates seem to accept that debate is about fighting, not consensus. When a dance metaphor arrives, it's a negative:

> Stephen Harper danced around Justin Trudeau's question.

In our age of technology, technological metaphors exist for human actions that are not technological. Consider this statement about an act by a government:

> The province downloaded the costs of social services onto the municipalities.

Downloaded works as a metaphor because we computer users immediately understand its implications. If we took a time machine back to the 1940s and used that term in conversation, people wouldn't understand. The *Oxford English Dictionary*, which catalogues the history of words, says *download* was first used in 1976. That's young for a word. Here's another technological example:

> The producer rebooted the Superman movie franchise.

The verb *reboot*—to restart a computer after a power failure or malfunction—is relatively young in the history of words. According to the *Oxford English Dictionary*, the first known printed evidence of *reboot* as a verb came in 1971 (*reboot* was not used as a noun until 1980). No inherent meaningful connection exists between the word for starting up a computer again and a series of movies. They are different realms. But most people today understand the word *reboot*. It makes clear sense and doesn't seem overused—yet.

> Metaphors have a way of holding the most truth in the least space.
> —ORSON SCOTT CARD

Metaphors may also personalize new objects. When a technical writer describes the company's devices as having *wake* and *sleep* functions, he or she is using figurative language. The words personify the computer, giving it human abilities (the author could have just said it will turn *on* and *off*, of course, but that wouldn't be as interesting). Original phrasing often comes from the creation of new comparisons between unconnected realms of experience.

A simile is a type of metaphor. While metaphoric language becomes so natural we don't even realize it, similes are more obvious. Similes overtly compare by using *like* or *as*. In the next set of examples, *like* and *as* tip off the reader explicitly that the sentences are metaphorical:

a) The decay of society was praised by artists as the decay of a corpse is praised by worms.

b) My words swirled around his head like summer flies.

c) A bad metaphor is like a dead rat behind a wall.

d) The drunk old man raged and raged like a hurricane.

For a metaphor to be effective, though, the reader has to be able to make the connection mentally. If the metaphor isn't understood or doesn't resonate as an acceptable comparison, then it fails. Some people—including war veterans—criticize the use of war metaphors in sports. Think about this extended metaphor:

> In the seventh game, the Detroit Red Wings battled to the death against the New York Rangers, eventually losing in overtime. Still, the Detroit Red Wings left with honour.

Veterans and other readers take issue with this war metaphor because they argue that sport is like war only superficially. The Stanley Cup final may be the toughest cup to win in sports, but nobody dies at the end.

Another problem with metaphors is that they demand a certain level of knowledge. What if a reader lacks the education or cultural experience required to understand a metaphor? Consider these examples:

a) David's prose made me feel like I ate a plate of hushpuppies.

b) The professor's mind was as sharp as an Ulu.

c) Sally hunted for the pen like a Griffon.

You may have to run to the dictionary to find out just what a hushpuppy, an Ulu, and a Griffon are. Only then can you understand what the author thought about David, the professor, and Sally. Metaphors that assume such knowledge fail to create the intended effect. They fail to make that connection between two realms of experience. Don't bother with metaphors unless you're certain they'll resonate with your target audience.

The following metaphors make more obvious sense for most readers. You don't need obscure knowledge to know what the authors mean:

a) Our relationship drips more often than it flows.

b) I crawled into my warm nest at bedtime: a large duvet and four down pillows.

c) I loved her like Marilyn Monroe loved blond.

d) Her theories resonated like a drum with her students.

> The essence of metaphor is understanding and experiencing one kind of thing in terms of another.
>
> —GEORGE LAKOFF AND MARK JOHNSON

All three metaphors make intuitive sense. They connect with most readers because they tap into general knowledge. Yet neither one is a cliché. We haven't heard this language before. The authors have put some thought into constructing these sentences. They didn't turn to easy cliché.

An explanatory simile can say a lot as well, on different meaningful levels. These similes deliberately attempt to clarify and explain. Consider these examples:

a) Grandpa's teeth are like the stars: they come out at night.

b)   True love is like a unicorn. You can read about it, you can dream about it, but you can never experience it.

c)   Like tiny chimes in the wind, my earrings tinkled.

d)   The men on the assembly line looked like captive beasts.

e)   I was as likely to succeed as a ballet dancer with a wooden leg.

Whether or not a metaphor will work with an audience depends on the writer's ability to know an audience. Ask the question: does the audience have the cultural knowledge to understand what I'm saying? If you're not sure, then it's best to revise the language or remove it, or else you'll confuse readers. If the audience doesn't have the cultural knowledge to get it, then they will overlook or resist the metaphor—and then you've lost them.

Many of the cliché examples earlier in the chapter contained mixed metaphors. Here are some more examples of mixed metaphors. These come across as overwrought and crass:

a)   The moon, a silver coin, hung in the draperies of the enchanted night.

b)   Her voice bounced like a basketball off the walls of the amphitheatre as the walls mocked her every note.

c)   The chef stood at the doorway to success but the food critic crushed his mountain of dreams.

Here the authors try too hard to use figurative language. We alluded to this problem earlier. When you focus too much on figurative language—as opposed to just expressing yourself as best as you can—you may end up with strange mixed metaphors that prompt laughs, not admiration. Use metaphors and similes appropriately and sparingly.

Irony, Overstatement, and Understatement

Three other useful rhetorical devices for original phrasing are irony, understatement, and overstatement. These devices play with literal meanings too.

Irony means to say one thing on the surface while actually meaning something else. Sarcasm is the crudest form of irony. The irony is clear in these examples:

a)   Our boss at the radio station had a face for radio.

b)   The drug dealer down the street said he hated drugs.

c)   The federal politician failed to pay his taxes for four years.

In each case, we see a gap between two meanings. In the first, the writer implies that the boss is so ugly that she or he is better suited to radio than to television. In the second, the man dealing drugs has a problem with his own product. In the final example, a reader would find it ironic that a person paid by taxpayers hasn't paid his own taxes.

The second approach, overstatement (also called hyperbole), deliberately exaggerates a situation or a thing:

a) I read the first sentence and I knew I was going to read the longest story ever written.

b) That dog would have looked less like death if it had been dead.

c) Thompson always thought his latest theory would change the world.

This overstatement calls great attention to a point. It emphasizes a point without necessarily coming out and telling us explicitly (the story was tedious, the dog was in poor condition, the theories were not as significant as the theorist thought).

The opposite, understatement, takes big moments or people and plays them down:

a) Among his family, he wasn't the Great One. He was just Wayne.

b) The birthday party had only a few thousand of Gary's closest friends.

c) The Nobel Prize winner said her latest research may change a few minds.

In each case, the writers suggest some other meaning. In the first example, the writer says practise that Wayne Gretzky's family treats him like anyone else, not like a star. In the second, the writer implies that Gary is popular. The final sentence suggests self-deprecation, but we know from the context that the prizewinner is more influential than she suggests. The language in all three examples evokes these meanings while being subtle.

EXERCISE 34 ▶ Figurative Language Approaches

To get a feel for these techniques of figurative language, you need to practise them. This exercise requires you to write a total of 10 sentences containing all five types of figures of speech described above:

- Write two sentences with metaphors not using *like* or *as*.
- Write two sentences with similes.
- Write two sentences with irony.
- Write two sentences with overstatement.
- Write two sentences with understatement.

Academic Writing and Original Language

Original phrasing through metaphor is not just for storytelling—it's commonly employed in academic writing as well. Here, though, the metaphor is not used to decorate language; it works fundamentally at the level of the concept. In technology and science, for example, fresh metaphors serve as a way to explain difficult concepts to the general public. The image of a spider web explains the structure of the Internet. Electricians talk of the current of electricity, like the flow of a river. Astronomers call our galaxy the Milky Way even though there's no milk up there. The concept of the greenhouse is used to explain how our Earth's atmosphere heats up. All of these metaphors bring together different, unrelated realms of experience to make the abstract more concrete.

If you're struggling with words and can't explain a difficult concept, turn to a metaphor. Metaphors have to resonate, but their explanatory power solves many writing dead ends.

Originality also comes into academic writing at the level of the idea. The best academic writing touches on ideas that have come before but doesn't copy or repeat them. The best academic writers know who's written what on a specific area of interest, and they join in—*they stand on the shoulders of giants*. The academic writer simply pushes previous thinking forward a step, or shifts it a bit with a new perspective, or provides new evidence for a position. The academic writer is not producing completely original not-before-seen work every time he or she writes; the academic writer must always inherently owe a debt to others. If you think nobody has written on your particular topic before, recheck sources and find out whether people in other related fields have written on the subject. Other scholars may have disregarded the topic for reasons you haven't discovered yet, or perhaps they've considered it in different ways, with different concepts and language.

Final Thoughts on Figurative Language and Originality

Coming up with figurative language is hard work. Consider it only after you've written your rough drafts. Before you jump into that *deep pool* of original figurative language, you can improve your writing significantly by removing only the dead figurative language. Don't get caught up in deliberately trying to create the next hot, new phrases. If you just avoid clichés and focus on the story or point you want to express, original phrasing will emerge naturally. Capture a moment, or an idea, or a concept, and communicate it clearly and precisely. Let creativity happen—don't force it. With this attitude, you'll create the next cliché without intending to.

> Metaphor, the life of language, can be the death of meaning. It should be used in moderation, like vodka. Writers drunk on metaphor can forget they are conveying information and ideas.
>
> —ROBERT FULFORD

Peer Models for Emulation

The next peer model deals with love relationships. Love relationship stories are often cliché territory. Be careful, as clichés for love abound: *We fell head over heels for each other, love conquers all, love is blind.* In reality, though, love relationships become complicated. Rather than write about fairytale love, good writers share those complications with us. As you read the first story, below, think about the originality of Adam Giles's language.

Christine

BY ADAM GILES

I turn my car onto Christine's street and roll toward her house. I see her white car in the driveway. I park on the road. I pick up the card and the flowers from the back seat. I hold them and stare at my steering wheel. I place the flowers gently on the passenger seat. I open my door and step out of my car. I walk slowly to her door. I stand there. I take a deep breath. I ring the bell. I wait. Her brother answers the door—he looks surprised to see me.

"Hey. Is Christine home?"

"Yeah, just a minute." He turns around. "Christine!"

I look back at my car. My hands shake. Christine walks to the door wearing a white T-shirt and plaid pajama pants. She bends her eyebrow and curls her top lip.

"Hey," she says.

"Hey. Can I talk to you?"

Christine looks side to side and back at me. "Uh. I guess. What are you doing here?"

"Can you come outside?"

"What's going on? We have company over right now. I can't talk too long."

Her eyebrow curls down again and her lips part. She steps onto the porch and closes the door.

"Okay. Please don't be shocked. But I came here to give you this." I hand her the card. I pause. I look at the ground.

"And to tell you that I love you."

I can't lift my heavy head. I stare at the porch's grey concrete. I force my head up and look at her face. I'd never seen that much of the whites of her eyes before. Her lashes flicker up and down and her mouth remains open. I look at her mouth and wait for words to come out. I wait and wait and wait. Silence.

Silence forever.

"Okay," she mutters. "When did this happen?"

"It's been here for a while, but I never had the guts to tell you."

"So you just show up here, unannounced, and throw this on me while we have company?"

"I'm sorry, but I just had to tell you now. I couldn't take it anymore. I know you're going back up to Lindsay tomorrow, and I had to tell you face-to-face."

Christine fires a blank stare at me.

I swallow some saliva. "I brought something for you. It's in my car."

"I don't know, Adam," she says. "I should be getting back in now."

"Please," I say. "Just come over here."

I lead her to my car. I open the passenger door. I pick the roses off the seat and turn around. I hand Christine the roses. "Here."

Her eyes widen, squint, then open again. She holds out the card. "No. I can't take these."

"Yes you can," I say quietly. "Please. Just take them."

"No!" she whines. "I've got company inside. They can't be seeing me walk in with flowers."

"So just hide them."

"No. Here." She holds out the card.

"At least take the card. You can hide that easily."

"Okay," she snaps.

"I hope you understand that I needed to tell you and I want to stay friends, no matter what, Christine."

She nods. "Okay. I'll send you an e-mail or something when I get back to Lindsay." I nod.

Christine runs back to her house, and I walk around to the driver's side of my car. I open the door, fling the roses into the passenger seat, sit down, and slam the door. I speed away. Tears blur my sight. I turn onto Credit Valley Road, past the Petro Canada gas station. I turn onto The Chase and, as I turn, I grab the roses off the passenger seat and throw them out the window.

I'm almost home when I shake my head and turn around at Sandown Road. I drive back to Petro Canada to buy cigarettes. I don't know which ones to ask for since I've never bought a pack before—I always just took some from my dad's open packs around the house when I felt like smoking. I ask the guy behind the counter for the DuMauriers in the grey package—my dad's brand.

The guy turns around and looks back at me. "The Special Milds?"

"Yeah, I think so," I say, looking at the floor.

"Can I see some ID?"

I look up at him and squint. I fumble though my wallet and show him my driver's license.

"King size?" he asks.

"Yeah."

"$4.73 please."

I hand him a five-dollar bill, and he hands me some coins. I grab my pack of cigarettes and walk back to the car. I drive to Erin Mills Town Centre, turn into the parking lot and look over a sea of open asphalt. Not one car in the lot. I pull into a spot and jam the gear selector into park. I turn the key backwards so my car's off and I can still listen to music. I listen to "Push" by Matchbox 20.

I wanna push you around
Well I will, well I will
I wanna push you down
Well I will, well I will
I wanna take you for granted
Yeah, yeah, yeah.

I rip the plastic wrapper off the cigarettes, open the pack, and rip out the silver foil that covers the cigarettes. I pull out a cigarette, place it between my lips, then fumble in the glove compartment for an old lighter. I light up, wipe the back of my sleeve across my eyes, and look across the empty parking lot. Dim, orange lights shine down on grids of yellow lines painted over the black asphalt. I breathe in some smoke and blow it out the window. I pool the saliva in my mouth, bend my tongue, and spit out the window. I look over city lights, cars driving along Erin Mills Parkway, and the empty parking lot. I smoke.

(Giles 116–19)

EXERCISE 35 ▸ Rhetorical Analysis

Write a rhetorical analysis of "Christine." Think first about what Giles does right, and then consider any missed opportunities and what you would edit. Consider one or all of the points and questions below to give you ideas for this exercise.

- How does Giles locate the story at the beginning?
- What role do strong verbs play in the story? List some strong verbs and explain their roles.
- How does Giles help us see Christine?
- List three pieces of original language in the story (language you have not seen used before).
- What techniques does Giles use to place us in the moment, as if we were there, during the key scene when he expresses his love?
- Evaluate the ending of the story—do you find it satisfying?

The next peer model, by Taylor Lush, is a research paper on a subject that may surprise readers: the financial problems of rich professional athletes. As you read, consider how Lush uses original language to explain his argument.

Financial Hardship among Former Professional Athletes and Its Contributing Factors

By Taylor Lush

Over the past three decades, professional sports leagues and the athletes who compete in them have grown immensely popular, turning athletes into household names. As a result, athletes in their teens and early twenties have been awarded lucrative, multi-million dollar contracts. Many athletes without the foresight to invest this money carefully have found themselves dealing with bankruptcies and home foreclosures less than a decade after retirement. The childhood dream of achieving financial stability through sport quickly turns into a financial nightmare; eventually athletes may experience the same financial hardship as people earning far, far less. In this paper I argue that three factors play into professional athletes' financial hardship: career brevity, obligations to provide for friends and family, and a lower socioeconomic background.

The annual earnings of professional athletes are substantial. In 2010, the average player salaries from the NFL, MLB and NHL were US$1.1 million, US$3.3 million, and US$1.9 million respectively (Agyemang 135). While these amounts may seem high to most people—almost like winning the lottery—they also reflect the reality that athletic careers are short. Michael McCann has shown that the typical career lasts only between four and six years and playing into one's thirties is rare (1490). This short period of time places tremendous pressure upon athletes to earn as much as possible and save for possibly more than 50 years of retirement.

The importance of conserving wealth for retirement, however, is often lost on young athletes. Wright argues that "often the young athlete has feelings of immortality. At the very least the athlete considers estate planning something that will only become important when he or she gets older" (28). Players in two professional leagues in particular are not heeding the advice of financial planners: 60 per cent of NBA players experience financial hardship within five years of retirement, while 78 per cent of NFL players experience financial hardship after their first two years of retirement (McDougle and Capers 72–3). These incredibly high rates show a financial short-sightedness that is perhaps a product of age, financial naiveté, and new circumstances athletes face.

While the brevity of athletic careers and poor financial planning are the most common cause of bankruptcy and financial difficulties among retired athletes, the obligation they feel to use their newfound wealth to provide for their friends and family amplifies the problem. Gifts and favours for loved ones, while coming from good intentions, cause financial problems too if athletes are not aware of the tax consequences on gifts, as Joseph Wright points out: "In many cases, young athletes make substantial gifts to family members and friends that are well in excess of the amount allowed under the annual exclusion of $10,000" (40).

Beyond taxation, some athletes have used their lucrative contracts to provide family members with substantial wealth. For example, Philadelphia Phillies player Richard Allen transferred $40,000 of his $70,000 signing bonus directly to his mother

(Brown 243). While these actions may seem admirable, generosity over the course of an athlete's playing career represents a substantial amount of money that could have been saved or invested.

Professional athletes also become targets of those who seek to exploit their new-found wealth, particularly "unscrupulous investment brokers" (Wright 37). These individuals lure young athletes into investments that have little to no chance of producing a tangible return on investment. The lack of success for professional athletes who choose to invest their money is well-documented, as Ruby Henry reports that among athletes "investment effort appears to increase the probability of bankruptcy" (13).

Finally, the class background of professional athletes plays a role in financial hardship. For children from lower socioeconomic backgrounds, "becoming a professional athlete is seen as an achievable career option and a ticket to prosperity" (McDougle and Capers 72). Having lived without wealth as a child, the sudden exposure to "large amounts of money can be troublesome for some athletes" (Agyemang 136). These athletes are much more likely to spend their money recklessly and develop an "expanded means of living" (Agyemang 137). Big purchases during athletes' careers—houses, cars, jewelry etc.—take money away from retirement and represent a lifestyle that's difficult to afford once salaries end.

With the factors of career brevity, paying friends, family and questionable investors, and the temptation to overspend large salaries, professional athletes face financial challenges that may be surprising to people with average salaries and 9 to 5 jobs. Yet athletes face their own unique challenges; if they do not meet those challenges, financial ruin is possible. Regardless of how long an individual plays professional sports, he or she must carefully invest, conservatively spend, and meticulously plan to ensure long-term financial stability. Even with the lucrative multi-million dollar contracts in today's professional sports leagues, if athletes are not dedicated to a long-term view and financial preservation, many of them will find themselves back where they started.

Works Cited

Agyemang, Kwame J.A. "Different From the Rest: An Interview With Nic Harris of the Carolina Panthers." *Journal of Management Inquiry*. 20.135 (2010): 135–139. Print.

Brown, Leonard G. "Compensation Planning for the Professional Athlete." *Southern University Law Review*. 235 (1980–1981): 235–54. Print.

Henry, Ruby. "Business, Bankruptcy, and Beliefs: The Financial Demise of NBA Stars." *IZA Discussion Paper Series*. 7238 (2013). Print.

McCann, Michael A. "It's Not About the Money: The Role of Preferences, Cognitive Biases, And Heuristics Among Professional Athletes." *Brooklyn Law Review*. 71 (2005–2006): 1459–1528. Print.

McDougle, Leon and Quinn Capers. "Establishing Priorities for Student-Athletes: Balancing Academics and Sports." *Spectrum*. 1.1 (2012): 71–77. Print.

Wright, Joseph D. "Skyrocketing Dollars and the Tax Reform Act of 1997: Estate Planning for the Professional Athlete in the New Millenium." *Sports Law Journal*. 27 (1991): 27–55. Print.

EXERCISE 36 ▶ Rhetorical Analysis

Write a rhetorical analysis of "Financial Hardship among Former Professional Athletes and Its Contributing Factors." Explain any opportunities you find for revising or editing. Some or all of the following points may help you analyze the paper.

- How does Lush map out the sections of the paper at the beginning?
- What role do strong verbs play in the paper? List some strong verbs.
- List three pieces of original language in the story (language you have not seen used before).
- Do you find the paper sympathetic to athletes or does it take an objective approach? Explain.
- The paper includes many strong nouns. Identify five strong nouns and explain their effectiveness.
- How does the paper transition from paragraph topic to paragraph topic?
- Examine the Works Cited and evaluate the appropriateness of the sources of evidence.

Assignment 6a

In this assignment, we suggest brainstorming a few options before freewriting one. Beginning writers often want to choose the story or topic that first comes to mind but those don't always make the best writing. Think about which stories and topics best satisfy the needs of readers, needs we've described throughout this book.

Suggested Topics:

1) Write a narrative about something you have experienced or observed in a romantic relationship.
2) Write a research paper that considers the factors that have led to the popularity of online dating sites—use academic sources.
3) Write a personal essay that answers this question: what makes relationships last?

Here are suggestions for writing your assignment:

- In stories, emphasize one incident. Love relationships produce many incidents, but you aren't writing a book here. Select the most poignant incident—one that you remember well. In academic papers, choose a fairly narrow argument to ensure specificity and detail.
- Resist the desire to idealize love and relationships. They have many dimensions. Show the subtle parts—the things we don't always see (good or bad).

- Details abound in the two peer models above. For stories, however, your memories may have faded. Consider some ways of prompting memory: refer back to diary entries or e-mails you've kept about the relationship; look at old photos and videos and note down appearances; ask friends or family members about their memories of your relationship; brainstorm some words that describe the relationship and the incident. This creative detective work may help you take your mind back to the moment. These strategies are no different in academic writing. Extensive research and brainstorming will help you find factual details and detailed arguments.

- In revision, remove wordiness, dead verbs, passive voice, vague pronouns, and clichés. It's natural to have these interfering factors in your rough drafts—even at this point. Removing them may spark new, fresh language.

- Some students ask: *What if my plot is cliché? What if my argument is cliché?* At this point, let's not worry about plot and argument cliché. Many writing scholars argue that only perhaps 7 to 10 basic plots exist (with variations). At the essential structural level, readers are not always so concerned with well-worn plots. We have cautioned above, however, that well-worn treatments of stories, particularly love stories, may bore readers. In academic writing, clichéd arguments usually develop out of a lack of research. Investigate the topic more deeply and become an expert on it. You'll learn the clichéd arguments and you'll find your fresh alternatives.

- Put the rough draft away for a week before revising it. Once you've had some time away from the story, you will come back to editing it rationally, not emotionally.

- During revision, you may suspect you've found a cliché—but you're not sure. In that case, Google the phrase and see if it pops up on cliché databases. If so, consider alternatives.

CHAPTER SUMMARY

This chapter raises awareness of originality in writing. Originality consists not of saying what has never been said, but of finding your own take on expression. But some language becomes overused to the point where it becomes cliché—everyone says it. Your job is to avoid saying what everyone else is saying.

People love original language. New catchphrases, sayings, and words amuse people. They *go viral*, particularly in this age of instantaneous media. The downside of this instant creativity is that such language eventually becomes old and stale. It may even become a joke.

If you see clichés, you know what's hot and what's not in language. If you cannot recognize clichés, you'll reproduce them. As a result, smart readers and editors may avoid your writing. To help you see clichés, we listed some examples such as *His back was against the wall* and *You should walk a mile in my shoes*. Some examples even combined clichés into one completely unoriginal sentence.

Clichés come from specific cultures and historical periods. *Groovy* sounds like a word from the 60s and early 70s, doesn't it? Clichés exist in any social realm, not just the realm of writing. Fashion has its clichés. Some people hope their fashions or their words become cliché—that means they're popular, although they were fresh when first introduced.

Sometimes we use clichés without having any idea of their origins. We showed that one cliché—*once in a blue moon*—probably came from a society more in tune with nature. Today many clichés come from the streets of big cities, like the word *swag*.

We pointed out that many writers use clichés. Why would they? Perhaps they just don't recognize a problem with using well-worn phrases and sayings. Maybe they don't read enough to know what's now overused. Or perhaps they do not know the clichés of the culture they're writing about—clichés are culturally specific. Some writers use clichés because they make writing easy—they make easy meaning and tap into populist ideas. Other writers use clichés to fill space (because making new meaning is hard). Finally, we think some writers use clichés to improve their style without realizing the negative effect. Avoid being the Egotistical Stylist.

Sometimes using clichés is acceptable—for example, when a writer is setting historical atmosphere. Writers also use them in dialogue—if that's how the person normally talks. Finally, some writers play with clichés for fun, winking at the reader. Advertisers do this for humour.

The chapter then turned to original phrasing. We showed examples of original phrasing related to one important element in good stories: a sense of place. The effective examples of place provided strong images through effective detail.

We suggested that beginning writers remove clichés and then focus on describing images well so that readers can see what they saw. Once you've mastered this, you may turn to creating new, fresh, figurative language.

The most common types of figurative language are metaphors and similes. These parts of speech compare one realm of experience to another. But writers have to ensure that the comparison resonates with readers. Obscure comparisons will not resonate.

Other forms of figurative language include irony, overstatement, and understatement. With irony, the surface statement doesn't match the reality. Overstatement usually takes a small situation and makes it bigger than it is, for emphasis. Understatement takes a big situation and plays it down, as if it's not a big deal. Readers who are aware and well read can derive meaning from all three types of figurative language. Metaphors and similes get readers involved in making meaning; they think *I see what you did there*.

▌Further Readings

For more about metaphors:

Lakoff, George and Mark Johnson. *Metaphors We Live By*. 2nd ed. Chicago: University of Chicago Press, 2003. Print.

Geary, James. *I Is an Other: The Secret Life of Metaphor and How It Shapes the Way We See the World*. New York: HarperCollins, 2011. Print.

For more about clichés:

Doyle, Charles Clay, Wolfgang Mieder, and Fred R. Shapiro, comps. *The Dictionary of Modern Proverbs*. Yale University Press, 2012. Print.

McLuhan, Marshall and Wilfred Watson. *From Cliché to Archetype*. New York: Viking Press, 1970. Print.

Parallelism

Reason may convince, but it is rhythm that persuades

—C.H. SISSON

So FAR IN THIS BOOK we've talked a lot about cutting and simplifying. This chapter and the next one will help you to bring back complexity and variance to your writing without returning to complicated structures that lessen readability. The enhancing factor of parallelism is one way to do this.

Parallelism is the use of two or more identical grammatical elements in a pattern. The metaphor of train tracks helps describe the concept of parallelism further: trains need two tracks that run exactly parallel; otherwise, the train runs off the rails. It's a deceptively simple idea rarely taught in schools these days. With parallelism, the writer repeats a set of verbs or nouns or adjectives or other parts of speech; an almost infinite number of patterns exist.

Parallelism solves readability problems. With some writing, we get tired when we read it. The writing is grammatically complex. Some writing meanders in structure, and we lose track of what the author means. Parallelism, on the other hand, is grammatically simple. Parallelism's simple structure makes understanding easier. Readers like parallelism for a number of reasons: it's easy to follow; it provides readers with stable sentence structure; and it reminds readers of connections between two or more related ideas.

Yet parallelism hides among hundreds of rules in grammar books. When grammar books mention parallelism, they often only discuss it as a negative, as faulty parallelism, which is our sixth interfering factor in writing. Faulty parallelism means a break in the consistency of the series of grammatical elements. We believe parallelism is much more important than a small point in a book—it's essential to good writing and deserves the long treatment we give it in this chapter.

Parallelism creates an underlying consistent beat, like the beat of a song. Effective speechwriters use parallelism to create a poetic rhythm in prose. Some memorable speeches provide excellent examples of parallel structure. One of the most famous examples is Martin Luther King's "I Have a Dream" speech. Notice the poetry-like repetition in this excerpt:

I say to you today, my friends, so even though we face the difficulties of today and tomorrow, I still have a dream. It is a dream deeply rooted in the American dream.

I have a dream that one day this nation will rise up and live out the true meaning of its creed: "We hold these truths to be self-evident: that all men are created equal."

I have a dream that one day on the red hills of Georgia the sons of former slaves and the sons of former slave owners will be able to sit down together at the table of brotherhood.

I have a dream that one day even the state of Mississippi, a state sweltering with the heat of injustice, sweltering with the heat of oppression, will be transformed into an oasis of freedom and justice.

I have a dream that my four little children will one day live in a nation where they will not be judged by the color of their skin but by the content of their character. (Bond and Smith 154)

King uses a great deal of parallelism in this short excerpt—some parallel structures are obvious and some are more subtle. We'll explain these structures in detail later in this chapter. Nonetheless, King's use of parallelism means nobody forgets the line *I have a dream*.

The poetry and order of parallelism remind us of a different time, a time when **orality**—not print—dominated human communication. The Greek study of rhetoric was not a study of how to write, but a study of how to speak. Greek orators did not read from a page—speeches were never copied down for posterity. Rather, orators used parallel structures to remember their speeches and to emphasize their points. In our time, in contrast, silent reading from pages and screens dominates. As a result, beginning writers tend to focus more on **semantics** than on the rhythms of writing. But rhythm affects readers too.

The Grammar behind Parallelism

The nature of grammar allows parallelism to work. When you write down a grammatical element such as a subject (a doer of the action in a verb) you open a gate. Imagine a farmer opening a gate for cows to pass. The gate opens and the cows stroll through, one after another, until the farmer closes the gate. It's the same in grammar. When you open the "subject gate" in an active voice sentence, the words that stroll through after it relate back to the subject. Grammar allows writers to condense grammatical structures to their smallest parts—that's economical. Consider these three separate and simple active voice sentences:

Terry screamed. Terry ran. Terry disappeared.

In each sentence, a gate opens—the writer introduces the subject, Terry, three different times. In each sentence, a verb strolls through the "Terry gate" next. As English readers, we know that each verb, each action, applies to Terry. These three sentences are thus parallel in structure when compared to each other. This is one kind of parallelism.

We can also use grammar's associative capabilities to condense these sentences into another kind of parallelism:

> Terry screamed, ran, and disappeared.

This is parallelism not between sentences but rather within a sentence, a parallelism of verbs in the same tense and number. The revised sentence is also more efficient. We don't need to repeat *Terry* two extra times. All three sentences in the original are a part of the same action sequence so combining them into a single series makes sense.

Surface and Under-the-Surface Parallelism

Parallelism may occur in two main ways: **surface parallelism** and **under-the-surface parallelism**. For the reader, the most obvious parallelism occurs with surface repetition (which repeats the underlying grammatical structure too, of course):

a) I ran and ran and ran away from the monster.

b) Mozart composed and composed and composed until the music sounded right.

c) The Ferrari drifted and drifted on the dirt road.

In each sentence, parallelism through explicit verb repetition implies continuation and emphasizes the great extent of the action. The writer shows a lot of running, a lot of composing, and lot of drifting.

Sometimes parallelism is less obvious to the reader. In under-the-surface parallelism, the meanings of the words vary while the parts of speech repeat. Consider these examples:

a) Sander ate and burped at dinner.

b) Priya walked and ran the marathon.

c) The theory circulated and then settled in the discourse of the academic field.

In each case, no surface verb meanings repeat. Instead, the repetition is more subtle—it's under-the-surface parallelism. We've just repeated the *type* of grammatical element: Verb + Verb.

> There is nothing more difficult to master than repetition. If you do it badly, it's clumsy, stupid. When it's well done, it's a little echo, like waves, poetry itself.
>
> —Laurence Cossé

Most readers don't see this as repetition at all but the orderliness and rhythm are just as strong.

Faulty parallelism makes writing difficult to follow. Consider these examples:

a) John was screaming, ran, and disappeared.

b) The topic of creationism and science was quite heated in the past few years. People on both sides of the debate are debating their sides, and furthermore argued vehemently in a way that does not help come to some conclusion.

c) Kat Thompson presents and explained the legal case.

These sentences all suffer from the same problem: the verb tenses aren't parallel. In the first sentence, the first verb (*was screaming*) doesn't match the form of the others: we see continuous action, past, and past. It should be *John screamed, ran, and disappeared*. The second sentence is more complicated but has the same errors: the verb *was* is in the simple past, and as such it isn't parallel with the present tense verb *are*. Then we switch back to the simple past—*argued*. Similarly, in the third example, the verb tenses are inconsistent: *presents* is in present tense, and *explained* is in the past tense. Attention to parallel structure—and correct grammar and verb tenses—will help you avoid these inconsistencies and turn grammatically wonky sentences into stable, consistent structures that readers can follow easily.

Now let's turn to the seven basic types of parallelism you can use in your writing to enhance its rhythm.

Single-Element Parallelism: Part I

Verb Series

The first and most important type of parallelism is a **verb series**. You've already read some of these above, on page 185.

Statistical analyses consistently show that the writing people like best tends to contain the highest ratio of verbs (not counting dead verbs like *was* and *have*) to total words. We have learned that verbs give writing its forward movement, energy, and the sense that something important happens. And that's why people read: they want to know what happens. Using verb series—combinations of two verbs or more—increases the ratio of verbs to total words in your writing. Be sure to make your verbs strong.

In practice, a verb series is a single subject followed by two or more verbs in a parallel list. The simplest series goes like this:

I laughed and cried at the same time.

The subject is *I*. *Laughed* and *cried* are the verbs. With two verbs, both in past tense, we have a parallel grammatical structure under the surface, even though the words in that structure are different. Here's a sentence with both surface and under-the-surface parallel structure:

> Larisa studied, studied, and studied for the calculus exam.

The three verbs (*studied*) stand consistently in the past tense, while the repetition emphasizes the meaning. Here, the writer could simply tell the reader that *Larisa studied a lot for the calculus exam*, but this phrasing is more elegant and interesting. The repetition creates implied meaning, and the reader is led to think *Gee, she studied a lot!*

Writers also extend and combine verb series. Let's extend the sentence about Larisa and her calculus exam:

> Larisa studied, studied, and studied for the calculus exam, and when the professor laid the exam on the desk in front of her, she trembled, shrieked, and bolted out of the lecture hall into the washroom, where she whimpered and shook for 35 minutes.

This long sentence includes three verb series of varying lengths. Can you identify them? Notice that this 44-word sentence has the same clarity and precision that we get with short sentences.

In the following shorter examples, the verb series convey repetitive action without the author explicitly telling the reader that the actions are repetitive:

a)   I write, edit, revise, and then write, edit, and revise again.

b)   John ate, drank, drank more, drank too much, and he talked, talked more, and said more than he ever should have said.

These repetitions force the reader to feel the continuous action.

If you change the last element of a series, you create a surprise, as in these examples:

a)   In the summer, we swam, hiked, laughed, and kissed. In the winter, we studied, worked, complained, and fought.

b)   Even the official biographer noted that Williamson studied, read, wrote, and drank.

The first sentence uses parallelism to condense six months of a relationship into 18 words. The second sentence makes us laugh when the punch line hits: the man is not just studious.

Novelist Cormac McCarthy used the noun series in his classic novel about cowboys, *All the Pretty Horses*. Describing the action of one cowboy, McCarthy writes:

> He lay there three days. He slept and woke and slept again. (204)

McCarthy's elegant approach is much more interesting than what the sentence implies, namely *He slept a lot*. Similarly, in her book *The Stone Angel*, Margaret Laurence employs a verb series to describe the flowing movements of a seagull:

> I feel the brush and beat of its wings as it swoops and mounts. (217)

The series *swoops* and *mounts* presents two related actions. Notice also that Laurence pairs a series of object nouns, *brush* and *beat*, with the verb parallelism. That's poetry in prose.

Noun Series

We argued in Chapter 5 that nouns are second only to verbs in their importance for visual, detailed writing. Strong nouns create vivid details that readers can "see." One problem: writing gets bogged down in long patches of descriptive detail. As with verbs, nouns work well in **noun series** to compress description and to relay lots of detail quickly and efficiently.

You may put a noun series in two grammatical positions: the subject position and the object position. Can you identify the noun series and their grammatical positions in the following sentences? If you're not yet sure about subjects and objects, identify the verb and then determine who does the action of the verb:

a) Julia, Tarn, Mark, Kuldeep, and Kwanza presented the sales pitch.

b) I saw on his desk a dictionary, a thesaurus, a pen, a disk, a computer, a cup, an Oreo, and an aspirin.

One reason to build a parallel noun pattern is to then shift it. The point where you shift the pattern becomes a point of emphasis. We can manipulate a list for effect, as in the examples below:

> The most basic way to get someone's attention is this: Break a pattern.
> —CHIP HEATH

a) The town had a church, a bank, a school, and just beyond the town line, a morgue.

b) Peterson's quantitative analysis project showed increases, decreases, and mistakes.

c) After the accident, I saw scattered on the highway a seat, a tire, a suitcase, a doll, and a head.

Novelist Toni Morrison used a surprise in a noun series in her book *Tar Baby* as she described a hungry man searching for food on a boat:

> He looked in the cupboards: glasses, cups, dishes, a blender, candles, plastic straws, multicoloured toothpicks and at last a box of Norwegian flat bread. (7)

As we read Morrison's list of objects, we follow the man along as he scans the cupboard. The reader feels his relief when he discovers the final noun—something to eat. Morrison's final element looks a bit different than the first six nouns: it has an adjective. It's not just *flat bread*, it's *Norwegian flat bread*. This is a small but interesting twist of detail.

In her classic extended essay *A Room of One's Own*, Virginia Woolf created a subject position noun series to show people seeking out knowledge:

> Professors, schoolmasters, sociologists, clergymen, novelists, essayists, journalists, men who had no qualification save that they were not women, chased my simple and single question—Why are women poor? (36)

This noun series works well because it reflects Woolf's meaning: a long list and a wide range of people have tried to investigate the problem.

EXERCISE 37 ▸ Single-Element Parallel Series—Part I

Now it's time for you to apply the lesson. Once you've tried simple parallelism, you'll start to see opportunities to add parallelism to your writing during revision.

Write five sentences that contain verb series (at least one with a surprise in the final verb).

Write five sentences that contain noun series (at least one in the subject position and one in the object position).

Single-Element Parallelism: Part II

The next three parallel series are less commonly used than verb or noun series, but they still find a place in much professional and academic writing.

Adjectives modify nouns and pronouns. **Adverbs** modify verbs. Both can be trouble spots in writing: they add subtle meaning but beginning writers often overuse them.

Note how adjectives, peppered all over, weigh down this paragraph:

> Xavi bought the red car with the blue trim. He drove it down the black asphalt road. He turned into his concrete driveway and parked next to the green planter. Then he walked up his stone walkway and placed his hand on the silver doorknob of the maple wood door.

> When you catch an adjective, kill it. No, I don't mean utterly, but kill most of them—then the rest will be valuable. They weaken when they are close together. They give strength when they are wide apart.
>
> —MARK TWAIN

Most of the adjectives the writer uses here, largely related to colour, are unnecessary because they describe unimportant and redundant things—do we need to know that the doorknob is silver or the door is wood? And isn't asphalt usually black? Good writers know how to include only details that are germane to the story and discard the rest. Too many adjectives blind the reader. Relevant adjectives, used sparingly and wisely, help the reader see.

The same, not surprisingly, is true for adverbs. Consider this example:

> David ran quickly down the sidewalk as he frantically chased his dog Bozo. Bozo charged aggressively towards another dog that galloped wildly and tried to escape quickly Bozo's charge. David caught up to Bozo finally and grabbed his collar harshly as Bozo whimpered softly.

Here, a surfeit of adverbs slows down our ability to process the verbs. And as with the adjective example, many of the adverbs used here are redundant—for instance, *quickly*. The sentences become comical. A good rule of thumb for writers is that if you've used a good verb, you usually don't need an adverb.

Adjective Series

While it's true that individual adjectives and adverbs should be used sparingly, it's also true that they can take on new life in the occasional parallel series, when you absolutely, positively must add more detail to a noun or verb. In the following adjective series, we get a quick shot of detail—like a shot of vodka at the bar—before the sentence moves on to the noun:

a) Grey, motionless, dull clouds hung over the picnic.

b) Detailed, coherent, well-argued writing makes Dr. Kilgour's book a pleasure to read.

c) She was attractive, smart, well-focused, soft-spoken, and dishonest.

These provide great details and spice up nouns and pronouns with important, additional detail. But just like with vodka shots, a good writer knows when to stop: don't pile on series after series or you'll wear your readers out.

Long-time editor of *The New Yorker*, David Remnick, uses a noun series and an adjective series effectively in an article profiling former NBA star Michael Jordan. Here, Remnick describes the site of Jordan's exploits, the Chicago Bulls' arena:

> The Bulls play their games now across the street at the United Center . . . and the place features all the new amenities: lots of bathrooms, nice parking, no rats. The United Center is huge, cool, and white: a mobster's mausoleum, the world's largest freezer unit. (289)

The noun series provides a surprise about the rats—reminding readers of the problems of old Chicago Stadium—and then the adjective series suggests the blandness and lack of character of its replacement. That's a lot of visual detail in just two sentences. The adjective series also gives Remnick's point force and presence. Adjective after adjective tells the reader *Hey, this is important!*

Adverb Series

Adverb series work in the same way as adjective series, but adverbs have more grammatical freedom to move within a sentence. You can place them in different positions, as in these examples:

a) Slowly, quietly, assuredly, the lioness circles closer and closer to a beautiful, peaceful, complacent zebra, who drinks his last drink at the watering hole.

b) I loved him wholly, unreservedly, blindly, and stupidly.

c) In the presentation, Dr. Gregson analyzed the argument completely and tirelessly.

All three series present valuable additional details. In the first example, the physical and spatial details of the adverbs do well to describe the lioness's hunt. In the second sentence, the person doesn't just love another—the person loves him in a complex way. The third example shows that the professor didn't just analyze the argument; he also did a thorough job.

In the following example, a short adverb series characterizes a man's voice:

His voice grew quickly and wildly.

In this case, the adverbs add extra meaning to the verb. A way to test the series' utility is to remove the adverbs and see if the verb holds the same meaning without them. If not, the adverb series is appropriate. Use these in the right moments but not all the time.

Preposition Series

Another effective type of series uses prepositions for effect. Prepositions are small linking words—for example, *on, under, beside, during*—that express relationships between subjects and objects according to space, logic, or time. Prepositions don't get much attention in the grammar and style books. Typically, they draw the most attention when they end a sentence—a grammatical no-no for some. However, we think prepositions deserve more attention.

Too many prepositions exist to list here, but some of the more common ones include:

above	beside	out	within
below	beneath	over	during
under	after	to	into
on	off	with	
at	on	without	

Refer to a good dictionary or website to discover others. Before we look at **preposition series,** here is a brief review of single prepositions in action:

a) The boy sits <u>on</u> the bike.

b) The boy sits <u>beside</u> the bike.

c) The boy looks <u>at</u> the bike.

d) The boy stands <u>over</u> the bike.

e) The boy rode his bike <u>after</u> school.

f) The boy thought of his bike <u>during</u> school.

All of these examples use single prepositions to situate a boy (the subject) in relation to a bike and to school (the receivers of his actions, or objects). To make a preposition series, then, we must combine two or more in a row. Can you identify the preposition series in these sentences?

a) In our country, government by, of, and for the people has become government over, around, and through the people.

b) We looked in, around, and under the shed for that cat.

c) I can't live with or without you.

Music fans will recognize the third example—it comes from the song "With or Without You" by the Irish rock band U2. The juxtaposition of the two opposite prepositions adds paradoxical meaning to the song.

When you need to describe complex time, space, or logical relationships, the preposition series is a useful tool to do it elegantly.

EXERCISE 38 ▶ Single-Element Parallel Series—Part II

Now it's time to attempt all three of the series types we've just studied.

a) Write three sentences that contain adjective series.

b) Write three sentences that contain adverb series.

c) Write three sentences that contain preposition series.

d) Write three sentences that combine two of these series.

Parallelism in Jack Layton's Letter to Canadians

In late August of 2011, after the death of federal New Democratic Party leader Jack Layton, thousands of people travelled to Toronto's City Hall and wrote messages of condolence in chalk on the pavement and walls around Nathan Phillips Square. Many of the messages expressed simple, heartfelt thoughts like *we will change the world*, *love is better than anger*, and *love hope optimism*.

The writers didn't invent these messages. Instead they found them in a letter Layton himself wrote, which his wife, Olivia Chow, released to the public shortly after his death. Widely published, the letter itself became famous. Its language about hope and collective political action resonated with many Canadians, and Canadians paid their respects by writing Layton's words on the concrete.

Layton's language resonated, first of all, because the content—the message of hope—spoke to many Canadians. Layton was a charismatic politician with a large following before the letter, too. But the letter's success wasn't only a product of its content or its writer's history.

The structural elements Layton used—particularly parallelism—made the content memorable. The proof is in the condolences: many people could easily remember and write Layton's words without a script in front of them.

In the letter, Layton begins an extended theme of optimism when he tells people to remain positive as they battle cancer:

> You have every reason to be optimistic, determined, and focused on the future.

This sentence's adjective series stands out. It encourages readers with three words: *optimistic*, *determined*, and *focused*. This encouragement theme—moving on to politics—continues near the end of the letter:

> Hope and optimism have defined my political career, and I continue to be hopeful and optimistic about Canada. Young people have been a great source of inspiration for me. I have met and talked with so many of you about your dreams, your frustrations, and your ideas for change.

Here, the first sentence begins with a noun series: *hope and optimism*. It serves as the subject of the sentence in the active voice. These two abstract ideas act: they *define* an object, which is Layton's career. Later in the sentence, Layton modifies the nouns slightly but the roots remain the same: *hopeful* and *optimistic*. The repetition in this noun series is subtle, reinforcing his point. The paragraph closes with a pronoun-noun series mirroring the one earlier in the letter. This time, however, the repeated pronoun isn't *my*. Layton turns it around: *your dreams, your frustrations, and your ideas*. This letter isn't about him but about his audience.

continued

Notice how Layton continues using the pronoun-noun series in these two sentences:

> I believe in you. Your energy, your vision, your passion for justice are exactly what this country needs today. You need to be at the heart of our economy, our political life, and our plans for the present and the future.

These two sentences continue the back-and-forth parallel series between Layton and the reader, completing a pronoun cycle of sorts: *my, your, our*. The pronouns represent a reciprocal relationship, like a dialogue between Layton and his audience that ends in consensus. The second sentence ends with *present* and *future*, a rhythmic pair of nouns.

Finally, the letter ends on a crescendo of parallelism, the exact words that the public echoed in their chalk writings:

> My friends, love is better than anger. Hope is better than fear. Optimism is better than despair. So let us be loving, hopeful and optimistic. And we'll change the world.

A lot goes on in these final five sentences. Layton employs a noun-verb-adjective-conjunction-noun series. That's the big technical term for it. The series occurs three times, each with a different pair of nouns. The nouns contrast: *love/anger, hope/fear, optimism/despair*. The second last sentence, an adjective series, plays with the root words: *loving, hoping*, and *optimistic*.

The final sentence contains no parallelism—that's fine. The lack of parallelism provides a contrast: Layton makes one point clearly and directly without ornamentation.

Notice we haven't said much about the content of the letter. Political scientists could say a great deal about the political and social philosophies embedded within it. But that's the typical focus of analysis—the surface meaning. We've shown how the form—which readers instinctively enjoy—creates effects, too.

The outpouring of love for Jack Layton was a product of many factors from his long political career. But the public's imitation of the language in his final letter likely owes credit to his poetic, rhythmic structures of parallelism.

Multiple-Element Parallelism

By now you should have a sense of how to parallel simple grammatical elements like verbs, nouns, adjectives, adverbs, and prepositions. Now we want to introduce more complexity to the idea of parallelism: combinations of grammatical elements. These series complicate things, but we think you'll figure them out quickly.

Adjective-Noun Series

The formula of the first multiple element series, the **adjective-noun series**, reflects its name: the formula is simply adjective/noun + adjective/noun and so on. Let's expand a simple noun series:

Mark wore a hat, a jacket, a vest, and a tie.

We can turn this into a slightly more complex and revealing sentence by putting an adjective in front of each noun in the series to create an adjective-noun series:

Mark wore a purple hat, a green jacket, a red vest, and a blue tie.

Compare the meaning that develops from the use of an adjective series versus a noun series. Mark changes from a conservative dresser to a wild dresser. We see him immediately. One sentence tells us all we need to know about Mark's look.

In his article about the aging of theatre audiences in Canada, Kamal Al-Solaylee writes this parallel series:

The competing wafts of perfumes, hair gels, and Bengay couldn't hide the stench of decay. Old people, old plays, old actors. (3)

Al-Solaylee's repetition of the adjective-noun series emphasizes the problem theatres face trying to get young people interested in live performances. You would not employ this kind of series often, but again, in the right moments it serves a purpose.

Subject-Verb Series

We can also combine subjects and verbs into a **subject-verb series**. Unlike verb series where the doer of the action is stated only once—at the beginning of the sentence—the subject-verb series repeats the subject element in each combination (the noun that serves as the subject may or may not vary). The subject-verb series allows for a greater complexity of meaning between connected parts, as in this sentence:

In Baxton's study of the town's history, he showed that the peasants protested, landowners complained, soldiers marched, and peasants died.

In the last nine words, the sentence expresses the complete history of a major event in a village. By putting these subjects and verbs together in one sentence, the writer connects the actions. One action leads to the next, which leads to the next, and so on. The writer doesn't say that the soldiers killed the peasants. The reader must make that conclusion—this means the reader becomes active. What's the less elegant, less parallel, way of writing this?

In Baxton's study of the town's history, he showed that the peasants protested, which caused the landowners to complain, and then the soldiers marched and shot the peasants dead.

We prefer the elegant parallel structure of the original, which is easier to follow and thus comprehend.

Perhaps the most famous and obnoxious subject-verb series is this ancient Latin phrase spoken by Julius Caesar: *Veni, vidi, vici*. Translated, it means simply

> I came, I saw, I conquered.

We could turn it into a verb series, but it just wouldn't have the same effect:

> I came, saw, and conquered.

The transformation neuters Caesar, as if he had just shrugged and said, *I just came, saw, conquered. No big deal!*

Use these series when you want to connect actions of different subjects without devoting whole paragraphs to their description.

Subject-Verb-Object Series

Extending the idea further, we can take the second type of active voice sentence explained in Chapter 4 and create **subject-verb-object series**. This type of series repeats the combinations of each grammatical element, as in this scientific example:

> Nichole purified the sulphur, Mary heated the acid, Kareem weighed the magnesium, and John combed his hair.

The surprise at the end of the sentence makes the most interesting point here. A group of people work diligently on a science experiment but one member slacks off. Each unit could have been its own sentence (just put periods in place of the commas and remove *and*). But we put the parts together to reflect their common work (or lack of it) on a science project.

In an essay about the horror genre, Stephen King uses a subject-verb-object series to make a point about the curious fact that people love being scared by horror movies:

> When we exhibit these emotions, society showers us with positive reinforcement. (King "Why We Crave")

King repeats no words in this series, yet the underlying structure repeats. *We* and *society* are subjects. *Exhibit* and *showers* are verbs, and *emotions* and *us* are objects. It also works well to show a **reciprocal** relationship between people and society. Structure mirrors meaning.

Verb-Preposition-Object Series

Our final multi-element series, the **verb-preposition-object series**, finds another use for prepositions. This series repeats only the combination of a verb, a preposition, and an object. It suggests movements through space, the passing of time, or the progression of logic. In this series, the subject doesn't repeat; it performs all the actions in the sentence. Let's look at three examples of this series:

a) The cat walked down the road, stopped on the sidewalk, strolled over to the yard, and stared at the dog.

b) The professor fumbled through his notes, fiddled with his glasses, looked away from the students, and talked to himself.

c) The study of semiotics centres on language, looks at signs, and attends to meanings.

In the first sentence, the cat moves and changes its relationship with four different objects, including finally a dog. In the second sentence, the reader gets a quick lesson on the professor's character. The professor acts in relation to four objects—*notes*, *glasses*, *students*, and *himself*. In the third sentence, *study* is the doer of all the actions in the verbs. The objects of that study are *language*, *signs*, and *meanings*.

In the book *Pilgrim at Tinker Creek*, Annie Dillard uses verb-preposition-object series to describe her own movement in nature:

When I slide under a barbed-wire fence, cross a field, and run over a sycamore trunk felled across the water, I'm on a little island shaped like a tear in the middle of Tinker Creek. (6)

Here, Dillard comes into spatial relationships with many objects. This is an apt use of a preposition series, as it shows how she lives and her connection with the natural environment—the overriding theme of her book.

These seven series represent ways of adding details quickly and compactly to your writing. Professional writers use them to create rhythm and solidity of structure, as we've seen in the examples above. Using parallel series helps writers to avoid the tendency to sprinkle many individual parts of speech—adjectives and adverbs in particular—around their writing.

These series may seem simple. That's the point. The simplicity of these series should help you see your sentences structurally. As you try out parallelism, you'll start to map out your sentences more clearly. You won't fall into the trap of long, confusing constructions that tire out readers. You won't fall into the dreaded run-on sentence.

We began with a few of the simplest parallel series because we wanted to introduce you to the topic. You may extend the idea and parallel any parts of speech we haven't discussed here. Your creativity is the only limitation. For example, Martin Luther King created a noun-preposition-pronoun-noun series in this memorable sentence:

I have a dream that my four little children will one day live in a nation where they will not be judged by the color of their skin, but by the content of their character. (Bond and Smith 154)

Did you see the parallel structure? *Color* and *content* are the first nouns he pairs in the series. He repeats *of* (a preposition) and *their* (a pronoun). Then he pairs the nouns *skin* and *character*. Audiences remember this sentence because King puts the surface meaning—about how humans should be judged—into identical parallel structure. The structure imprints itself on our minds, and so too does the content.

EXERCISE 39 ▸ Multiple-Element Parallel Series

Complexity returns in these four series. The bonus for you as a writer is that they will help ensure that readers will find your sentences easy to follow.

a) Write three sentences containing adjective-noun series.
b) Write three sentences containing subject-verb series.
c) Write three sentences containing subject-verb-object series.
d) Write three sentences containing verb-preposition-object series.

▌ Academic Writing and Parallelism

Good scholarly writing regularly employs parallelism. Parallelism helps present information clearly and directly. Scholarly writers are particularly fond of the rhythm of the verb series. Take this example from an oft-cited article by communication theorist James Carey on journalism history:

> Journalism has changed as it has reflected and reconstituted human consciousness. (*James Carey* 92)

The verb series *reflected* and *reconstituted* is used appropriately here. Carey means to suggest that journalism both influences and is influenced by human consciousness. The verb series allows Carey to connect two related abstract processes.

In his classic writing on the history of books and reading, Roger Chartier employs a useful series:

> We must also keep in mind that reading is always a practice embodied in acts, spaces, and habits. (3)

The noun series *acts*, *spaces*, and *habits* condenses a number of key practices into one list, which both classifies the types of practices themselves and draws a comparison between practices and other concepts not mentioned in the sentence. These words define the objects of study in Chartier's writing.

Duncan Koerber uses noun series in a study of the social construction of fan identities in newspaper coverage of early Canadian sports:

> In the amateur age around the turn of the 20th century, sports writers in the *Globe* and *Star* did not call fans customers. . . . Instead, sports writers predominantly called viewers of sports then "spectators" and "crowds." In addition, viewers of sports were called "baseball lovers," "supporters," "the bicycling public," "the hockey loving public," "lovers of pure amateurism," and more plainly, "visitors," "persons," and "people." These identities did not evoke connotations of the marketplace; they suggested "pure" participants in the community of sport untouched by the corrupting influence of money. (*Constructing the Sports Community* 132)

Koerber's close reading of hundreds of sports articles helped him to gather these nouns. The nouns work best in series to list quickly all the ways sports writers described fans. Rather than explaining each noun in its own sentence, Koerber uses the series to provide a quick "snapshot" of his research results before going on to assess the meaning of this naming.

▌ Interview-Based Articles

So far in this book we've presented personal narrative and academic writing. Another essential form is the **interview-based article**. Much professional and academic writing requires interviewing. Indeed, it's an essential task of many writers who want to discover untold stories and information. Interviewing gets you directly to the witness of an event or the creator of an academic study. Interviewing is a difficult task but the rewards are enormous: first-hand knowledge and experience.

Readers love interviews. They abound in print and also on TV during morning talk shows, midday news programs, dinner-time news, and late-night comedy news shows. A great deal of academic writing—particularly sociology and history—develops from the authors' interviews with people to discover how great economic and political forces have affected people's lives.

Writers decide to interview someone for one of two main reasons. One reason is to access that person's expertise or special experience. The other is to show readers an interesting person. You may choose to interview someone who

- has a special experience you'd like to know more about (a tattoo artist, a detective, a mountain climber)
- is an interesting character (a comedian, a natural storyteller, a criminal)
- observed a past event (9/11, a hurricane, a sports final game)
- holds expertise in social life or politics (a professor, a politician, a crisis care worker)
- has an interesting job (an oil rig worker, a dog walker, a crane operator)

The person need not be famous. Regular people interest readers too. In 2011, a *Columbus Dispatch* reporter noticed a homeless man holding a sign by the off-ramp of a highway. The sign bragged about the man's great voice. The reporter stopped in front of unkempt and unshaven Ted Williams and offered money if he spoke. To the surprise of the reporter, Williams spoke in a deep, refined voice characteristic of radio announcers. Standing on the side of the road in worn-out clothes, Williams's first words were

> When you're listening to nothing but the best of oldies, you're listening to Magic 98.9 . . . And we'll be back with more right after these words. And don't forget tomorrow morning is your chance to win a pair of tickets to see this man, live in concert!
>
> Source: www.youtube.com/watch?v=jaGLDKBE8Ho

The reporter got out of his car and interviewed Williams, and then he posted the video on YouTube. Millions of YouTube viewers were amazed at his voice. They wanted to know more about his story of a radio career cut short by drug and alcohol abuse. Stories like these exist everywhere around you—find them.

Doing the Interview

If this is your first time interviewing, you may be nervous. That's normal. Interviewing is a strange human interaction. How often do you call or approach strangers and ask them to answer your questions, answers that you'll publish for an audience of thousands? Your job is to make the interview process feel less strange.

On the positive side, the interview is so rewarding. We get new perspectives on life. We get fascinating details about a person or a city. We get examples of personal struggle and personal success. We get all of these things by drawing detailed stories out of other people—but that's also a problem. When you write personal narratives, you have direct access to all the details in your memory. Your interview must extract the same level of detail, the same engaging stories, from the memories of other people.

Chemistry in interviews matters. **Rapport** with the interview subject doesn't necessarily happen right away, if at all. Interviewing can be awkward—even for experienced professionals. You get better at it the more you do it. Awkwardness and shyness will decline over time.

The best interviews are ones that don't seem like interviews. They seem like a conversation. But conversation can die if you don't prepare. Preparation shows respect. Interviewees feel good, and will say lots of interesting things, when you respect them. If you respect them, you'll get a great deal of detailed content.

Good, well-researched, **open questions** allow interview subjects to elaborate and tell stories. **Closed questions** are fine for discovering facts you cannot find anywhere else, but they won't garner much more than that. Here are some examples of open and closed questions, the open ones naturally progressing from the closed:

Closed Questions	Open Questions
Where were you born?	What do you remember about your birthplace?
Is religion important to you?	Can you tell me about your religious observances?
When did you arrive in Canada?	What did you see first when you arrived in Canada?

The best questions ask about key moments in a person's life. Key moments are a first date, the first day of school, the moment the car crashed, graduation day, wedding day, marriage proposals, the day the Berlin Wall came down, September 11th, the day the bombs dropped. People don't preserve memories of what they ate for breakfast last Monday, but they do preserve memories of emotional, important days. Try to excavate those important memories with good questions.

> There's only one interview technique that matters. . . . Do your homework so you can listen to the answers and react to them and ask follow-ups.
> —JIM LEHRER

The Questioner and the Listener

Many beginning interviewers think their job is simply to ask questions. That's the job of what we call The Questioner. The Questioner simply asks a question, writes down the answer, and then asks another question. Instead, you should think of yourself as The Listener.

The Listener asks questions too, of course. But The Listener is much more focused on a person's answers. This is a subtle but important difference. The best interview-based articles spark from an interview where the interviewer listened intently to everything a person said.

You may think *Of course I listen. I have two ears. This is obvious.* But many people hear without truly listening. In unusual and stressful situations—the nature of an interview for many—people focus so much on their feelings and their questions or comments. They ask questions and transcribe, ask questions and transcribe, until the time is up. The interviewee could say anything at all and it wouldn't matter to the interviewing process. Interviewing becomes robotic.

To focus on listening, you can't worry about what to say next. You can't worry about how the interviewee will react. Just listen. Then think about what to say next when they stop talking. Our brains work quickly enough to formulate something to say in milliseconds. And if silence ensues, enjoy the silence. Interview subjects will try to fill that gap while you decide what to say next. You are in control.

The by-product of good listening is improvised follow-up questions. Follow-ups can be as simple as *What happened next?* or *Tell me more.* They are sparked by what the interview subject says. When an interview subject says something unexpected or unusual, the skilled interviewer does not turn to the next prepared question but moves onto the new path. Let's look at an effective interviewer's conversational style, a style that begins with careful listening and includes follow-up prompts. Here, PBS interviewer Charlie Rose talks to comedian John Stewart of *The Daily Show* about how Stewart comes up with jokes:

STEWART: Our viewership is somewhat young. And they're not clamouring . . .

ROSE: What are you talking about, 12, or 20 or what?

STEWART: Eight. They go right from rugrats to us. But they're not clamouring for more financial justice jokes.

ROSE: What kind of jokes are they clamouring for?

STEWART: They enjoy a good legalized pot joke—always have, always will.

ROSE: How about anthrax, are they clamouring for anthrax?

STEWART: They were. Anthrax is over, man. We don't follow anthrax anymore.

ROSE: What's the barometer you use and your comedy writers use? I mean you know the sensibilities of your audience so therefore . . .

STEWART: No. We actually—and this may or may not be a good thing—don't think about them in any way, shape, or form, until they are in the audience either yelling at us or clapping. We go by sort of an internal barometer and intuition that we all have as people who have done comedy for a long time. That's all we've ever gone by.

ROSE: All you can do is say "Does this make me laugh or not?"

STEWART: Does this make me laugh? Do I feel creepy saying it? Do I not feel creepy saying it? Is it the right target? Do we feel like we're choosing our point without being didactic? Is there enough balance in the show—silliness versus something that might be more pointed? Will it be interesting to watch? Are we changing the pace? Those are the things we'll think about sometimes. But we don't ever think "Well, how's that going to play at Theta Delta Kai?"

ROSE: They're too old for you at Theta Delta Kai.

STEWART: Yeah, I don't understand their world anyways.

ROSE: It's always instinctive in terms of what you think.

STEWART: I believe so.

Source: www.youtube.com/watch?v=DE8XeBcnx7s

Here, Rose chats with Stewart, prompting him here and there, but letting Stewart lead the way. Rose must judge when to prompt and when to shut up and let Stewart talk as much as he wants. Rose didn't plan out all of these questions but he was prepared. He improvises based on what he's heard from Stewart. The result is a more natural interview and greater rapport with Stewart. Stewart knows Rose is listening and that Rose cares.

> The art of conversation is the art of hearing as well as of being heard.
> —WILLIAM HAZLITT

EXERCISE 40 ▸ Effective Interviews

Go on YouTube and find an interview video that you like. In 200 words, explain what you like about the interviewer's style, delivery, questions, and so on.

Listening can sometimes be hampered by the technology of recording an interview: the pen and the recording device. Either method is fine for getting words down, but recognize that each one has its strengths and weaknesses. When using a pen, you can sometimes forget to look up at the person and create rapport—instead, you scribble down words frantically. Some interviewers choose to write down only the key words of a sentence and fill in the rest later. Alternatively, many interviewers use a recording device as a primary recording method or as a backup to the pen. Interviewers find the recorder frees up their eyes to look at the interviewee and respond to them immediately. The downside is that recorders can fail, and transcription of the recording can take hours longer than the interview itself. Experiment to discover which method works best for you.

> Listening is a magnetic and strange thing, a creative force. . . . When we are listened to, it creates us, makes us unfold and expand.
> —BRENDA UELAND

█ Writing Interviews

Once you've completed the interview, you either have pages of handwritten notes or a transcription of a recording. Now it's time to assess the material. The material you have will determine the focus you take and the structure of the article.

If the quotations reveal fantastic character, then you'll emphasize the person in the article. If the person spoke in long, detailed narratives, then you'll emphasize one good story in the interview-based article. If the person's quotations reveal data, information, and opinion, you'll probably focus on some greater social or political topic.

An interview-based article can take any number of structures. We boil these structures down to three basic types:

1) monologue;
2) informal;
3) formal.

The structure of each is defined by the presence or absence of the author. Up to this point in this book, you've regularly used *I* in personal narratives to reveal your subjectivity. With the interview-based article, the presence or absence of the author becomes a key question driving the way you structure it.

Monologue Structure

The **monologue structure** is perhaps the most difficult to put together. The monologue shows character by letting people speak extensively directly to the reader without mediation or context from the writer.

Monologue structure depends on what the interviewee said and how he or she said it. If an interviewee speaks in story then you may transcribe it as a complete monologue. The reader experiences the interview as if he or she had sat there and listened to the person speak. The interviewer disappears.

If the person doesn't speak in story form, imposing a monologue structure makes the article seem disjointed. If the interview subject rambles, the monologue will ramble. Writers may compress, as author Lee Gutkind calls it, the interview, moving sentences around to create a better flow. (This is contentious, however, as inexperienced authors may misrepresent what the person said.)

The interview context, such as the details of location and appearance, is not included in monologue—there's just no place for it.

Informal Structure

The **informal structure** sees the writer as a character in the article. The writer might use phrasing such as: *I sit here in Starbucks with the richest man in the world and nobody realizes who he is.*

Another common informal structure is the question-answer format, which foregrounds the writer's questions. If you choose a simple question-answer style, it's important to publish only the question-answer units that fit together on a theme. Developing continuity between each question and answer unit may require you to remove some of the units that just don't fit into the interview flow.

In either form, the writer becomes another voice in the interview encounter. The informal structure gives the interview context—details of location, people's appearances, and so on.

Formal Structure

In the **formal structure**, any one person being interviewed is less prominent in the article. Some greater topic, perhaps social or political, defines the article. The author exchanges the first person *I* for the third person. Multiple voices from multiple interviews speak to those larger issues. This structure suggests formality, distance, and pseudo-objectivity. This is most common in newspapers and magazines.

These three structures map out the possibilities for organizing the structure of an interview-based article. Your interview-based articles need not adhere only to one. Mixing and matching structures—such as employing an informal style with an extended monologue—can work effectively.

EXERCISE 41 ▸ Interview Article Structure

Interview-based articles exist everywhere. Find an interview-based article in a magazine or newspaper that you enjoy reading. At the top of the page, write down the name of the structure the article uses. Highlight or underline the interesting quotations. Cross out the uninteresting quotations. In 100 words, comment on how effective the article's structure and quotations are.

▋ Peer Models for Emulation

The next piece of peer model writing is an interview-based article. In Joyce Ong's "Two Hard Years," we feel like we're listening directly to her father tell his story. Think about the coherence of the monologue form.

▋ Two Hard Years

BY JOYCE ONG

This story comes from a set of interviews I have done with my father about his life as a teenager and a young man in revolutionary China of the 1950s, 60s, and 70s. The narrative voice in this story—the "I" who tells the story—is the voice of Mr Angus Ong, my father.

As head of the Shenyang Transformer Research Institute and the Liaoning Overseas Chinese Association, and as a member of the Political Consultation Committee, my father enjoys high political status. Membership in a political organization connects you to the Party like an umbilical cord. Dad is well-liked in his plant and in his overseas Chinese association, but his European education and his marriage to a western woman make him vulnerable to attacks. Party members in the Institute want to nail Dad as a spy. After my brother Eddie's letter in 1968 reveals Dad's comment to his work unit—he equated The Bible to Mao's Little Red Book—the Party cuts Dad's cord.

In his letter, Eddie attacks Dad's "anti-Mao comments" and Dad's special privileges. He says Dad gets bread, meat, vegetables, sugar, and eggs our neighbours only dream of eating. Neighbours and workers all know of Dad's food privileges. Eddie says Dad spends most of his day looking for food. Eddie says Dad not only gets the highest salary at the institute, but he also has the nerve to ask for income supplements from the government. Eddie says this bourgeois lifestyle runs counter to the Communist ideology of selfless sacrificing for the benefit of the people.

If you catch a spy, the Communist Party praises and recognizes you as a loyal pro-Mao Communist. Eddie exposes Dad to get a coveted Communist Party membership.

The Worker's Propaganda Team from Shenyang Transformer Research Institute comes into Shenyang Mechanical and Electrical Engineering College to weed out bourgeois "bad elements." The Ministry of Heavy Industry allocates five students to work in the research institute. Sniffing around the family backgrounds of five students, the Propaganda Team smells out two bad elements. My name is on that list. The head of the Propaganda Team signs me and another student up for two years of farm work.

My farm lies in a remote part of China, three to four hours southeast of Shenyang by train. Six guys and four girls from my university class leave with me for two years of farm duty. Students from colleges all over China get sent to these big farms for "re-education."

The farm is not like the peasant farm I went to nine years ago in high school. This is a strategically placed military farm. The People's Liberation Army runs its own farms, stockpiles, colleges, industries and research institutes. The army is self-sufficient.

I live in an ugly, brown, cracked mud house. I sleep on a straw mattress covering a layer of ugly, brown, cracked mud. This layer of mud sits on a bed of hard bricks. The brick bed extends all the way down one wall of the mud house and repeats on the opposite side. A hollow cavern runs inside the brick beds. The cavern conducts baking heat from a stove down one wall of brick beds. In my mud house, six men roll and snore on one wall of baking beds, and another six roll and snore along the other wall. Early in the morning, before we leave for farm work, we must fold our blankets like square boxes on our mattresses. Hand-sized busts of Mao must sit in the middle of all the mattresses. We can't move the busts from our mattresses during the day. The army does not want us to remove the busts and nap on our mattresses in the afternoon. After the 7:00 a.m. line-up, breakfast, and Mao songs, we march to the field.

We plant rice and weed rice paddies and spray fertilizers on rice paddies and drain water from rice paddies and cut rice and bundle rice and haul bundles of rice, using thin bamboo sticks on our shoulders, all the way to the end of the field and beat and shake off grains of rice and stack useless rice stalks for horse feed. We sweat our asses off doing all this work with four army lieutenants sweating beside us.

These lieutenants are heroes. Two lieutenants braved the biting cold in the trenches high up in Tibet during the India War. Another lieutenant waged war against the Americans in Vietnam. When the sun's heat blasts down on the growing rice, the lieutenants run political discussion groups on hardship and Mao. Local farmers come to run more discussions on hardship and Mao. The local farmers remind us how miserable life was in the old days. From the lieutenants' war experiences we get stories of superhuman survival, complete with appropriate references to Mao. The lieutenants tell us we don't know anything about hardship.

Other Chinese students can carry eight to ten heavy bundles of rice with the thin bamboo sticks pressing deep into their shoulders. I can muster only two rice bundles on my bamboo stick, with lots of stopping along the way.

Good food, some pay, and Sundays off are our rewards for hard labour. But Sundays off to where? Off to the nearby small village, half an hour away by foot.

In the middle of the growing season, the lieutenants decide to drill us. They send all two hundred students on a week's march. With bed sheets, boots, jackets, toothbrushes, cups, and spoons dangling from our backs, we march all day long. We eat in houses along the way and we sing Mao songs to pass time. As the sun descends, we reach the next village. The head of the local People's Commune comes out, gives a speech, and assigns us to some farmer's mud house for the night. When I get to the farmer's mud house, I can't say I'm tired. I can't dump my dangling load off my back. I can't drop my aching and tired body on a straw mattress. No. I must sweep his courtyard, fetch him some water from the well and eat with his family. That's what Lei Feng does, that's what Mao's Little Red Book says, and that's what the lieutenants tell us to do.

For two months I leave the warmth and hardness of the brick beds to spread Mao's word to two small villages, miles away from the military farm. All two hundred students and four lieutenants spread out in a fine weave across a county in northern China to preach Mao's philosophy of hard work and sacrifice in local farming villages. The local authorities, what's left of the local authorities after the Cultural Revolution, fight among themselves for control of the communes. The farmers and their broods sit in their houses and smoke cigarettes all day. Rice sits and rots in the fields.

I have to run two small villages of six hundred people, three walking hours apart. I have to get the farmers out of bed and out working in the fields. I also have to run political meetings, explaining to the smoky room of farmers why Mao wants them to work hard. I have to inspire the smoky room of farmers to collect the rotting rice. My speech lacks zeal, and I get a dead fish reaction from the farmers.

Every two weeks I walk up and down two hills to meet with the other students and our lieutenants at a central hub. We have to detail the progress, if any, of our small villages in rice harvesting. The county officials know we can't inspire the farmers to action. They just want us to provide them details on our villages. In other words we spy on the farmers.

Two years end. I board the train out of this remote region of northern China in 1970. At the train station, some guys from the farm, Communist Party members and others close to the army, tell me the report coming out from the farm boot camp says that I should not be trusted and that I should not work sensitive jobs. I cry on the train all the way back to Shenyang. Two years of hard labour end with one bad report.

(Ong 251–255)

EXERCISE 42 ▸ Rhetorical Analysis

Write a rhetorical analysis of "Two Hard Years." Your rhetorical analysis could go in many directions. Maybe you'd like to talk about content. Maybe you'd like to talk about form. Consider some of these points as you write:

- What's the most compelling part of Ong's tale? What details make it compelling?
- List some open-ended questions that you guess Ong used to elicit certain details from her father.
- Can you find parallelism in the language of Ong's father? Provide examples.

The next peer model, a research paper by Nicole Brewer, presents an argument about changes in forms of music delivery and music consumption. In one of our classes, Brewer wrote an interview-based article on record shops and then, for the final assignment, turned the topic into a research paper. As you read the paper, look for how she weaves in a part of that interview among the secondary sources and uses parallelism to connect points and make reading easier.

Solace in Obsolescence: Vinyl in the Age of Free Music

BY NICOLE BREWER

When music was first recorded and reproduced for personal use, the nature of music changed. Music became a commodity to have and hold and show off, not just a social, interactive event. The introduction of sound recording and music reproduction in the late nineteenth century marks "the end of music as a significant social discourse and initiates its relegation to the status of a mere commodity like any other" (Auslander 78). This first major paradigm shift in musical culture began with Emil Berliner's gramophone and moved through 78 r.p.m, 45 r.p.m., and 33 r.p.m. records, cassettes, 8-tracks, and CDs. These material forms of music finally hit the digital wall in the late twentieth century with the rise of intangible MP3s. Here occurs the second paradigm shift, when people no longer consume recorded music through material objects. This shift, called the "dematerialization" of music (Auslander 77), removed recorded sound even one step further from its origins in live events—the "disappearance of specific physical objects" transformed music into "a commodity in itself, unmoored from physical support" (Auslander 82). Still, many people crave and appreciate the physicality of records, and a strain of modern day musical culture finds solace in obsolescence, seeking the comforting tangibility of music in the form of vinyl LPs.

In 1887, Berliner's paradigm shifting flat disk design, the kind we now associate with vinyl records, departed from Edison's cylindrical phonograph. The disks sounded nearly unbearable, but by 1893 Berliner had improved the design enough to go into business, and by the early twentieth century the gramophone became an integral part of social culture (Ober 38–39). Berliner's gramophone and his related business ventures—Victor Talking Machine Company, London Gramophone Company, and the Columbia Phonograph Company—saw the development of a consumer market newly interested in the recordings of singers, bands, and musicians ("Phonograph" 56). Suddenly, music was available to consumers, and they wanted it.

Commercial music reproduction then began with the 78 r.p.m. record and has since faced a relatively constant stream of reconfiguration; each new development claims to be the best yet. In the 1940s, Columbia Records and RCA each introduced new forms of the record: the 33 r.p.m. disk and the 45 r.p.m. disk, respectively. These two new formats eventually phased out the 78s—the 33 taking its place as the LP still sold today, and the 45 being perfectly suited to singles—but as record players ran at different speeds to run the new formats, it was a slow and rocky transition (Gorman 132).

Technological developments spearheaded the slow and rocky transition, much the same as the later transition from LP to cassette to CD. The 78 r.p.m. record was born of a need to capture sound using acoustic recording, but "the development of electronic recording and playback heads made possible fine recording, and repro-duction at much lower speeds" (Gorman 133). When technology improved con-sumer access to higher quality music, the industry found a way to make the market accommodate it.

This appearance of higher quality sound reproduction in a mainstream mar-ket changed how the public perceived music. Recording technology first "brought about a crucial change in the sensory economy of music consumption" (Auslander 77); that is, it made *hearing* the most important sense in the consumption of music, rather than *seeing* a performance. With high-quality music, though, music consump-tion became an even more heightened and individual experience, more rooted in consciousness than entertainment. Marshall McLuhan argues that "a depth approach to musical experience also came in. . . . Depth means insight, not point of view; and insight is a kind of mental involvement in process that makes the content of the item seem quite secondary. Consciousness itself is an inclusive process not at all depend-ent on content" (McLuhan 282–283). With the increased quality and availability of music, musical culture became unto itself a physical and auditory experience, a ritual in which the medium of the music—the LP—was as much a part of the music as the music was.

When the CD hit shelves in the 1980s, listeners found themselves once more fac-ing a technological dilemma. Turntables had to be replaced by CD players and retailers either had to find new shelf space, or relegate the disk that seemed on its way out to back walls and dark corners in favour of the shiny new incomer. Like the 45s and 33s, the CD boasted its technological improvements: "The unprecedented audio clarity, disc durability, and storage capacity made the CD a more attractive format than vinyl.

And in keeping with the design of most new technologies, CDs featured certain con-veniences that transcended the other available modes" (Plasketes 112). Critics have suggested that the mobile, automatic, small, and detached CD, combined with the mobile cassette, caused the momentary decline in the LP (Plasketes 112).

Today, listeners find it easy and inexpensive to get music. This reality existed first with Napster and Limewire, then with torrents and iTunes, and now with streaming sites like Rdio. Digital music has been completely separated from its physical origins, whether that refers to LPs or the original performance. Digital music has become strictly an auditory experience, and a free and high-quality experience at that.

A curious development that the major players of the CD game and the inventors of the MP3 did not foresee, though, was that some listeners actually enjoy the hands-on attachment of vinyl. One 1992 article noted that "specialty shops and used record stores have become havens, or museums, for the vinyl subculture. In a survey of sev-eral major metropolitan LP-only and used record stores, owners indicated that their sales have increased—not decreased—during the past three years" (Plasketes 116). Even as music reproduction changed, as MP3s left CDs behind, the LP persisted. A com-bination of overzealous retailers, confused customers, and determined distributors swept vinyl far under the rug in the late 1980s and 90s. By the time of the early 2000s, however, someone had started to lift the rug and sweep it back out. By 2007 LPs rose again, with a 15 per cent jump in sales from the year before (Van Buskirk)—and they are still on the rise, with another 16 per cent increase between 2011 and 2012 (Thurm).

This dedication to a physical object today demonstrates the value of the medium over the value of the content. In a 2001 article that examines the physicality of the vinyl record, the author observes that "since . . . most consumers own more musical recordings than they have the time to listen to, the recording becomes an object of exchange and contemplation: an image of music that substitutes for music itself" (Auslander 78). This observation supports McLuhan's assertion of the medium as the message; that is, although LPs are collected, one thinks, for their content—the music recording—the medium is still the most important part of the collection.

The LP lingers because some listeners want to own something and want to show something off. They want to have a physical object of importance or value, importance or value that is difficult to attach to a digital product: "Collecting is about the thrill of the hunt, the accumulation of expertise, the display of wealth, the synesthetic allure of touching and seeing sound, the creation and cataloguing of memories, and the pleasures (and dangers) of ritual" (Katz 11). The consumption of music is not, and has never been, solely about the consumption of sound as with digital music, and many modern-day consumers are still searching for a way to satisfy the senses of both sight and sound when searching for music recordings.

The modern-day music-listener has many options for consumption and ownership but the LP remains powerful because it allows consumption and interaction that the cassette, CD, and MP3 do not. Walter Benjamin states "the unique value of the 'authen-tic' work of art has its basis in ritual" (224), and every development in music recording since the LP has served to remove the ritual from the musical experience—MP3s are instant and intangible, and "CDs simply contain music, while the medium of the vinyl record is part of the listening experience" (McCarthy).

Patrick Grant, a manager of the popular record store Kops on Queen Street West in Toronto, suggests that the comeback of the LP is a result of how easy it is to access music now. "Music is essentially free," he says, "but people invest differently in physical stuff. Having a tangible object, where the sound is created by the scraping of two objects together, it registers with your body differently than when you're just listening to a digital file. A vinyl listening experience feels more important, so the records that are more important to you, you're more likely to buy on vinyl" (Grant). Many modern-day listeners seek to find no music listening experience quite as appealing as the vinyl record.

Although other forms of music have transcended vinyl records, the tangible ritual of finding, buying, and playing an LP serves as a reminder of the physicality of music at its roots, as a performance and an interactive experience. Vinyl records allow music an importance not afforded by the phantom MP3, and they invite an intimacy and appreciation for music that seems easy to lose in an increasingly digital environment.

Works Cited

"A Phonograph Album." *Music Educators Journal.* 64.4 (1977): 52–59. Print.

Auslander, Philip. "Looking at Records." *The Drama Review.* 45.1 (2001): 77–83. Print.

Benjamin, Walter. "The Work of Art in the Age of Mechanical Reproduction." *Illuminations.* Ed. Hannah Arendt. New York: Schoken Books, 1969. Print.

Gorman, Robert. "What's What in the Platter Battle." *Popular Science.* 154.5 (1949): 132–133. Web. 20 Mar. 2013.

Grant, Patrick. Personal Interview. 26 Jan. 2013.

Katz, Mark. *Capturing Sound: How Technology Has Changed Music.* Berkeley, CA: University of California Press, 2004. Print.

McCarthy, Alison. "Living With Digital, Resurrecting Analog, and Our Shifting Search for Sound." *gnovis.* 10.2 (2010). n.p. Web. 21 Mar. 2013. http://gnovisjournal.org/2010/04/25/living-digital-resurrecting-analog-and-our-shifting-search-sound

McLuhan, Marshall. *Understanding Media: The Extensions of Man.* London: The MIT Press, 1964. Print.

Ober, Norman. "You Can Thank Emil Berliner for the Shape Your Record Collection Is In." *Music Educators Journal.* 60.4 (1973): 38–40. Print.

Plasketes, George. "Romancing the Record: The Vinyl De-Evolution and Subcultural Evolution." *Journal of Popular Culture.* 26.1 (1992): 109–123. Print.

Polt, Richard. "Typology: A Phenomenon of Early Typewriters." *Back to the Things Themselves!* 21–13 Mar. 1990. South Illinois University, Carbondale, IL. Ed. Anthony Steinbock. n.p. Print.

Thurm, Eric. "People Still Buy Music: Vinyl and digital sales are up even as overall music sales are down." *A.V. Club.* Onion Inc. 4 Oct. 2012. Web. 10 Feb. 2013. www.avclub.com/article/people-still-buy-music-vinyl-and-digital-sales-are-86255

Van Buskirk, Eliot. "New Vinyl Sales Rose Fifteen Percent in 2007." *Wired.* Condé Nast. 21 Jan. 2008. Web. 10 Feb. 2013.

> ### EXERCISE 43 ▸ Rhetorical Analysis
>
> Write a rhetorical analysis of "Solace in Obsolescence: Vinyl in the Age of Free Music." You may consider the following points and questions or think about some of your own. Write this analysis in a clear style—the style we've described throughout this book.
>
> - What's the overall argument of Brewer's paper? Explain it in one sentence.
> - What kind of evidence does Brewer use to defend her argument? If you're not sure how to answer this question, review the examples of evidence in Chapter 1.
> - List four examples of parallelism in the paper.
> - Do you find the paper economical? Explain why or why not.
> - How does Brewer enter an academic conversation that came before her but also make a new contribution?
> - What's the value of the interview element to this paper?

Assignment 7a

Now it's your turn to use interviews in your writing. They may serve as the appetizer or the main course. Prepare for your interview well to get the most out of it.

Suggested Topics:

1) Do an interview (or multiple interviews) and then write an interview-based article using one of the three structures we have discussed.
2) Interview an expert at your school in an area of study you find interesting and write an interview-based article that is focused primarily on either the person or the research. Make sure you explain the research in a clear way for non-experts.
3) Take an academic paper you've already written and consider an expert you could interview to add research to it. Contact the expert and set up an interview. Interview the expert and include quotations from him or her in your paper.

Here are some tips for this assignment:

- The topic should be manageable and focused. An interview-based article cannot be about everything. Do not interview a physics professor about what it's like to be a professor. Interview a physics professor about her controversial new theory about black holes.
- Always identify yourself and your project and publication (if you have one) before you interview someone. Publishing an interview with someone without their knowledge of your role or purpose is unethical.

- The interview location matters. Some subjects talk best when they are in their homes or their offices. Some subjects censor themselves in the presence of family members. Some people will talk best in a restaurant with a glass of wine in hand. If you visit them, take note of details of the place—those may spark conversation or provide colourful details for your article.
- Do not edit quotations for interfering factors like wordiness and passive voice. Capture the way people talk. If you think the quotation style will embarrass the interviewee, use a different quotation. Writers often debate whether they should fix up a poor quotation. Many find fixing up this to be an unethical practice unless it corrects only a small problem without changing the meaning of the sentence. Be careful with other people's words.

CHAPTER SUMMARY

Writing can be overly complex in structure and difficult to read. This chapter presents an solution: parallelism. When we attend to parallelism we attend to the repetition of grammatical elements, which makes writing easier to read. Martin Luther King's "I Have a Dream" speech is a famous example of effective parallelism.

Thinking of writing in this way reminds us of the ancient times before print. Orators used techniques like parallel structures to remind them of what to say. Today, we read silently, so we don't feel the rhythms of prose as much as orators do.

On pages 184 and 185, we showed a simple example of Terry performing three actions. Parallelism existed between the sentences (subject + verb) and, once the sentences were combined, within the new sentence (verb + verb + verb).

One way to understand parallelism is to think of sentences as having surface and under-the-surface elements. Surface parallelism is a repetition of the same words. Under-the-surface parallelism means that the grammatical structure repeats, even if the surface words do not. Faulty parallelism occurs when the parallelism in a sentence breaks down.

We suggested seven useful forms of parallelism, called series. First we presented the simplest series: verb series, noun series, adjective series, adverb series, and preposition series. These series look like lists. Writers sometimes shift the last element in these series to create surprise. We then turned to multiple-element parallelism. These parallel series—adjective-noun, subject-verb, subject-verb-object, and verb-preposition-object—combine grammatical elements.

The chapter then turned to the next form of writing, a staple of professional and academic writing: interview-based articles. Writers interview people to access their experiences or to show their fascinating characters. Interesting interviewees can be famous or not—it's about the story they tell, not their status.

We suggested you prepare thoroughly by researching the person, event, or job and then coming up with some good questions. Questions should be mostly open-ended as close-ended questions can be answered with a simple yes or no—you need more from the interviewee than that.

The beginning writer of an interview-based article thinks of himself or herself as The Questioner. But the best interviewers take on the role of The Listener. A product of good listening is the development of conversation. An interview should be like a conversation, not a formal question-and-answer session. Good listening helps you to develop follow-up questions, questions you never could have prepared about comments you never could have expected.

We then turned to writing up the interview. The quotations you have to work with will drive the focus of your piece. Then you have to decide how to structure it. Three main structural types—monologue, informal, formal—hinge on the extent to which you are a character in your article. You can mix and match these forms.

▌ Further Readings

For more about article structure:

Gutkind, Lee. *The Art of Creative Nonfiction: Writing and Selling the Literature of Reality*. New York: John Wiley & Sons, 1997. Print.

For more about interviewing:

Gerard, Philip. *Researching and Crafting the Stories of Real Life*. Long Grove, IL: Waveland Press, 2004. Print.

Sentence Variation and Sound

> A good sentence in prose should be like a good line in poetry, unchangeable, as rhythmic, as sonorous.
>
> —GUSTAVE FLAUBERT

A GOOD DRUMMER KNOWS a key aspect of good writing: variation. Drummers hold the band together with a consistent beat but also break out for emphasis, varying speed and volume for effect. Soft hits and hard hits, starts and stops—these are techniques good writers understand too.

The drummer's unit of measure is the drum stroke, while the prose writer's unit of measure is the sentence. This chapter is about the final enhancing factor for good writing: variation in sentence structure, length, and sound. In Chapter 7, we examined how writers can impose a consistent rhythm on their writing using parallelism—like a beat—within and between sentences.

Good writers use sentences that vary in structure for a change of pace. Good writers vary the length of sentences to speed up and slow down the reader's experience of the content. Good writers attend to the sounds of the words in their sentences. These three techniques emphasize and mimic meaning, creating sentences that resonate more deeply.

The interfering factor in variation and sound is monotonous sentences. Unless they are deliberate, monotonous sentences bore the reader. Imagine a public speaker talking in a monotone voice—the same can happen with the printed word too. To get a sense of the problem, read the following paragraph out loud:

William entered the grocery store. He looked around for candy. He walked over to the chocolate bars. The store owner said hello. William grabbed a chocolate bar. He walked over to the counter. He placed the chocolate bar on the counter. The owner rang up the price: $1.20. William handed the man the money. He stepped out the door onto the sidewalk.

The paragraph is not particularly bad. Each sentence is grammatically correct. Each sentence employs economy, active voice, strong verbs, strong nouns, original language, and even some parallelism between the sentences. It does everything we've told you to do in this book. The effect of reading the paragraph, however, is a mind-numbing drag.

This is an extreme example of a collection of **segregated sentences**. Segregated sentences stand on their own, focusing on one point. They're typically used in description or narration. They start with subjects and verbs. Segregated sentences are oriented towards events. They don't deal so much with what goes on in the mind but focus instead on the external world. When we hear this type of sentence we tend to picture something that's outside of ourselves.

Segregated sentences are the building blocks of good writing, but they too can be overused, as in the paragraph about William, above. All it takes to fix the problem is to vary the length of the sentences. Read this revised version out loud to feel the sentence variation:

> William entered the grocery store and looked around for candy. He walked over to the chocolate bars and the store owner said hello. William grabbed a chocolate bar, walked over to the counter, and placed it down. The owner rang up the price: $1.20. William handed the man the money and stepped out the door onto the sidewalk.

Always be a poet, even in prose.
—CHARLES BAUDELAIRE

The sentences vary in length from 7 words to 14, breaking the monotony of the original. It feels more natural, less rigid, after revision. Now let's look at some other sentence patterns that will help you change the way you "drum" in your rhythms of prose.

▌ Sentence Patterns

Our examples of parallel series in Chapter 7 showed how to set down a consistent beat within and between sentences. When you want to vary that beat, you can alter the internal order of the words in one sentence or the relationship between two sentences. Many of these patterns have names in classical rhetoric. Rather than list those names, we prefer to describe them according to their internal structure. Below, we list the equation for the structure under each name.

Intrusive

Sentence A—Sentence B—Sentence A.

The first example of internal order variation is the **intrusive sentence**. The punctuation around an intrusive sentence is two dashes. The dashes set off a complete, grammatically correct sentence from another complete, grammatically correct sentence that continues after the second dash. Consider these examples of the intrusive sentence:

a) He did not deserve his father's hatred—does any four-year-old deserve its father's hatred?—but he faced abuse regularly.

b) The birthday greeting—Daniela sends the same card to everybody— reads "Happy Birthday to my closest friend."

c) The condition stimulus—this part of the evidence is crucial—failed to produce the anticipated results.

Why would a writer use the intrusive sentence? To give more detail on general observations made in Sentence A. In each example above, Sentence B could stand alone—it has all the parts of a grammatical sentence if we look at it on its own. All three intrusion examples work well because they give us important extra information right where it's needed, after the opening element of Sentence A. Readers often enjoy that change of pace.

End/Beginning

Clause + Repeating Element. Repeating Element + Clause.

This form of sentence variation works between two sentences. The **End/ Beginning structure** repeats the end of one sentence (however many words you want to repeat) in the start of the next sentence:

a) What you have described is life. Life is tough.

b) Markevitch wanted Smith to reveal the evidence. Reveal the evidence Smith did.

c) Robinson turned on the electricity and his invention hummed. His invention hummed and changed his life forever.

What's most valuable about the End/Beginning Repeat construction is that it creates coherence—it links one sentence meaningfully to the next. The structure tells the reader to consider these two sentences together.

Beginning/Beginning

Repeating Element + Clause. Repeating Element + Clause.

The **Beginning/Beginning structure** places the repeating element at the beginning of two sentences. The beginning of any sentence is a natural emphasis point:

a) The door slammed and the house shook. The door slammed and our marriage ended.

b) Smith's theory seemed original to himself. Smith's theory seemed unoriginal to the committee.

c) The court system sends the guilty to jail. The court system sends the innocent to jail.

Readers of these three sentences cannot fail to make the connection—the repetition of the opening elements is obvious. The writer implies *Hey reader, think of these two sentences together*. This isn't simply repetition for repetition's sake. It's a relational repetition. One point clearly leads to the next one, raising the significance of the writer's meaning. Use this pattern wisely. If you use it too much, it becomes obvious. Overdoing it kills the effect as it becomes monotonous.

End/End

Clause + Repeating Element. Clause + Repeating Element.

The **End/End** structure repeats some number of words—your choice—from the end of the first sentence at the end of the second:

a)   He was a snivelling, whiny little brat. I wanted to kill that whiny little brat.

b)   Before we had money, we worried about money. After we got money, we still worried about money.

c)   The price of a car was high. The cost of a banana was high.

In sentence (a) the repetition of the adjectives and noun emphasizes the child's behaviour. This is one bad kid. Sentence (b) makes an interesting point in an elegant way: *the more money you have, the more you spend*. The final example shows a city where inflation—or at least scarcity—has set in. The End/End repetition is particularly strong because the repeating element closes out the sentences. The last words of a sentence stick in a reader's mind.

Beginning/End

Repeating Element + Clause + Repeating Element.

The **Beginning/End** sentence structure repeats elements at the beginning and end of one sentence. These constructions remind us of old sayings. The structure creates the poetic sound of a proverb:

a)   Forever is a long time and I intend to live forever.

b)   Sam, whatever you say about him, is still Sam.

c)   Problems led to more problems.

Beginning/End repeat will probably occur only occasionally in your writing. These structures draw too much unnecessary attention to themselves if used often.

EXERCISE 44 ▸ Sentence Patterns

The way to feel the variations in these sentence patterns is to create some of your own.

    a)   Write two examples of the Intrusive type.
    b)   Write two examples of the End/Beginning type.
    c)   Write two examples of the Beginning/Beginning type.
    d)   Write two examples of the End/End type.
    e)   Write two examples of the Beginning/End type.

EXERCISE 45 ▸ Pattern Paragraph

It's one thing to create patterned sentences. It's quite another to apply them in full paragraphs on specific topics. Write a paragraph of about 150 words on any topic that contains at least three different sentence patterns (the other sentences may be segregated sentences). Integrate meaning with repetition.

▋ Short Sentences

The variation so far has dealt with structure inside a sentence and relationships between sentences. Now let's turn to the length of sentences. Length affects a reader's comprehension.

The short active voice sentence, which we explained in Chapter 4, works particularly well for depicting physical actions or single points. It mimics an action's sharpness and quickness and lack of continuity. It mimics the clarity of one thought. The **staccato effect** of one short sentence after another also reflects a disjointed consciousness or a moment of emphasis. Consider the effect of the short sentences in this example:

> I punch. He jumps back. He lunges at me. I grab his arm. I throw him down on the mat. I hold him. The referee smacks the mat. One. Two. Three. I win the championship for the first time.

In real life, punches, jumps, lunges, grabs, and throws all occur as short, quick movements. Short, quick sentences replicate that surface meaning and create a symbiosis of form and content. Notice how the final sentence above, longer than any of the other five, is a nice change of pace. The reader speeds through the short sentences and slows down, and lingers, on the expanded final sentence.

Short sentences for variation are also valuable in any writing when you want to ensure that the reader doesn't miss your point. Readers can lose track of, or overlook, a part of a long sentence, particularly in academic writing where we try to pack in many points. A sequence of short sentences in the right moment makes points no reader can overlook. Consider this sentence:

> During wartime, they thought traitors lurked everywhere. Your dentist could be a Communist. Your butcher could be a Communist. Your father could be one too.

The longest sentence in this paragraph contains just seven words. Each sentence makes a single point, without *ands* or *buts*. Nothing gets lost. David Remnick, editor of *The New Yorker*, uses two short sentences to end a profile about Michael Jordan:

> Three weeks later, at the United Center against the Knicks, Jordan did not need to play half as well as he had in New York. This time, he shared the ball with Pippen, and the two of them destroyed New York. Jordan is right. He's back. (305)

Certain brief sentences are peerless in their ability to give one the feeling that nothing remains to be said.

—JEAN ROSTAND

Remnick makes a telling point that no reader can miss with the two short closing sentences. The sentences work like exclamation marks at the end of a sentence. Combining them into a longer sentence, such as *Jordan is right about the fact that he's back* wouldn't emphasize those points as well.

EXERCISE 46 ▶ Short Sentences

To feel the effect of sentence variation with short sentences, you need to write some of your own. Think about a situation you experienced that had action: a school fight, a car race, a sporting event, or some other suitable moment. Write a paragraph of about 75 words that shows the moment's actions. Describe only one action per sentence. Your writing will seem choppy—that's fine. The form will mimic the choppiness of the content.

█ Long Sentences

Long sentences have their own unique effect. They're loosely structured so they're inherently ambient and atmospheric. They're **impressionistic**. They're useful for depicting dreams, experiences of drug and alcohol abuse, intense emotions, and observational scene-setting. They're often called **freight train sentences**. If you've ever stood on the side of a railroad track, you've seen a whole series of cars pass with a coupling between each. In a freight train sentence, grammatical units repeat, coupled with conjoining words, conjunctions like *and* or *but*.

The freight train sentence is particularly good for depicting dreams because dreams don't stop and start abruptly the way fights do. Dreams move smoothly, from location to location, with **juxtapositions** of places and people. Consider this dream sequence:

> I floated off the ground and looked around and saw sand for miles around, and behind me I saw a man on a Harley Davidson riding my way, so I started to fly in the opposite direction, but I moved slowly and he gained on me, so I turned to look for an escape route and suddenly I floated over a cliff and flew down into the canyon below, where I landed softly on the ground and looked up to see the man on the bike, and he looked angry.

The reader experiences the dream not just in the meaning but in the form. The key to writing this long sentence is the connectors. Long sentences come together best when you join active voice sentences with conjunctions like *but*, *so*, or *and*. Connectors can't be complicated or else the sentence becomes hard to follow. Without the proper connecting words, though, it becomes a run-on sentence, a train wreck.

When placed under the pressure of intense emotions, people lose their train of thought. Stress increases, heartbeats accelerate, and blood runs hot. They can't think straight. In the next example, thoughts rush through a bullied boy's mind:

> I see Randy over by the see-saw and want to run, but he's already spied me and he turns away from his friends and lurches across the grass, his arms hanging like a monkey's by his side, and sweat rolls down my back and my face feels hot and my hands tremble, but I can't seem to move and I just see his eyes locked onto mine, like Superman's eyes, and he strolls right up close to me, face-to-face.

In this example, the writer never tells the boy's feelings. Instead we sense what he feels from the physical details. The freight train sentence mimics his emotional state.

Authors sometimes use a freight train sentence at the beginning of a story to help us look around and set the scene:

> Terry stood at the top of the Great Mountain and looked down at the greenness of the valley, the yellow dandelions marking the grass, and he saw a fawn strolling along and sniffing the ground, and then the fawn's mother ushered it away, and Terry looked over to the peaceful lake, and a swan floated with another, and he enjoyed the silence, the silence of home.

This scene-setting creates images in our mind in the same way a movie camera pans. The corresponding camera in our mind's eye moves around the landscape.

Long sentences work in essays too. Veteran journalist Richard Gwyn used a Freight Train sentence to open his political essay about Liberal Party leader Justin Trudeau:

> When Justin Trudeau announced his candidacy for the federal Liberal leadership last October, the near-universal assumption of columnists, pollsters, backroom types, political scientists, historians, and others of that ilk was that he and the party were engaged in the political equivalent of a Hail Mary pass—in other words, an act of desperation. (26)

This sentence is 53 words long but as clear as a sentence half its length. Gwyn sets up a point he's going to delve into in his essay, and the freight train sentence relays that point elegantly. Notice that he also uses a noun series to list the commentators on this political issue.

You'll rarely write a sentence as long as some of these examples. Indeed, a freight train sentence need not be excessively long. The strength of a freight train sentence is its flowing structure, not some absolute measure of length. Consider this example from Mark Twain about Mississippi in the nineteenth century:

> The town drunkard stirs, the clerks wake up, a furious clatter of drays follows, every house and store pours out a human contribution, and all in a twinkling the dead town is alive and moving. (2)

At 35 words, Twain's sentence isn't that long (and it is much shorter than some sentences found in academic writing!). But it has the same rambling, flowing feeling of the longer examples. In your own writing, use a sentence length that you find appropriate.

EXERCISE 47 ▸ Long Sentences

Now we want you to write extremely long sentences. This exercise has two parts: dreams and reality.
1) Write a single long sentence of around 75 words describing a dream or fantasy.
2) Write a second long sentence of around 75 words about a real experience (i.e., not a dream).

Variation of Long and Short for Effect

In terms of sentences, neither short nor long is inherently better. A succession of short sentences may become choppy and monotonous. A succession of long sentences weighs your writing down. The point is to vary your sentence lengths for certain effects.

The contrast of a short sentence after long sentences makes a resounding point that no reader will overlook. Consider this example:

> The Canadian newspapers of the early nineteenth century were quite different than the Canadian newspapers of today. Newspapers back then were small-time operations, and the editor worked as the printer too, sending papers by mail to a small readership of a few hundred. Editors often printed nasty, vitriolic comments about their political enemies, the kind of comments we tend to find today on the Internet. Partisanship reigned.

This paragraph on early Canadian newspapers includes three reasonably long sentences. What stands out, however, is the final short sentence. In only two words—the simplest active voice sentence—the author emphasizes one point: the importance of partisanship in early Canadian newspapers. It acts like an exclamation point on the sentence and a welcome break from the longer ones.

> You have to do tricks with pacing, alternate long sentences with short, to keep it vital and alive.
> —THEODOR GEISEL (DR. SEUSS)

When you want to slow down a reader's experience, use long sentences. When you want to speed up a reader's experience, use short sentences. In the next example, Remnick uses sentence length to chance pace when he describes rookies watching baseball star Reggie Jackson in spring training:

> They studied his easy looping warm-up swings, his murderous slashes at the ball, even the vicious way he spit through his teeth after every pitch, and as they watched him, they may have remembered seeing the same motions a decade ago on television or, if they were lucky, from a seat in the upper deck. Jackson was a part of their boyhood. (133)

Remnick first pulls along the reader in a kind of romantic vision of Jackson now and then. He jolts the reader with the short sentence, a single point, about the rookies' boyhood.

Your variation need not be this extreme. Just a slight difference in sentence lengths can have a similar effect. Readers will appreciate your change of pace.

Academic Writing and Sentence Variation

Does sentence variation matter in academic writing? Yes, but not much attention gets paid to it. Even good academic writing tends to be pragmatic in sentence structure, not poetic and musical. Sometimes academic writers move from just relaying information to making a bigger, stronger case about their subject. They use variation to emphasize that bigger, stronger case.

Communication scholar James Carey concludes his famous journalism history article with an extremely long sentence punctuated by a short sentence fragment for effect. Consider the poetry in this passage:

> When we do this the presumed dullness and triviality of our subject matter evaporates and we are left with an important corner of the most vital human odyssey: the story of the growth and transformation of the human mind as formed and expressed by one of the most significant forms in which the mind has conceived and expressed itself during the last three hundred years—the journalistic report. (93)

Carey uses noun series with *dullness* and *triviality* and *growth* and *transformation*, and uses verb series in *formed* and *expressed* and *conceived* and *expressed*. He deliberately chooses to hold back the object of the second clause—*the journalist report*—the way a comedian holds back the punch line. This is one of the few instances when the editor would not change the passive to active. The *journalistic report*, set off by a dash, works like a short sentence to emphasize the object he describes. Carey's sentence length and variation match his content and elegantly drive home his point.

EXERCISE 48 ▸ Variation of Long and Short for Effect

Write one long sentence of about 75 words on any topic. Then write a short sentence of 8 words or fewer that makes some emphatic point about the first sentence.

▌ Sound

Without variation, writers get into a rut with monotonous sentences and sounds. During a speech, the sound of a monotonous speaker's voice grates on us and annoys us. In writing, it's no different. Even when reading silently, readers do hear the sounds of our words. Paying attention to the "sound" of your words on the page can help you, as a writer, avoid annoying your reader and create positive effects.

Canadian novelist Timothy Findlay would read his manuscripts aloud—hundreds of pages—to his partner, both of them listening to the sound of the prose. We've encouraged you in this book to read your work out loud to catch errors. When you've done your revisions for everything we've talked about in this book, you may conclude by listening to the sounds of your words and the effects they create. Read your work out loud.

> Somewhere along the line the rhythms and tonalities of music elided in my brain with the sounds that words make and the rhythm that sentences have.
> —E.L. DOCTOROW

The acoustic effect may be harsh or smooth or soft or loud—or it may even rhyme. Below are some suggestions about how to attend to sound in your writing.

Euphony

Writing that uses soft consonants and vowels has a **euphonic** feeling—it sounds pleasing to the ear. Here are some examples of soft consonants and vowels and their sounds:

- S as in snake
- F as in free
- Sh as in shake
- R as in reed
- L as in less
- W as in water
- FL as in flower
- OH as in low
- A as in hat
- AH as in car

We can combine these sounds the way we linked together parallel elements in the last chapter. Read the following sentences slowly out loud, and feel the effect of softness:

a)   She licked her lips and I loved their luminous wetness.

b)   The sensitive subject deserved a soft touch in the essay.

c)   Wind whirs through murmuring pines.

d)   Shimmering in the morning sun, the lake looked pristine.

Notice that the form matches the content of the sentences. On the surface, we process the words and understand their meanings. But the words resonate much more deeply because they sound like what they describe.

> Writing and music are two different mediums, but musical phrases can give you sentences that you didn't think you ever had.
> —BARRY HANNAH

Cacophony

The opposite of softness, **cacophony**, means hard sounds. Hard consonants that create this effect include

- C as in critter
- B as in butter
- D as in danger
- G as in gargle
- T as in traitor

Notice how these examples sound much harsher than the sentences with soft consonants and vowels:

a)   A fist of knuckled flesh tore skin, broke teeth, and whacked cheekbones.

b)   The torrents thundered down.

c)   The BMW crashed in the ditch and exploded.

d)   She trashed the changing room.

e)   The jury treated the testimony with skepticism.

Cacophony works particularly well in showing harsh physical actions. The connection of sound to meaning emphasizes the point of the words.

Alliteration

Alliteration means the repetition of words, usually with opening cacophonous sounds. You must be delicate with alliteration—too much of it becomes obvious and annoying. Not surprisingly, many clichés rely on alliteration—*tattle tale*; *far-flung*; *tried, tested, and true*—and as we learned in Chapter 6, clichés are something we want to avoid as writers.

The next paragraph includes much more subtle and effective examples of alliteration. Can you hear them?

> The test driver raced the Porsche down the Montreal track. The car's wind whipped up the dirt on the asphalt. A few fellow drivers—looking like tourists—stood in the stands under the hot sun. The car disappeared down the track after the first turn.

Here the alliteration sometimes occurs with words close together and sometimes with words that are farther apart. The alliteration serves the meaning of the sentence—it's not misused or overdone.

Assonance

In the same way a writer constructs alliterations by repeating consonants, he or she can also repeat vowel sounds to create assonance. Many familiar expressions use this technique: *cat nap, brotherly love, jail break, nitpick, fly-by-night, hothead*. In each one, the repetition of the vowel sound makes them memorable. Here's a longer example:

> The teen grips the thick leather steering wheel as he speeds through the police stop on the highway. The chase lasts an hour. The captain's car catches up with the teen, finally, at the exit to Edmonton.

This paragraph contains obvious and subtle examples of assonance. Can you hear them? The repetition provides an aural connection between words and sentences that readers find resonant and poetic. Another fact about vowel sounds: open vowels like *oh* slow the experience of the writing down; short vowels like *i* speed it up.

Attention to these four types of sound variation can make your writing more pleasing to the reader's ear. But don't think about sound when you're freewriting or drafting. You can waste hours hunting for alternative words in a thesaurus to create sound repetition. And as we've said, excessive repetition can lead to awkward combinations of words. Our advice is simple: become aware of the sound of your words at the editing stage and use these four examples of sound variation appropriately and sparingly.

EXERCISE 49 ▸ Prose Sounds

Give sound in writing a try. Be a "musician of words." Trying out sound will raise your consciousness of this important aspect of prose.

Write four short paragraphs (three or four sentences each) on any topic. Write one paragraph for each of the four sound types we described above: euphony, cacophony, alliteration, and assonance. Read your finished paragraphs out loud to test their effects.

▍ Personal Essays

At this point in the book you've written personal narratives, research papers, and an interview-based article. You found the content in your mind or the minds of others. You told simple, direct, detailed, focused stories about your life and the lives of others. You took other people's research and indirect experience and used them as the basis for your own clear, precise academic writing.

In this chapter we want you to try a hybrid form of writing, one that combines elements of personal narrative with elements of academic writing. In the personal essay, you move outside your own history to, in a sense, research your communities. You observe what goes on around you.

The word *essay* comes from the French word *essayer*, meaning a short written piece of subjective writing. In school, the word *essay* gets mixed up with research papers—but they are not the same. The essay presents an inherently tentative, short, focused observation using arguments and relates those arguments to everyday life. It is not a mode of writing suited to extensive, broad topics.

Essays may include narration, description, and illustration (you've done all three already in the personal narrative assignments). Its structure is more fluid and organic than that of a rigidly organized school paper. This is no hamburger-style paper as is often taught in high school.

The Power of the Personal Essay

At first glance, a personal essay may seem like insignificant piece. How could a writer influence or affect anyone with an essay? But a well-written essay can be used to influence admission committees, consumers, citizens, and politicians.

Think of the personal essay as your small contribution to a larger public conversation. Our society's truths develop out of billions of conversations that define good and bad and right and wrong. In this light, the essay writer who defines, for example, what it means to be a woman in the twenty-first century or how people should act while driving is performing a significant task.

Audiences read, reflect on, and respond to those propositions by agreeing or disagreeing with them. Out of this come ideas some see as truths: work hard, respect others, love hockey. And these truths in turn develop and change through further discussion, agreement, and disagreement.

You may choose to write about preserving a cultural practice (e.g., respect for the military). Maybe you want to change a deep-seated belief that some people hold (e.g., gay marriage is wrong). Maybe you want to shed light on an injustice (e.g., unequal pay for equal work).

Some major shifts in cultural practices and beliefs over the past few decades about same-sex marriage, recycling, and healthy eating illustrate the point. Thirty or forty years ago, few writers said much on these subjects. Those who did faced opposition from traditional thinkers, who asked: Shouldn't only a man and a woman have the right to marry? Do I really need to go through the effort of separating my garbage every day? Doesn't healthy food taste worse than hamburger and fries and greasy pizza?

> The drama of the essay is the way the public life intersects with my personal and private life. It's in that intersection that I find the energy of the essay.
>
> —RICHARD RODRIGUEZ

But cultural and legal upheavals don't happen because one person requests change in an essay. They happen because thousands of writers publish their ideas in the public sphere, time and again, until their voices become loud and unified and they catch the attention of the mainstream. Writers identify problems, step forward, and speak out. Writers outline consequences and circulate solutions. They argue passionately and ethically and logically. They show how people can live their lives and still allow change.

In the case of the three examples above, writers argued for rights for same-sex couples, provided simple solutions for protecting the environment, and suggested diet changes for people interested in moving away from hamburgers, fries, and greasy pizza.

This collective writing effort changed the lives of millions of readers. Readers influenced friends and family. Friends and family convinced other people that change was good too. This slow process—over many decades—ended with millions of people thinking and acting differently.

Over your writing life you'll take on many different roles in making public meaning: academic, journalist, historian, and so on. Two roles that stand out in particular in essay writing are the Writer as Cultural Observer and the Writer as Activist. Let's take a look at how these roles work.

> A good essay must have this permanent quality about it; it must draw its curtain round us, but it must be a curtain that shuts us in not out.
>
> —VIRGINIA WOOLF

Writer as Cultural Observer

The cultural observer writes a personal essay from a somewhat detached position or stance. The essay isn't so argumentatively strident or forceful. Some of the best professional writing stands back and observes society, showing people details they've never noticed. Pulitzer Prize–winning movie columnist Roger Ebert—one of the inventors of the two-thumbs-up movie grading system—was a cultural observer of movies without equal. His movie observations became important to millions of people.

When you observe your culture, you often discover ideas that many people feel are true but that they haven't written or spoken about. Other times you discover something nobody else knows. Writing about one's culture can be amusing as well, if you have a knack for humorous writing.

What people do every day, what they watch, and what they buy are often affected by the words of opinion leaders, people who tell others about new and interesting things. If you know a topic well enough, and if you communicate its details effectively in essay form, you too can become an opinion leader in any community—a community of comic book fans, of moviegoers, of soccer spectators, and so on. Readers then learn from your work, and you develop authority. Cultural observers include reviewers, critics, scholars, columnists, bloggers, and tweeters.

> A writer, I think, is someone who pays attention to the world.
>
> —SUSAN SONTAG

EXERCISE 50 ▶ Cultural Observation Trends

Writers should always be aware of their surroundings. In this exercise, list 10 interesting trends you've observed lately. For each trend, explain its significance in only one sentence. Trends may be found in fashion, food, architecture, video games, music, cars, relationships, media, or some other social realm. Make sure your trends really are fresh. Tell readers something they don't know. The challenge here is to know your audience—your readers—well enough to know what they don't know.

■ Writer as Activist

The second major role that essay writers take on is writer as activist. In that role, the writer does everything the cultural observer does, but with an additional element. The activist writes about his or her observations but also demands change.

> I think that almost every important advance in American environmentalism has coincided with, sprung from, some piece of writing, some book.
>
> —BILL MCKIBBEN

A person becomes an activist to combat a power imbalance. An activist speaks for those without a voice, whether a human, an animal, or the natural environment. Unfair power imbalances hurt people or natural things. If successful, activism rebalances relationships.

Writing becomes one way to raise awareness of problems, suggest the significance of those problems, and provide concrete solutions. If you alter people's perceptions through writing, you exert influence.

Here are steps for activist writing:

- Describe the problem, whether local, national, or global (or a combination of all three).
- List credible evidence, like in academic writing, to prove the problem exists.
- Explain the significance of the problem—why should the average reader care?
- Describe clear solutions for the problem, solutions the average reader can do.

> The point of the essay is to change things.
>
> —EDWARD TUFTE

Activists in the environmental movement mastered the art of describing a problem like overfilled garbage dumps, providing evidence of damage to the Earth, explaining why the problem mattered to people, and suggesting simple day-to-day solutions, such as home recycling boxes.

EXERCISE 51 ▶ Activist Causes

Maybe you already support a cause, such as cancer research or anti-bullying. For this exercise, we'd like you to list three causes you support directly (either small or big). For each cause, write one sentence—not a paragraph—that argues some change you'd like to make on behalf of that cause. Think about the cause in a new way—don't parrot the same old arguments other people have made. Avoid generalities.

Activist Writing: The David Suzuki Method

Environmental activist David Suzuki is best known for his long run as the host of the CBC environmental show *The Nature of Things*. The show has brought environmental issues into people's homes, created awareness of a growing environmental movement, and made the former University of British Columbia professor a household name. Suzuki includes commentary, personal views, and stories in his work to humanize often abstract and distant environmental causes.

Beyond his documentary TV work, Suzuki has written over 40 books and hundreds of personal essays. *The David Suzuki Reader* brings together his personal essays to celebrate their significance for the environmental movement. His approach to activist writing is highly effective and deserves a close look.

Suzuki engages readers by telling stories just like the ones you've read throughout this book. In one personal essay about the pollution of Canadian land, he describes an experience he had as a boy:

> In London, we lived on the northwest edge of town next to the railway tracks, along whose banks I would pick asparagus in the spring and hunt for insects in the summer. . . . Bicycling west on Oxford Street, I would quickly run out of pavement and hit the gravel road. In about twenty minutes, I'd be at my grandparents' 4-hectare (10-acre) farm at the end of Proudfoot Lane. But first I'd always stop at the large swamp beside the road to look for frogs, snakes, and damselflies. . . . In the thirty-five years since my boyhood, the Thames River has been saturated with industrial effluent and agricultural runoff accumulating along its length. The river was too convenient for dumping garbage and chemical wastes. Now there are few clams, crayfish, or minnows to be seen. Londoners today recoil at any suggestion of eating fish from the Thames or asparagus from the tracks. ("London in My Life" 15)

Suzuki's personal tale has authority—he has seen the environmental change with his own eyes. Readers in turn are able to see his experience through his detailed storytelling. He contextualizes that narrative with a few telling points about the effects of industrialization. In this way, readers empathize with Suzuki's story and clearly understand its point.

Suzuki also doesn't fear his opposition. Indeed, opposing arguments should not be seen as negatives or obstacles. They can help modify and bolster an argument, the way a chess master predicts an opponent's next few moves. This approach requires the writer to read widely and know thoroughly those concerns. Consider this example from a personal essay Suzuki wrote called "Global Warming":

> Some people question the seriousness of the dangers. The greenhouse effect is exaggerated, they argue. Fluctuations in global temperatures have occurred in

continued

the past, and extinction is normal, since 99 percent of all species that ever lived are now extinct. These two points fail to consider the rate of change. The warming that ended the last Ice Age occurred at the rate of about a degree every millennium. The coming rate of change could be several degrees per century. (60)

In this passage, Suzuki considers and references the arguments of the other side—that makes him look fair and reasonable. Writers cannot ignore such objections and hope they just go away. In the public sphere of debate and discussion, people read these objections from other writers, and Suzuki works them into his writing. His arguments push forward the debate in an honest way.

In one personal essay, Suzuki even admits—and this admission may surprise some readers—that "our ignorance about the factors that influence weather and climate is so great that it is impossible to make a realistic scientific prediction" (61). Some writers may be unwilling to admit this hole in the science on global warming. But Suzuki's opponents know the hole and they write about it; Suzuki must address the concern. However, his admission doesn't paralyze his argument. Instead, he describes the clear and copious scientific data on human-made gas emissions, warming oceans, rising sea levels, and more intense and frequent storms. He argues inductively that storms and flooding will lead to massive economic costs.

In a more strident personal essay titled "Why We Must Act on Global Warming," Suzuki ties a personal anecdote to these objections. After a particularly cold Canadian winter, a friend says sarcastically "So much for global warming" (66). Suzuki then admits that even the succession of hot summers in the 1980s didn't, by itself, prove global warming. These kinds of observations aren't clear proof of anything and we still need more studies of the subject, he writes. But he warns against inaction on greenhouse gases as we wait for more and more studies. Instead, he calls for the precautionary principle—that is, the idea that we should take precautions to stop releasing chemicals into the environment before it's too late.

Suzuki's careful, measured, subtle arguments for environmental protection also educate rather than scold the reader. People like to learn, but talking down to people turns them off. In activist writing, the writer isn't trying to convince his or her fervent enemies about the truth of the cause or attack them personally. The activist writer is trying to convince the large, mushy middle of society, the unsure and the uncommitted, to join the cause. Writers who use a welcoming and educational approach bring the unsure and uncommitted to their side, developing a powerful political bloc to make change.

Finally, Suzuki's personalization of environmental issues and his approach to argumentation has contributed to his cultural credibility. This credibility helped him co-found a non-profit environmental organization called the David Suzuki Foundation that promotes environmental policy change across Canada, an organization that's a legacy of his activist writing.

Personal Essays and the Truth

Good personal essays defend or challenge what we know as true and right. What people accept as true and right isn't necessarily fact, the way the sky is blue is fact. To a great degree, we create our truth. The philosophical arguments around reality and truth are too complex and difficult to discuss here. But a problem—or an opportunity—exists when you jump into public debates as an essay writer on unsettled topics. Many public writers today state truths that, upon further investigation, fall apart. Consider these statements:

a) Homeless people are just lazy bums.

b) Politicians always waste money.

c) Technology makes us a better society.

All three of these examples of common essay arguments are unequivocal about their truth statements. There's no *maybe* or *perhaps* or *possibly* here. These writers take a strong stand in a way that sounds like fact. Being unequivocal isn't a bad thing—we do it in this book, even in this sentence. But that's not always the case. And sometimes knowing this helps writers argue better.

Let's look at the three examples above. People who work with the homeless know that many homeless people want to work—they aren't lazy. But circumstances intervene: job loss or mental illness, for example. Politicians don't always waste money (we see roads and bridges and water treatment plants and parks built on time and on budget). *Waste* is also a debatable term, depending on your ideological bent—one politician's waste is another's community valuable funding. Finally, we revere technology so much these days that many people assume new technology is always better. Examples abound, though, of technologies that foul the Earth or reduce our privacy.

Good essay writers always remain sceptical of broad truth statements— *X and Y are always this or always that.* Truth statements influence the nature of a public debate by providing the boundaries of meaning that we must all accept just to have a conversation. Consider these classic examples of the concept of assumptions-as-facts:

a) The current president of Canada is bald.

b) Jane no longer writes fiction.

In the first example, the assumption is that there is a president of Canada (in reality, there is not). The second assumption is that the president is bald (if Canada doesn't have a president, then this point is obviously untrue). This statement seems obviously untrue to Canadians. Those less familiar with Canada may accept it as unquestionable. In the second sentence, the assumption is that Jane once wrote fiction. If she didn't, then the assertion also starts from a false premise.

The reader needs prior knowledge to determine the truth of these examples. Without prior knowledge, most readers accept willingly a writer's assertion. Unethical political writers take unfair advantage of this fact with naive or uninformed readers.

In writing an essay, you want to know what assumptions your readers hold if you want to make change. If you can undercut the assumption, you can undercut the resistance to your fresh, new ideas.

This struggle for truth, of course, never ends. Change is never complete. Some people continue to reject same-sex marriage, toss recyclables in with regular garbage, and eat pizza, hamburgers, and fries daily until they die. Their own ideas remain true to them. But let's not forget that 150 years ago in Canada, neither men without property (renters) nor women could vote for their elected leaders. Today we laugh at the people who upheld those so-called truths. Truth changes.

> The truth is rarely pure and never simple.
>
> —OSCAR WILDE

EXERCISE 52 ▸ Truth Statements

Recognizing other writers' truth statements is the first step towards careful consideration of an argument. In this exercise, find an opinion column in a newspaper or magazine. Underline the truth statements. Do you agree or disagree with what the writer suggests are facts? Are those statements rooted in undeniable facts or in stereotypes? If you have trouble finding a truth statement, look for verbs like *is* or *are*. Those verbs often indicate these statements.

Three Rhetorical Elements

Writers of essays and research papers alike want their ideas to resonate with the most readers. The best writers reach wide audiences because they use language that appeals to all three elements of classical rhetoric. A set of three principles from an ancient philosopher, Aristotle, helps essay writers increase the effectiveness of their writing.

Aristotle said the best rhetoricians combined pathos (emotion), ethos (ethics), and logos (logic). The combination produced the most effective communication. Let's consider emotion, ethics, and logic in your essay writing.

Emotion

All good writing engages the emotions on some level. You saw in the personal narrative readings in this book how a short piece of writing can make you smile, cry, or laugh. Academic papers can make you wonder. Emotional appeals work best if the writer expresses emotion through story and evidence, not through simply telling readers the emotion.

Emotional appeals annoy audiences if too overt. Think about those commercials for animal and child welfare: they overdo emotion with pictures of abused animals and starving children.

Nonetheless, essays that only argue rationally and logically can be too abstract and distant to affect readers. They don't help readers care. If you find yourself falling into the abstract in your essay, a return to narrative can bring the reader back to the concrete, feeling world.

> If emotion without reason is blind, then reason without emotion is impotent.
> —PETER SINGER

Ethics

Many unethical essay writers exist in the public sphere. The columnists of populist newspapers may twist and spin facts to rile up readers with offensive and loaded language. Other writers, like environment activist David Suzuki, argue carefully and ethically.

Suzuki is fair and reasonable, and he considers other points of view while remaining passionate about his causes. He pushes dialogue further along by anticipating the objections of his audiences; this means not pretending those objections don't exist, which requires deep knowledge of the discourse surrounding his causes.

Suzuki's ethical writing has developed a large and loyal readership. That readership has given him authority, authority to speak on environmental issues that deeply concern his readers. If he'd taken the unethical approach—by ignoring or misrepresenting his opposition's position—people would have found him out. His enemies would have publicized his ethical breaches. In your writing, respect the audience; don't twist and turn the facts in your favour. Readers will respect you in turn.

Logic

Logical reasoning is just as important as emotion and ethics, Aristotle said. People in our age expect appeals to logic. When someone tells you *You're not making sense*, he or she expects logic.

Two approaches to general reasoning are useful both for essays and academic writing: inductive and deductive. **Inductive reasoning** works from the bottom up while deductive works from the top down. Inductive reasoning identifies specific individual points or cases of evidence, and argues from those. Consider this inductive argument:

The Earth is getting warmer.

The rate of warming is increasing.

There's an increased variability in weather patterns.

Specific argument: Global warming is happening.

Deductive reasoning requires no such cases or evidence leading to a point. Instead, a deductive argument moves from a general statement to more specific ones that logically follow. For example, consider this deductive argument:

Global warming affects all countries.

Canada is a country.

Specific argument: Global warming affects Canada.

Most writers start with inductive reasoning, as it works from the evidence to a major point: they know their point will match the evidence at the end. However, some may employ deductive reasoning within the body of a piece to make a point as well. The success of deductive reasoning depends upon the accuracy of the premises, but this kind of logic can be correct even if the premises are factually false. In the deductive example above, a lack of evidence of global warming would make the whole argument moot. Evidence still matters.

Fallacies of logic, however, abound in essay writing in the public sphere. Unethical writers use fallacies as a tool. They want to demean an opponent or trick unaware readers into believing their point. Some writers fall into fallacies without realizing it.

Argumentative fallacies are not just academic concerns. In your day-to-day life, you argue often. You argue with your mother or father, your sister or brother, and your teachers. You have argumentative experience already. You may recognize some of these fallacies in everyday arguments:

Ad Hominem (attacking the person):

"I can't trust any person that believes in socialism."

Hasty Generalization:

"Justin Bieber fans don't know what good music is."

Either/Or Fallacy (providing only two options):

"You're either with me or you're against me."

Straw Man (mischaracterizing your opponent's argument):

"All you pot smokers want is a licence to sit around all day and get wasted."

Slippery Slope/Domino Effect Theory (the worst will happen):

"If the government allows gay marriage, soon enough people will want to allow siblings to get married."

Post Hoc Ergo Propter Hoc (simple cause and effect, no other factors):

"He got into a fight because he watched that violent movie."

False Analogy (incorrect comparison):

"The hockey game was like a war."

Avoiding these most common argumentative fallacies strengthens your writing's logic—which readers appreciate—and avoids providing easy counterarguments and ammunition for the other side.

No argument, however, is airtight. Even the smallest assumption—the meaning of a word, for example—could be a source of disagreement between readers. But at the very least, the arguments you make should be reasonable. Most readers aren't philosophy professors testing your logic—they're willing to give you a chance if you respect them and others.

EXERCISE 53 ▶ Logical Fallacies

Logical fallacies lurk everywhere on the Internet. See if you can find them.

Log on to an Internet forum and find a discussion thread (7–10 messages) where people are arguing about a topic. Print out those messages. With a pen, underline the logical fallacies. In the margin of the page, write the names of the fallacies.

Peer Models for Emulation

The following peer model personal essay by Petura Burrows shows how one individual dealt with a problem in her family. As you read it, think about sentence variation in her writing. As well, do you think her argument is clear?

I Wear My Too-Black Skin with Pride

BY PETURA BURROWS

At 11 years old, I discovered my blackness.

My uncle, an exotic pearwood skin tone, called me Blackie and Darkie for the first time. My cousins, some as yellow as antique cherry wood, others as pale as maple, crowned me Mama Africa. My choir members, a perfect symphony of cedar woods and mahoganies, called me Shadow.

With these new titles, I received new limitations. My mother bought me only brightly coloured clothing, saying, "Black isn't your colour." The grandmother of the boy on whom I had a crush told me two dark-skinned people should not date. They "won't look good together," she warned.

As friends, associates, family, and strangers reinforced these restrictions, I reluctantly accepted my place as an ebony-skinned girl. I wore too-black skin.

This attention to one's shade of black skin pervades black society in a phenomenon called "colourism." Though not a new practice, the term recently emerged as a way for society to address discrimination and segregation among blacks in the United States, where people claim lighter-skinned blacks gain better economic opportunities and more social advantages than darker-skinned blacks.

Colourism hinges on "pigmentocracy," a term coined by Chilean sociologist Alejandro Lipshutz, which refers to a hierarchy based on skin hue and extends to features such as hair texture and the size and shape of the nose and lips.

Colourism mirrors slavery, which pitted whites against blacks. But slavery also created rifts among blacks and became the birthplace of colourism. House slaves, typically the product of sex between a master and a female slave, had lighter skin tones and worked inside the house. They ate better, learned to read and write, and reportedly looked better than the field slaves.

While slavery is no longer practised, colourism persists. It matured after emancipation with the "Blue Vein Society," a group of freed slaves of mixed African and European heritage who granted membership to those whose skin was light enough that they could see the veins at the wrist. Then, in the 1960s and 1970s, the "brown paper bag test" became a common practice in the fraternities and sororities of upper-class black America. Leaders granted admission only to people whose skin resembled or was lighter than the standard brown paper bag.

In the 1980s, colourism reached mass audiences in works by black authors and filmmakers. *The Color Purple*, by African-American author Alice Walker, emerged as an illustration of colourism (among other issues). The protagonist, dark-skinned Celie played by Whoopi Goldberg in the 1985 movie, faced constant abuse from her husband who was not much lighter in skin tone, and encountered ridicule because of her "blackness and ugliness." The husband was in love with Shug Avery, a lighter-skinned female.

Black filmmaker Spike Lee followed in 1988 with *School Daze*, a musical drama that explored tensions between light-skinned and dark-skinned students at a black college. In one scene, dark-skinned women ("jiggaboos") battled with the light-skinned girls ("wannabes"). Controversy surrounding *School Daze* showed that some black communities were not ready to accept brutally honest social commentary.

Blacks may deny illustrations of colourism in their movies, but research notes an undeniable disparity. In a 2007 article, "The Persistent Problem of Colourism: Skin Tone, Status and Inequality" in *Sociology Compass*, Margaret Hunter noted that lighter-skinned African-Americans earned more than their darker colleagues.

According to Evelyn Glenn's "Shades of Difference: Why Skin Colour Matters," allegations between people of the same minority group represent 3 per cent of the 85,000 discrimination allegations the U.S. Equal Employment Opportunity Commission (EEOC) receives annually. The EEOC also saw a substantial increase over the past 15 years in discrimination allegations based on colour—climbing to 1,241 in 2006, from 374 in 1992.

Even the government is not exempt from colourism discussions. In *Game Change: Obama and the Clintons, McCain and Palin, and the Race of a Lifetime*, it was revealed that during the 2008 U.S. presidential election, Nevada Democrat Harry Reid, the U.S. Senate majority leader, said then-Senator Barack Obama made a good candidate for president because he "is light-skinned" and "speaks with no Negro dialect, unless he wanted to have one."

What if Obama spoke with a heavy Negro accent? What if he wore too-black skin? Would America have placed limitations on him and restricted him from the presidency?

At 25, I rediscovered my blackness. My uncle still calls me Darkie. I ignore it. I embrace Mama Africa. Shadow still follows me. Limitations do not. I wear clothing of all colours. Black looks beautiful against my skin. I attract men of all hues. We look great together. I accept my place as an ebony-skinned woman. I reject the margins of colourism. I wear my too-black skin with pride.

(Burrows IN1)

EXERCISE 54 ▶ Rhetorical Analysis

Write a rhetorical analysis of "I Wear My Too-Black Skin with Pride." You may consider both the content of Burrows's writing and the form of the essay. Skim back through this book to find points to write about. We have some suggestions for inquiry below:

- Is Burrows a cultural observer or activist or both? Explain with examples.
- How does the personal essay weave personal narrative with research? Is this weaving effective?
- The ending of the personal essay returns to the story at the beginning. Do you think this was a good choice of conclusion or would you have liked a different approach to ending it?
- List five examples of variations in sentence length or sound.
- Are there any logical fallacies in the essay?

In the following peer model research paper, Nick Zabara relates research on human psychology to recent trends in community organizations. As you read the paper, think about how he varies his sentences. Consider, as well, the argument and the kind of evidence used to defend it.

Saints and Monsters: The Psychology of Altruism and Malice

By Nick Zabara

The once only philosophical debate over altruism and malice in human nature has, over the past fifty years, moved into the realm of social psychology and empirical experimentation. Scholars have established that no single factor causes pro- or anti-social behaviour. Instead, a combination of both nature and nurture—personality and situation—determines whether we choose to help or hurt others. This paper presents examples of such differences in human nature, a short gloss on foundational psychological studies into human behaviour, and then shows how new organizations are influencing human behaviour for good. Effectively, these new organizations marry the past research done by social psychologists with a goal of improving the way we behave in social settings.

History shows us startlingly different kinds of human behaviours even in similar situations. For example, on the morning of March 13, 1964, Kitty Genovese—she was a 28-year-old barmaid working in Queens—arrived back at her New York apartment before being robbed, raped, and murdered by an unfamiliar man (Krajicek 2011). Thirty-eight witnesses saw or heard some part of the assault. None offered help. None called the police. In contrast, between 1941 and 1944 residents of the French village of Le Chambon actively resisted Nazi occupation and elected to hide and protect Jews and other political refugees at grave risk to themselves, acting out of pure compassion to save over 5,000 lives (Rochat and Modigliani 1995, 198–201).

Psychologists have determined that what governs human behaviour in these cases is the nature of the actor and the situational circumstances (Wilson 1976, 1084). While situational variables better predict behaviour in familiar situations such as waiting in line at the store, personality traits better predict behaviour in a typical situations such as when someone attempts to rob the cashier at the store (Benjamin & Simpson 2009, 16).

Psychologist Stanley Milgram ran a controversial yet classic study that tested people's behaviour in situations of harm to others. Milgram wondered what caused Nazi war criminals like Adolf Eichmann to commit their atrocities; Milgram sought to answer whether people like Eichmann were regular people thrust into bad situations or true monsters that relished their evildoing (Benjamin and Simpson 2009, 12). Milgram's initial experiment—there have been many subsequent variations of Milgram's work since—recruited volunteers for a study on, he said, learning (Milgram 1965). In the experiment, participants had the power to control a machine that shocked learners if learners answered questions incorrectly. All of this was a ruse, however, and Milgram asked learners to answer incorrectly on purpose and scream in pain, demand release, and eventually fall silent.

The results showed interesting human behaviour. Despite undeniable symptoms of stress when hearing people apparently in pain, 65 per cent of participants gave the full range of shocks, and many follow-up experiments have since obtained similar results (Blass 1991, 398–402). What, then, is responsible for making us feel so secure in our own beneficence while simultaneously driving us to hurt others at the command of a person in a lab coat?

It turns out that the lab coat—and the rest of the situational setting—played a significant role in participants' behaviour (Blass 1991, 402–403). That is, the perceived authority of the institution and of the experimenter played a major role in determining how many people obeyed until the end. Other mitigating factors included the physical proximity of the experimenter and the distance of the learner (400–401). But personality factors of the participants came into play as well—after all, each variation of the experiment saw a minority of individuals disobey orders (402–403). Analysis of this dissenting group's personality characteristics revealed that traits such as low authoritarianism, low conventionalism, low interpersonal trust, high moral judgement, and high social responsibility produced subversive results.

Not all psychological experiments focus on harmful behaviour. Following Kitty Genovese's murder, Darley and Latané (1968, 378–379) staged a series of experiments to determine what influences our choice to help others in distress. Participants were led into separate rooms and told to anonymously discuss troubling aspects of their lives over intercoms. Soon after the conversations began, one of the speakers—an associate of the experimenters—demonstrated difficulty speaking, noting that he or she was prone to epilepsy. The speaker would then plead for help and later go silent, with sounds of thrashing being audible over the intercom.

Experimenters found that when participants believed themselves to be the only listener, 85 per cent actively sought help, whereas of those who thought that four others were also listening, only 31 per cent did so (Darley and Latané 1968, 380). This phenomenon has since been dubbed the "bystander effect," which dictates that one of the most important situational influences on helping behaviour is the diffusion of responsibility within groups (Bereczkei et al. 2010, 238; Wilson 1976, 1079).

Other situational variables that influence our chances of helping include how likeable and attractive we perceive the other to be, how physically similar we are them, and whether we interpret the situation as an actual emergency (Batson et al. 1986, 216; Daley & Latané 1968, 383). Researchers have also uncovered a number of personality characteristics, such as high empathy, high contentiousness, high agreeableness, and low masculinity, that all contribute to a greater probability of helping (Bereczkei et al. 2010, 240; Tice & Baumeister 1985, 424). Other studies have since found that later-born individuals and people raised in urban environments are consistently more helpful than first-borns and rural-raised people (Batson et al. 1986, 218–219; Weiner 1976, 120).

These studies raise questions about how we can increase people's chances of helping others in need and reduce the likelihood of them falling prey to ways of thinking that can injure their fellow citizens. Already, numerous organizations have sprung up to take charge of reinstating humankind's humanity. Some charitable organizations, such as Amnesty International and the Red Cross, focus on providing relief to those in dire need through material aid obtained through donations.

Other organizations focus on changing attitudes and behaviours of those living comfortably in the first world. *Improv Everywhere* (2013) is an American group that stages comical situations all over the world, getting people to laugh and play with events like pants-less subway rides and boardroom meetings held in Staples show-rooms. In addition to the fun, *Improv Everywhere* seems to recognize the ill effects of high conventionalism and authoritarianism, which they challenge by "break[ing] store policies or park regulations." *People for Good* is a Canadian organization that is using ads and social media to increase our emotionality and empathy:

> When was the last time you saw someone give up their seat, or hold a door open? When was the last time you looked up from your phone and had a conversation with a real person? We get so caught up in our own lives that we forget about each other. We're out to change that. (2013)

Improv Toronto is trying to establish interpersonal closeness and a norm of reciprocity by doing good deeds for Torontonians, such as providing umbrellas on rainy days and handing out snacks to hungry commuters (2013).

The concept of group pressure is being used by *CopWatch*, an organization "intended to both promote public safety and to ensure that police officers remain accountable for their actions" (2013). They operate by asking the public to film or sim-ply watch any arrests that they witness to deter police misconduct. Many other organ-izations are also promoting the concept of mindfulness—teaching people to enter into a state of "awareness that arises when paying attention to the present moment" (Mindfulness Everyday 2013). This way of thinking helps people develop attitudes such as "acceptance, patience, non-judgement, and compassion" (Mindfulness Institute 2013), augmenting altruistic and caring qualities and limiting negative thought pat-terns that may lead to harmful behaviour.

Though past research has shown that people often lack empathy and embody authoritarian attitudes, there have always been pockets of resistance. The difference today is that these new organizations, beyond the laboratory experiment, are working together to turn such resistance into the norm. In the past, researchers first discovered the "banality of evil" (Jones 2009, 280) but soon developed the complementary con-cept of the "ordinariness of goodness" (Rochat and Modigliani 1995, 204–205). In the same way today, psychologists have revealed to us the dual influence of personality and the situation over both helpful and harmful behaviour, and it now falls to those who have listened to institute a union of science and action—to challenge our mind-sets and replace vice with beneficence.

Works Cited

Batson, C.D., Michelle H. Bolen, Julie A. Cross, and Helen Neuringer-Benefiel. "Where Is the Altruism in the Altruistic Personality?" *Journal of Personality and Social Psychology*. 50.1 (1986): 212–220. Print.

Benjamin, Ludy T., and Jeffry A. Simpson. "The Power of the Situation: The Impact of Milgram's Obedience Studies on Personality and Social Psychology." *American Psychologist*. 64.1 (2009): 12–19. Print.

Bereczkei, Tamas, Bela Birkas, and Zsuzsanna Kerekes. "The Presence of Others, Prosocial Traits, Machiavellianism." *Social Psychology*. 41.4 (2010): 238–245. Print.

Blass, Thomas. "Understanding Behavior in the Milgram Obedience Experiment: The Role of Personality, Situations, and Their Interactions." *Journal of Personality and Social Psychology*. 60.3 (1991): 398–413. Print.

Copwatch. Web. 1 Nov. 2013. www.copwatch.org

Darley, John, and Bibb Latané. "Bystander Intervention in Emergencies: Diffusion of Responsibility." *Journal of Personality and Social Psychology*. 8.4 (1968): 377–383. Print.

Improv Everywhere. Web. 1 Nov. 2013. www.improveverywhere.com

Improv Toronto. Web. 1 Nov. 2013. www.improvintoronto.com

Jones, Kathleen. "Eichmann in Jerusalem: A Report on the Banality of Evil." *International Feminist Journal of Politics*. 11.2 (2009): 279–282. Print.

Krajicek, David. "The Killing of Kitty Genovese: 47 Years Later, Still Holds Sway Over New Yorkers." *New York Daily News*. 13 Mar. 2011.

Milgram, Stanley. *Obedience*. 1965. Film.

Mindfulness Everyday. Web. 1 Nov. 2013. www.mindfulnesseveryday.com

Mindfulness Institute. Web. 1 Nov. 2013. www.mindfulnessinstitute.ca

People for Good. Web. 1 Nov. 2013. www.peopleforgood.ca

Rochat, François, and Andre Modigliani. "The Ordinary Quality of Resistance: From Milgram's Laboratory to the Village of Le Chambon." *Journal of Social Issues*. 51 (1995): 195–210. Print.

Tice, Dianne M., and Roy F. Baumeister. "Masculinity Inhibits Helping in Emergencies: Personality Does Predict the Bystander Effect." *Journal of Personality and Social Psychology*. 49.2 (1985): 420–428. Print.

Weiner, Ferne H. "Altruism, Ambiance, and Action: The Effects of Rural and Urban Rearing on Helping Behavior." *Journal of Personality and Social Psychology*. 34.1 (1976): 112–124. Print.

Wilson, John. "Motivation, Modeling, and Altruism: A Person x Situation Analysis." *Journal of Personality and Social Psychology*. 34.6 (1975): 1078–1086. Print.

EXERCISE 55 ► Rhetorical Analysis

Write a rhetorical analysis of "Saints and Monsters: The Psychology of Altruism and Malice." The analysis may consider the points we've made in this chapter, or you may want to consider lessons from previous chapters. Don't fall into some perceived academic style of writing—write clearly, precisely, and directly for a regular reader. You may consider some or all of these points and questions:

- List four examples of sentence variation in Zabara's paper.
- Determine Zabara's overall argument and then explain how he links each paragraph to that overall argument.
- What similarities and differences do you see, whether in approach or appearance, between Burrows' personal essay and Zabara's research paper?
- Describe the academic conversation Zabara enters and then explain how he brings in cultural observations.

Assignment 8a

The final assignment of this book requires you to take on the role of cultural observer or activist. This is a good time to go back through the book and review the previous chapters' enhancing factors—everything we've said applies to both essay and academic writing. You may find it helpful as well to go back and look at your previous assignments and revise them for sentence variation and sound. That way, you'll tackle this final assignment with that experience in mind.

Suggested Topics:

1) Write a 1000-word personal essay about a cultural trend that interests you.
2) Write a 1000-word personal essay about an activist cause that interests you.
3) Write a 3000-word research paper that considers a cultural trend or activist cause in an academic way—include the elements of academic writing discussed in Chapter 1. Reread Di Luca's research paper in Chapter 2 to see an example of this writing.

Here are suggestions for writing your essay or research paper:

- Choose trends or causes that interest you deeply. If you don't care about the topic, the reader won't either. If you don't like writing about fashion trends, then don't write about fashion trends. If you prefer to write about social causes, write about social causes.

- Ideas for essays come from your personal life. Relationships, chance meetings on the street, a newspaper article, graffiti on a wall—these all provide ideas of trends and causes. Look at how Petura Burrows turned her day-to-day experience into an essay.

- Stay fresh. What's fresh and new in the capital punishment or abortion debates? Nothing. In choosing what to write about, recognize that a fresh angle is vital to breaking through the din of public commentary. A writer who reads magazines and newspapers regularly gets a sense of what's cliché and what's not.

- Apply all the enhancing factors discussed in the previous chapters: economy, strong verbs, active voice, strong nouns, and original language. Revise for emotion, ethics, and logic too.

- Dive right into the essay or research paper from the first sentence. Avoid broad, general first sentences. The traditional school essay begins with this vagueness:

> The world has had many conflicts in its history. Conflicts come about usually because of economic and political disagreements. Conflicts can lead to the deaths of thousands of people.

The first sentence is so general that the essay could be about any conflict. By sentence three we still don't know exactly what this essay is about. Draw the reader in with a specific first sentence.

- Whether you're writing an essay or a paper, make sure you research and understand the arguments of the other side. Your argument should play off theirs. This pushes public and academic debate along, rather than polarizing it.
- Pretend you're writing for the uniformed or unaware readers. Try to bring them to your side respectfully. Do not antagonize or disrespect any readers, even if they hold a different opinion.
- For research papers, start your writing in the middle with the body paragraphs. Writers who start with the first sentence of the introduction often feel paralyzed by the daunting task ahead of them. Get the bulk of the paper done first before writing the introduction and conclusion. That way, the introduction won't promise anything that isn't in the body.
- Reveal the bones of your essay or paper's structure during drafting. It's fine to say *This paper will examine . . . I will look at . . . In this section . . . The three parts of the paper will discuss . . . I will show how . . .* Some teachers and editors disagree on this. But the structure will help you see your paper's flow and order. You can always remove it later.
- When you write your paper's introduction, make sure your argument is stated clearly and specifically.
- You can get lost writing essays and research papers. Many bad pieces of writing meander away from the argumentative line. Ensure that every paragraph and every quotation serves your specific, overall argument. Any part that doesn't serve the purposes of the argument—even if you absolutely love the part—must be removed. That creates coherence. Coherence is important in any kind of writing.

Chapter Summary

We equated the techniques in this chapter with the techniques of a drummer. Drummers keep a consistent beat but then mix it up a little here and there. This chapter is about how to mix it up.

Monotonous sentences present a problem—there's no variation in structure or sound. We introduced a grammar term: the segregated sentence. Segregated sentences are used in description and narration. These clear sentences have one main point but when combined with too many others, they lack poetic rhythm.

We then described four new sentence patterns: Intrusive, End/Beginning, Beginning/Beginning, Ending/Ending, Beginning/End. These patterns allow you to vary phrasing and create coherence by inserting sentences into sentences or repeating one element of a sentence in another.

We then showed the power of short sentences. They mimic actions and emphasize points. Long sentences create a different effect. They're ambient, atmospheric. They mimic dreams, drug and alcohol experiences, and emotional moments. Perhaps most importantly, the contrast of long and short sentences provided the most interesting variation. A short sentence after a long one is like an exclamation point.

The chapter then considered something often overlooked in writing: the sound of the prose. We listed four main ways that you can consider sound in your writing: euphony (softness), cacophony (hardness), alliteration (consonant repetition), and assonance (vowel repetition).

We then moved to the next genre in the book: personal essay. A personal essay is a short piece of subjective writing. Writing an essay isn't insignificant. Every day humans engage in making meaning about their world, often producing great but slow change over decades. Essay writers have two different main roles: Writer as cultural observer, someone who is reserved and writes about trends, and writer as activist, someone who observes trends but suggests changes in the way people think or act. The line between these roles is blurred.

Essay writers often tackle common truths. We showed how many statements writers make are packaged as truth but upon investigation are wholly subjective. Identify the truth statements of writers and you'll come up with essay ideas and have ammunition to combat stereotypes and faulty thinking.

A good essay has three elements rooted in classical rhetoric (indeed, all good writing has these elements): emotion, ethics, and logic.

▌ Further Readings

For more about cultural observation writing:

Zinsser, William. *On Writing Well: The Classic Guide to Writing Nonfiction.* 7th ed. New York: HarperCollins, 2006. Print.

For more about activist writing:

Kahn, Seth and Jong Hwa Lee. *Activism and Rhetoric: Theories and Contexts for Political Engagement.* New York: Routledge, 2011. Print.

Research and Citations

IN THE SEVENTEENTH CENTURY, one of the meanings of the word *research* was "To seek (a woman) in love or marriage" (*research, v.1*). Today, definitions of research still include the seeking part, while the love or marriage part has drifted away. The *Oxford English Dictionary* describes research now as "Systematic investigation or inquiry aimed at contributing to knowledge of a theory, topic, etc., by careful consideration, observation, or study of a subject" and "The act of searching carefully for or pursuing a specified thing or person" (*research, n.1.*).

These definitions suggest that research is not simply for research papers. You research even when you write a personal narrative. Personal narrative demands a careful consideration of an event in your past, and many writers jog their memories by systematically tracking down and looking at old photographs, documents, e-mails, and diary entries to gather detail. While personal narrative doesn't require a Works Cited or References list, personal narrative does include source attribution, whether it's simply the *said* after a quotation or a statement of reputation in the Hierarchy of Detail like *People at the office thought Samuel worked hard every day*. The interview-based article investigates the lives of other people and interviews are a great way to discover new information. The personal essay researches communities, whether to describe a trend or to argue for change.

Starting Research

Starting research is often the hardest part—even the smallest project seems large and unwieldy. Your instructor's expectations, such as word and page counts, will help limit your scope. One of the most common problems instructors cite in students' writing is an overly broad topic. Many students attempt to do too much, such as writing about the whole history of NHL hockey in 2000 words (that's a topic for books). As you think about a topic and start to formulate a hypothesis—a tentative argument or overall point about the topic—you'll want to zoom in on the topic as much as you possibly can. This may mean choosing to write about a small slice of the topic rather than the whole pie.

You may find it hard to get started on research if the topic isn't your choice. A topic assigned by an instructor may seem uninteresting. To begin, try to find an aspect of the topic that does interest you. If the specific topic is open, choose an avenue that interests you personally. Maybe you've wondered why so many houses are for sale in your city, or why so many people are losing their jobs in a local industry—these observations may lead to research. If you choose a topic you care about, you're more likely to put in a good effort.

Researchers often think about topics and tentative arguments while doing preliminary reading. They skim books or articles on the subject. When you start, find the most recent books and articles on the subject and consider how they've dealt with the topic. All the while, keep thinking about your own opinions on the topic—you don't want to just repeat what everyone else has said. Where do your ideas fit into the previous research? Develop a tentative overall argument from this reading. You can always modify the argument later.

Primary and Secondary Sources

When you've got a tentative overall argument in mind, you may turn to reading your sources more deeply. Two main types of sources exist in research: primary and secondary. Primary sources are original documents or objects, while secondary sources are other people's writing about primary sources. Secondary sources provide guidance and a great deal of useful ideas and commentary.

While students usually use only secondary sources, students who track down primary documents—such as old letters, historical newspapers, or diaries—develop greater insights into a topic than those who simply work a step removed from them. You may also create your own primary sources, for example by conducting interviews with academics or surveys of citizens.

Researchers must ensure that primary sources are legitimate, not fake, and that secondary sources are peer reviewed. Peer-reviewed writing has passed a careful process of review by experts in a field. Our society values expert opinion; experts devote their careers to careful study of specific topics. Through peer review, work is tested by other academics and you can trust its accuracy.

Information from websites is typically not peer reviewed and may be inaccurate or misleading—use them with caution. You should assess the credibility of the website before using its research data. For example, academic, government and public organization sites provide information that's more credible than the information on a site created by a regular citizen. Some partisan political sites will avoid providing the whole truth on a topic, stacking up research that provides consideration of only one side. If you cannot determine the creator or the funding organization of the site, avoid using the site's information. You can, of course, still use it as an example of a type of Internet content.

One particular website, Wikipedia, presents both possibilities and problems for students today. Wikipedia has a significant amount of useful and easily found content. But that ease of use troubles some instructors who think students depend upon it too much. Some instructors question the accuracy of Wikipedia and prefer that students use other sources. As well, some instructors and institutions ban the use of Wikipedia as a source—check with your instructor before starting your research

The problem with Wikipedia, however, is not so much accuracy over time as accuracy in any given moment. Studies have shown that Wikipedia articles are about as accurate as articles in traditional printed encyclopedias. The bigger problem with Wikipedia, however, is vandalism—nefarious users can and do modify Wikipedia pages to add errors.

Rather than citing Wikipedia or other reference sites, then, you may want to simply use them in your initial stages of research to get a sense of your topic. Wikipedia requires citations for all information so you can collect those and then find the sources at your library. Indeed, that's how scholars work—they mine other scholars' bibliographies. Mining bibliographies of recent articles and books helps you understand what's important and current to read and what's not.

In many cases, a better online option for research is your institution's electronic resources portal. Found on the library website of your college or university, this portal provides access to thousands of academic journals, encyclopedias, Statistics Canada data, dictionaries, and so on. Much of this material is peer reviewed and thus highly credible. Increasingly, libraries are ending print subscriptions to academic journals, so you'll only find them online. If you're not sure how to use the online portal, check with your librarian.

One word of caution: don't try to read everything on the topic before you start writing. This leads to paralysis. Just read enough to get started. During the writing process, you'll always face dead ends and have to research more—rarely do writers complete all their research and then just write.

Documenting Citations

Having a documentation system in place before you begin your research is vital for accuracy and efficiency. Research and citation are not two different tasks, one done after the other. Instead, they should be considered together.

Without a documentation system in place before you begin your research, you'll lose details of your sources. Here's a worst-case scenario: you write down page after page of quotes and facts without documenting the sources completely. In that case, and often at the last minute, you then have to track down the books and articles to find that citation information. This is a tedious, time-consuming process.

Before taking notes, determine which citation style, such as MLA (Modern Language Association) or APA (American Psychological Association), your instructor expects. Some styles need information that others do not. Grab that information from your sources right before you start taking notes.

▌ Note-Taking

Note-taking and citation have evolved from the old days of writing notes and sources on recipe cards. Recipe cards are still useful, but many writers now choose to take notes and record citations in new ways aided by technology. For example, you may divide a Microsoft Word file into sections and drop in notes, quotations, and citations as you go. Other software packages such as Zotero, RefWorks, EndNote, and OneNote, among others, automate the documentation process, formatting citations and bibliographies with one click.

With a system in place, read sources carefully and take detailed notes—include the author and page number for easy reference if you need to return to the source. The best research notes are in point form, in your own words. Fill them out into full sentences later when writing the paper. By putting other ideas into your own words, you digest the information and prove to yourself that you understand it. Write down direct quotes only if they are wonderfully said. These two approaches will help you to avoid plagiarism—refer back to our discussion of plagiarism in Chapter 1. Writing down digested notes is particularly helpful later on, weeks after you've finished the research. When you sit down to write, you will know which parts of your notes are your own words and which are not. Writing down direct quotations in quotation marks ensures you won't inadvertently plagiarize.

Don't take too many notes, though; you're not trying to document everything in the book or article. We suggest you avoid using pens to highlight or underline large sections of your sources. Highlighting or underlining simply points to key passages for later reference but it doesn't require you to digest and truly understand them.

▌ MLA and APA Citation Styles

Many different citation styles exist. Check with your instructor or the governing association of your field for the appropriate one to use in your work. Citation style requirements may seem tedious, but they serve a purpose in helping other scholars find the sources you've used. Any missing or incorrect information may make that search difficult or even impossible. Other scholars cannot check the accuracy of your work or build on it without correct citations.

If you're not using software for automated formatting, see the samples of the main citation types below in two popular styles: MLA and APA. Humanities researchers typically use MLA while social science researchers and many science researchers use APA. We cannot list all the permutations of each type here—the basic types below should cover most situations. See the MLA 7th edition handbook (2009) and APA 6th edition manual (2009) for more details.

▌ In-text Citations

MLA style

When you bring someone else's material into your writing, you must cite it in the text using parentheses. The in-text citation lists the basic details of the source so that readers can find more information in your Works Cited section.

If you're writing generally about a single source, with no specific page number reference, you do not even need an in-text citation. Simply put the full citation of the author's work in the Works Cited and mention the author's name in your writing.

A Single-Author Work with a Page Number

For this simple type of in-text citation, the author and page number are all you need:

> As an idea, Canadian nationalism developed through and by the mass media (Rancourt 10).

Notice that, unlike in other citation formats, no comma is used after the author's name and the sentence's period goes after the last bracket. If instead you mention the author's name in the sentence, you do not need it in the citation—just include the page number in brackets before the period.

A Work by Multiple Authors

MLA style recommends listing up to three last names for a work by multiple authors:

> Two recent studies show a trend toward greater inequality (Gregory, Kumar, and Troft 299).

Notice that these citations of two and three authors spell out the word *and*; as well, they include no commas before the page number. If you want to cite the work generally, rather than citing a specific page, simply do not include a page number.

If the work has more than three authors, MLA recommends listing the first author and then the Latin abbreviation et al., which means *and others*:

> The groundbreaking study revealed the problem was more widespread than previously known (Gable *et al.* 380).

Multiple Works by a Single Author

If you're citing more than one work by an author, the in-text citation becomes a bit more complex. Simply listing the author's name and page number will, of course, lead to confusion as to which source you're referring to in the Works

Cited. In that case, you need to add a bit of the title, italicized, to the in-text citation:

> Few knew the ramifications of the political accord when it was signed (Porter, *Canadian Politics* 44)

This in-text citation distinguishes Porter's *Canadian Politics in Review* book from the other books by Porter in the Works Cited.

To keep citations short, it's often best to mention the author's name or the author's name plus the title of the work within the sentence. That way, the bracketed citation becomes nothing more than a page number, which is less intrusive.

A Work without an Author

For articles within works without an identified author, a word or a few words of the title of the work set off by quotation marks can serve the same function as the author's name:

> Newspaper editors circulated political news to like-minded partisans in the early 1800s ("Newspaper" 5).

For whole works without an author—not parts such as individual articles—a single word (or a few words) from the title is italicized:

> The commissioner regarded the complaint as vindictive (*Report* 54).

Multiple Sources in One Citation

If the citation refers to multiple sources, link them together with a semicolon:

> Scholars believe the problem hasn't been resolved (Kumar 94; Darnton 23).

A Work within an Anthology or Edited Collection

If you're citing an article or chapter in an anthology or edited collection, use the authors' names, not the editors' names (the Works Cited citation will include the editors' names):

> Some writers have considered the topic in depth, publishing detailed accounts (Montane 2006; Preston and Fareed 2010).

An Online Source

In-text citations for online sources are tricky since many web pages lack all the required information. If the page you're citing has an author—for example, an article posted online—then the citation looks exactly like the one for a book:

> The article caused a stir in the writing community when it was posted (Jackson).

If the online source doesn't have an author listed, then you turn to the title of the article or page itself:

> The article caused a stir in the writing communication when it was posted ("Composition").

Personal Communication, Including Interviews and E-mail

Personal communication usually comes in the form of an interview or an e-mail. In either case, the in-text citation looks like the one for books, without page numbers. The author of the interview is the person you interview, while the author of the e-mail may be you or someone else. Consider these examples:

> We discussed the variability in the concept (Smith).

> His e-mail stated the purpose of the campaign was to make change (Lavois).

APA style

The general APA style for in-text citations looks similar to the MLA style. APA uses parentheses as well and divides sources with a semicolon. Like MLA, if you refer to the author in the sentence, you don't need the author's name within the parentheses. Page numbers are not always required—you may sometimes refer to the work as a whole without needing a specific page.

A Single Author Work with a Page Number

The first difference between APA and MLA is subtle: APA requires a comma between the author's name and the date of publication:

> The debate between the two became heated (Pereira, 2007, p. 25).

A Work by Multiple Authors

A multiple-author citation also uses an ampersand (&) not the word *and*, as in this example:

> Figures show a year-over-year increase (Ibrahim & Sante, 2005, p. 60).

APA treats multiple-author citations differently than MLA does depending on the number of authors. If the citation has three, four, or five authors, list all of their names the first time you mention them; subsequent references only mention the first author followed by *et al.*:

> The theorem proved incorrect (Johnson, Peters, & Toth, 2007, p. 87).

> Theorists have provided a corrective that has satisfied reviewers (Johnson *et al.*, 2007).

If the work has six or more authors, APA requires only the first author even in the first reference to the source, keeping the citation simple:

> She revitalized the field with his fresh ideas (Pereira *et al.*, 2013).

Multiple Works by a Single Author

Another difference comes in how APA deals with multiple studies by the same author published in the same year. Multiple studies require a suffix letter—a, b, c, d, and so on—to indicate the correct source. Works must be alphabetized by title. For example, if the References include three journal articles by Pereira in 2009, then the date of publication for them would be 2009a, 2009b, and 2009c:

> Recently, scholars have turned towards new methodologies (Pereira, 2009a, 2009b, 2009c).

The suffix letter must also be attached to the years of publication in the references list for readers to find the right source. Notice that sources are placed in alphabetical order within the parentheses.

A Work without an Author

If your source has no author listed, the title becomes the key information at the head of the in-text citation. APA style prefers quotation marks surrounding a few words of the title of an article or chapter or web page. In the case of a whole periodical, book, or report, APA style prefers a few italicized words from the title:

> The data showed an increase over time ("The Report," 2009).

> In five years the media landscape changed considerably (*The Media Factbook*, 2011).

Don't forget the commas after the title—in the case of the article, chapter, or web page, the comma comes inside the final quotation mark.

A Work within an Anthology or Edited Collection

For a work, like an article, within an anthology or edited collection, the authors' names—not the editors'—appears in the brackets, just like in a book citation:

> Some writers have considered the topic in depth (Montane, 2006; Preston & Fareed, 2010).

The major difference between APA and MLA here is the use of the ampersand and the comma.

An Online Source

In-text citations for online sources are often difficult since many web pages don't have the required information for the parentheses. If the web page you're citing has an author—for example, an article posted online—then the citation looks exactly like the one for a book:

> The article caused a stir in the writing community when it was posted (Jackson, 2012).

If the online source doesn't have an author listed, then you use the title of the article or page itself:

> The article caused a stir in the writing communication when it was posted ("Composition," 2012).

Personal Communication, Including Interviews and E-mail

APA treats personal communication citations differently than MLA does, both in text and in the references at the end. APA notes that the reader cannot recover these sources anyway, so a citation in the references page is unnecessary. The communicator of the e-mail (the sender) or interview (the interviewee) is listed with initials, last name, and the words *personal communication*. Consider these examples:

> In our discussion, G.K. Harcourt mentioned the variability in the concept (personal communication, August 16, 2013).

> His e-mail stated the purpose of the campaign was to make change (T.P. Lavois, personal communication, July 5, 2005).

▍ Works Cited and References

MLA style

The Modern Language Association requires a section titled Works Cited at the end of the paper. This section is double spaced with the first line of each citation flush with the left margin. If the citation extends more than one line, the subsequent lines must be indented one inch—this is called a hanging indent.

Let's now look at some basic MLA citation forms:

A book by a single author

This citation is the simplest, beginning with the author's name with surname first. Periods divide the major elements. The title is italicized. The location of publication leads into the name of the publisher with a colon before a comma and the year of publication. Unlike APA style, MLA style requires some indication of the source's medium. Here, Chartier's book is listed as Print. But a common medium type today is Web for sources on the Internet.

> Chartier, Roger. *The Order of Books*. Stanford: Stanford University Press, 1992.
> Print.

A book by more than one author

For a book with more than one author, the second author's name is written in regular order. Don't forget the comma after the first author. Edition information goes after the title:

> Kolln, Martha, and Robert Funk. *Understanding English Grammar*. 9th ed. Boston: Pearson, 2012. Print.

A book by an editor or editors

Like the ones for books, this citation includes a short form *eds* for editors. For a single editor, it would be *ed*.

> Boyd, Alex, and Carmine Starnino, eds. *The Best Canadian Essays 2009*. Toronto: Tightrope Books, 2009. Print.

A work in an anthology or edited collection

Above, we described how to cite an edited book; these books are often called anthologies or collections. An anthology or collection has editors and includes works by many authors. Sometimes you want to cite the specific article, as in the following citation:

> Al-Solaylee, Kamal. "Too Poor to Send Flowers." *The Best Canadian Essays 2009*. Eds. Alex Boyd and Carmine Starnino. Toronto: Tightrope Books, 2009. 3–6. Print.

Notice that here the title of the individual work is placed in quotation marks while the book title remains in italics. This citation requires a list of the editors but the names are not in reverse order. This citation also includes a page range before the medium type.

An article in a scholarly journal

Journal articles represent an individual work within a longer periodical. Journals are typically peer reviewed and come out a few times each year. As with works in anthologies and collections, the title of the article goes in quotation marks with the italicized publication title afterwards. The next two numbers, separated by a period, represent the volume and the issue. Usually, journals advance the volume number with each year, and they print two or more issues per volume. The year follows in brackets, and then the page range of the whole article comes after the colon:

> Allen, Gene. "News Across the Border: Associated Press in Canada, 1894–1917." *Journalism History* 31.4 (2006): 206–216. Print.

A magazine or newspaper article

In MLA style, magazine and newspaper citations look similar to journal article citations, with a different format for the date. Short months like July are written out in full, but longer months like November are shortened to Nov.:

> Barber, John. "Judge's unsparing censure of municipal sleaze wildly exceeds expectations." *Globe & Mail* 13 Sept. 2005: A1. Print.

An online source

Online sources present a particular challenge for writers. Often, little information exists beyond a URL. Try your best to find all the information listed below, including the author of the page, the date it was written, and the publisher or site name in italics. The MLA Handbook notes that you may have to improvise with whatever information is available. What's added to the online citation is the medium type *Web* followed by the date you accessed the site. Finally, include the URL of the site.

> Wolff, Jonathan. "Literary Boredom." *The Guardian* 4 Sept. 2007. Web. 5 Nov. 2013. www.theguardian.com/education/2007/sep/04/highereducation.news

Personal Communication, Including Interviews and E-mail

Interviews you conduct and e-mails you receive are each formatted differently in an MLA Works Cited. The author of the e-mail goes first, like in other types of sources. The subject header of the e-mail is listed within quotation marks. Then a statement beginning with *Message to* states the receiver of the e-mail. If it's you, then write *the author*, not your name. The date follows, and then the medium form concludes the citation:

> Tran, Anthony T. "Re: Statistics." Message to Sarah S. Presley. 22 July 1994. E-mail.

> Davenport, Augusta. Message to the author. 17 Aug. 2001. E-mail.

Interviews that you conduct require perhaps the simplest citation style. The unique element here is the indication of personal interview or telephone interview. There is no medium type after the date:

> Preston, Robert G. Personal interview. 22 Feb. 2007.

> Macy, Reed. Telephone interview. 8 July 2013.

APA style

The APA style requires not a Works Cited but a References list at the end of the paper. Like MLA style, APA References pages are double-spaced with hanging indents. Let's examine some of the basic types:

A book by a single author

All APA citations, including this simple one, require abbreviated first names. The date also comes near the start of the citation in brackets:

> Chartier, R. (1992). *The order of books*. Stanford, CA: Stanford University Press.

A book by more than one author

For sources with more than one author, the last name comes first—even for the second author. The second author's first name is abbreviated too. APA requires ampersands, not *and*, between the author names. Any information about the edition of the book arrives after the title of the book, in brackets. Notice that a period comes after both the title and the edition information:

> Kolln, M., & Funk, R. (2012). *Understanding English grammar* (9th ed.). Boston, MA: Pearson.

A book by an editor or editors

An edited book citation places the editors up front in the author position, but requires a bracketed short form for editors:

> Boyd, A., & Starnino, C. (Eds.). (2009). *The best Canadian essays 2009*. Toronto, ON: Tightrope Books.

A work in an anthology or an edited collection

If you're citing a piece of writing in an anthology or edited collection, the title of the article is simply placed after the date without quotation marks or italicization. The editors' first names are abbreviated but they are listed in regular order after the preposition *In*. Like MLA style, the page range is included, but APA style prefers it in brackets with *p.* or *pp.* representing page or pages (no period comes between the italicized title and the bracketed page numbers):

> Al-Solaylee, K. (2009). Too poor to send flowers. In A. Boyd & C. Starnino (Eds.), *The best Canadian essays 2009* (pp. 3–6). Toronto, ON: Tightrope Books.

An article in a scholarly journal

With a journal article, APA style presents the volume number after the title and then the issue number in brackets. The page numbers are not bracketed and don't require *pp.* in front.

> Allen, G. (2006). News across the border: Associated Press in Canada, 1894–1917. *Journalism History*, 31(4), 206–216.

A magazine article

Magazine articles require the volume and issue numbers like a journal article:

Gwynn, R. (2013, July/August). The contender: The appeal of Justin Trudeau's emotional intelligence. *The Walrus*, 10(6), 26–30.

A newspaper article

The style for a newspaper article is similar to the one for a magazine article, except for a slight difference—the inclusion of *p.* or *pp.* abbreviations for page or pages:

Barber, J. (2005, September 13). Judge's unsparing censure of municipal sleaze wildly exceeds expectations. *Globe & Mail*, p. A1.

An online source

Online sources in APA style look similar to other sources. Authors go first; if the page has no author, the title goes first before the date, which is usually the year of publication. If no date is listed, use (n.d.). For online periodicals, include the month and day. The title of the article or web page comes next. The citation concludes with the URL prefaced with *Retrieved from*. APA advises to include only the retrieval date (Retrieved November 5, 2005 from) if the page is likely to change, such as with Wiki entries. Don't place a period after the URL, as some readers may type it in and cause an error.

Wolff, J. (2007, September 4). Literary boredom. *The Guardian*. Retrieved from www.theguardian.com/education/2007/sep/04/highereducation.news

Personal Communication, Including Interviews and E-mail

APA style does not require an entry for personal communication in the list of references.

Glossary

abstract: the realm of ideas, concepts, and theories. They aren't tangible things we can see, feel, touch, smell, or taste.

academic discourse: the unique ways of speaking, writing, and acting that we learn through socialization in schools.

academic writing: general term for forms of writing done for academic courses. Academic discourse demands that academic writing have certain unique elements, including credible evidence and citations.

active voice: a way of ordering sentences that places the doer of the action or the condition/state of being at the head of the sentence or clause.

adjectives: words that modify nouns and pronouns. They may occur before or after the word they modify.

adjective series: two or more adjectives in a list.

adjective-noun series: two or more adjective-noun units in a list.

adverbs: words that modify verbs. They may arrive before or after the verb they modify. The –ly suffix often indicates an adverb, but some adverbs have other suffixes.

adverb series: two or more adverbs in a list.

alliteration: the repetition of the same first consonant in multiple words.

analytical argument: presents an assessment of a problem.

antecedent: what comes before.

assonance: the repetition of hard or soft vowel sounds.

attributives: words that assign dialogue or quotations to people.

auxiliaries: little words that add meaning to a verb, such as tense or modality.

beginning/beginning structure: the repetition of the same word(s) at the start of two separate sentences, one after another.

beginning/end structure: the repetition of the opening word(s) of a sentence at the end of the same sentence.

cacophony: a hard sound.

classical rhetoric: the ancient study of public persuasion, usually intended for face-to-face audiences.

cliché: a condition when an aspect of social life becomes overused or widely known.

closed questions: a question that can be answered with a simple yes or no or a statement of fact. Closed questions do not allow elaboration.

commentary: a personal opinion stated on a topic.

concrete: the real aspects of our lives: we can see, feel, touch, smell, and taste the concrete.

condition or state of being: the state of existence. Right now, you are alive. You exist. You also exist with conditions or states. You are happy; you are sad; you are anxious. None of these conditions or states acts.

conditional perfect continuous: a verb tense for describing an action that hypothetically occurs in the future.

continuum: a range of possibilities, not an either/or choice.

conversion: the ability of words in English to change from one part of speech to another; also means an editing technique to turn passive voice to active voice and vice versa.

dead verb: a verb that creates no image or action in the mind of the reader.

deductive reasoning: a process of logical reasoning that begins with a broad statement followed by smaller statements that are subsets of the broad statement.

dialogue: conversation between people. Don't confuse dialogue with quotations. Quotations show speech but do not necessarily represent a conversation between people.

discourse: the expectations for how to think, speak, write, and act in any social domain defined by spaces and socially constructed meanings.

economy: using only the number of words necessary to make meaning and no more.

elevated language: language that attempts to impress through often obscure words and jargon. Elevated language doesn't attempt to communicate to a wide and general audience. It speaks above the general reader.

end/beginning structure: the repetition of the last word(s) of one sentence at the start of the next sentence.

end/end structure: the repetition of the last word(s) of one sentence at the end of a second sentence.

enhancing factors: stylistic elements found in all good writing.

essay: a short, tentative piece of prose writing from the personal perspective of the author.

euphonic: referring to a pleasant sound.

fallacies of logic: weak or incorrect reasoning. An argument that uses a fallacy is wrong by the rules of logic.

faulty parallelism: sentence constructions of similar meanings that do not have similar grammatical forms.

figurative: a meaning beyond the literal.

formal interview-based article structure: a structure of an interview-based article that focuses on a topic or issue and includes more than one interviewee. The quotations are usually short and tell information and opinion more often than story. The writer disappears from the text.

fragments: grammatically incomplete language.

freewriting: writing freely without judging your writing until you feel all your ideas are on the page.

freight train sentences: long but grammatically correct sentences that evoke ambience, atmosphere, and emotion.

future perfect continuous: verb tense describing an action that will occur continually in the future.

grammar: a set of rules that governs how people form meaning through language.

Hierarchy of Detail: a list of details required in different forms of writing according to a ranking from most important to least important.

impressionistic: a style less about capturing reality than about presenting subjective impressions of reality.

inductive reasoning: a process of logical reasoning that begins with points of evidence leading to a greater conclusion.

informal interview-based article structure: a structure of an interview-based article that includes the author and possibly the context of the interview in the text.

interfering factors: stylistic elements that come in the way of good writing.

internalize: when a lesson becomes second nature.

interview-based article: a short article based around an interview or interviews that presents other people's opinions and ideas in a journalistic style. A staple element of professional writing.

intransitive verbs: verbs that don't require objects.

intrusive sentence: one sentence placed inside another.

jargon: specialized language of a specific community, field, or discipline. Often readers from outside the community, field, or discipline do not know, or are not allowed to know, the jargon.

juxtapositions: combinations of unlike elements.

metaphor: a statement that compares two normally unconnected realms of human experience to make a point.

monologue interview-based article structure: a structure of interview-based article that allows interviewees to speak at length while the author and the context of the interview remain out of the text.

monotonous sentences: sentences without variation of structure or sound.

narrative: a story. Narrative shows connected actions and events.

noun: a person, place, or thing. Nouns often give or receive the action of the verb. That is, they can be a subject or an object of the sentence.

noun series: two or more nouns in a list.

open questions: questions that allow people to elaborate answers. These questions don't close down conversation. In particular, good open-ended questions allow narrative answers.

oral age/orality: the time before the invention of writing and the printing press. Scholars show that storytellers in the oral age depended heavily on memory techniques such as narrative. Used to describe societies that communicated completely or primarily through speaking. Societies think, act, and organize differently in an oral culture than in a print culture.

orality: human thought and speech that's not heavily influenced, and often not influenced at all, by writing and print technology.

overall argument/thesis: a specific, detailed, explicit statement about the point or purpose of the piece of academic writing.

parallelism: the repetition of two or more identical grammatical elements.

participle: an often irregular form of a verb, such as *broken* or *stolen*.

passive voice: a way of ordering sentences that places the doer of the action or condition/state of being at the end of the sentence or clause or doesn't include the doer at all. Often used to hide responsibility.

past perfect continuous: verb tense describing an action that occurred continually in the past.

personal essay: a short, tentative, persuasive piece of personal writing that may or may not include research.

plagiarism: the representation of someone else's words or ideas as your own. Many people regard the copying of an exact short sequence of words from another author, even with credit, as plagiarism too.

planned redundancy: deliberate repetition to emphasize a point.

plot: a sequence of actions.

plural: more than one.

populist: to appeal in language to the general public, not to elites.

prepositions: words that link subjects and objects in a sentence, suggesting time, space, or logical relationships between these two parts of speech. Prepositions include *after*, *before*, *with*, *without*, *to*, *up*, *down*, etc.

preposition series: two or more prepositions in a list.

profluence: flow or movement. Writing must go somewhere: it must flow along like a river flows.

pronouns: small words that take the place of nouns.

prose: regular language that people use in communication, usually in full sentences. Prose is usually contrasted with poetry, which emphasizes fragments in a regular metric.

psychic space: borrowed from psychology, this term means a created world that invites but doesn't force meanings on the reader. The reader becomes active in the making of meaning, instead of remaining passive.

rapport: a French word meaning chemistry between two people.

readability: a formal term to describe how easy readers find a text to process. Researchers have looked for factors in writing that make it easy to read.

reciprocal: shared, felt, or shown by two sides.

recursive writing: writing as a back-and-forth dialogue between text and research or text and further thinking. The text may come together in myriad ways, not necessarily in a logical order.

research paper: a longer piece of objective writing on a topic that presents research evidence, citations, and an overall argument or thesis.

rhetorical analysis: a close reading of some text or artifact to explain how it works and affects an audience.

rhythm: a recurring element, sometimes strong, sometimes weak.

right-branching sentences: sentences that begin with the doers of verbs. Verbs and objects follow. Readers find these sentences easy to read compared to more complex sentences.

segregated sentences: sentences that present one point, often of description or narration.

sentence: a set of words that is grammatically complete.

semantics: the study of the different meanings of words. Compare this to *grammar*.

sequence writing: writing as a logical process from initiation to completion.

series: a list of items.

simile: a statement that compares two normally unconnected realms of human experience using the words *like* or *as*.

social domain: a community upheld by both language and real spaces or places. Within these communities, people create and maintain language and rules. This process forms discourses.

spatial: our sense of location in space.

staccato effect: a musical term that refers to short notes that are separated from others.

stereotype: the perception of certain consistent, regular, repeating aspects of human life.

stream of consciousness: a writing approach that presents the flowing thoughts of the author as they happen. It lacks any clear order or sequence.

strong nouns: nouns that create images in the mind of the reader. Strong nouns are usually everyday words that most readers know well.

subject: the element of a sentence that does the action of the verb in the active voice.

subject–verb agreement: occurs when the number of a verb matches the number of the doer of the action.

subject-verb series: two or more subject-verb units in a list.

subject-verb-object series: two or more subject-verb-object units in a list.

suffixes: a combination of letters added to the end of a word. A common suffix to verbs is the *–ed* to express past tense.

surface parallelism: the repetition of identical words.

tense: the position of a verb in time. An act or state of being that exists in the past requires a verb form in the past tense. An act or state of being that exists in the present requires a verb form in the present tense.

transitive verbs: verbs that require objects.

unclear pronouns: pronouns that do not have a clear connection to a noun.

under-the-surface parallelism: repetition of grammatical elements without necessarily repeating identical words.

verb series: two or more verbs in a list.

verb-preposition-object series: two or more verb-preposition-object units in a list. The subject does not repeat.

wordiness: using more words than you need to, words that the average reader doesn't understand, long difficult words, and/or long sentences.

CREDITS

Chapter 1

Page 1, quotation by Jacques Barzun
Barzun, Jacques. *On Writing, Editing, and Publishing: Essays, Explicative and Hortatory*. 2nd ed. Chicago: University of Chicago Press, 1986. 8. Print.

Page 2, quotation by Philip Pullman
Pullman, Philip. *Latest Q and A's. Philip Pullman official website*. n.d. Web. 25 June 2013. www.philip-pullman.com/q_a.asp?offset5160

Page 5, quotation by Madeleine L'Engle
Rosenberg, Aaron. *Madeleine L'Engle*. New York: The Rosen Publishing Group. 74. Print.

Page 6, quotation by Peter Elbow
Elbow, Peter. *Writing with Power: Techniques for Mastering the Writing Process*. New York and Oxford: Oxford University Press, 1998. 13. Print.

Page 7, quotation by Julia Cameron
Cameron, Julia. *The Artist's Way: A Spiritual Way to Higher Creativity*. New York: Jeremy P. Tarcher/Putnam, 2002. 10. Print.

Page 22, quotation by Wendy Belcher
Belcher, Wendy Laura. *Writing Your Journal Article in 12 Weeks: A Guide to Academic Publishing Success*. Thousand Oaks, CA: SAGE Publications, 2009. 84. Print.

Page 24, quotation by Joanna Russ
Russ, Joanna. *How To Suppress Women's Writing*. Austin, TX: University of Texas Press. 137. Print.

Page 26, quotation by Vladimir Nabokov
Nabakov, Vladimir. *Strong Opinions*. New York, Vintage Books, 1990. 4. Print.

Page 26, quotation by Bernard Malamud
Malamud, Bernard. *Talking Horse: Bernard Malamud on Life and Work*. New York, Columbia University Press, 1996. 35. Print.

Page 29, quotation by Kelly Barnhill
Brown, John. Interview with Kelly Barnhill. 3 February 2011. Web. 20 May 2013. http://johndbrown.com/2011/02/interview-with-author-kelly-barnhill

Page 29, quotation by Henry Green
Green, Henry. Interview by Terry Southern. *The Paris Review*. n.d. Web. 5 June 2013. www.theparisreview.org/interviews/4800/the-art-of-fiction-no-22-henry-green

Chapter 2

Page 34, quotation by Stephen King
King, Stephen. "The Horror Writer Market and the Ten Bears." *Writer's Digest*, Nov. 1973. Print.

Page 35, quotation by Thomas Jefferson
Pine, Joslyn, ed. *Wit and Wisdom of the American Presidents: A Book of Quotations*. Dover Publications, 2001. 10. Print.

Pages 35–6, excerpt from Judith Butler
Butler, Judith. "Further Reflections on Conversations of Our Time." Diacritics 27.1 (1997): 13–15.

Page 36, quotation by George Orwell
Orwell, George. *A Collection of Essays*. New York: Harcourt Books, 1981. 170. Print.

Pages 39–40 excerpts from Denise Bellamy
Source: City of Toronto

Page 42, quotation by Truman Capote
Hart, Jack. *A Writer's Coach: The Complete Guide to Writing Strategies that Work*. New York: Anchor Books, 2006. 23. Print.

Page 44, quotation by William Strunk Jr.
Strunk Jr., William and E.B. White. *The Elements of Style Illustrated*. New York: The Penguin Press, 2005. 39. Print.

Page 44, quotation by Mark Twain
Graves, Heather and Roger Graves. *A Strategic Guide to Technical Communication*. 2nd Ed. Toronto: Broadview Press, 2012. 107. Print.

Page 47, quotation by George Orwell
Orwell, George. *A Collection of Essays*. New York: Harcourt Books, 1981. 170. Print.

Page 48, quotation by Gloria Steinem
Denes, Melisa. "Feminism? It's hardly begun." *The Guardian* 17 January 2005. Web. 6 May 2013. www.theguardian.com/world/2005/jan/17/gender.melissadenes

Page 49, quotation by Thomas Mann
Keren, Michael. *The Citizen's Voice: Twentieth-Century Politics and Literature*. Calgary: University of Calgary Press, 2003. 23. Print.

Page 49, quotation by Albert Einstein
Nairn, Alasdair. *Engines that Move Markets: Technology Investing from Railroads to the Internet and Beyond*. New York: John Wiley & Sons, 2002. 449. Print.

Chapter 3

Page 63, quotation by Stephen Fry
Bryant, Andrew and Ana Kazan. *Self-Leadership: How to Become a More Successful, Efficient, and Effective Leader from the Inside Out.* McGraw-Hill, 2012. 86. Print.

Page 65, quotation by William Zinsser
Zinsser, William. *On Writing Well: The Classic Guide to Writing Nonfiction.* 7th Ed. New York: HarperCollins, 2006. 68. Print.

Page 68, quotation by William Zinsser
Zinsser, William. *On Writing Well: The Classic Guide to Writing Nonfiction.* 7th Ed. New York: HarperCollins, 2006. 68. Print.

Page 70, excerpts from *Of Mice and Men*
By John Steinbeck, copyright 1937, renewed © 1965 by John Steinbeck. Used by permission of Viking Penguin, a division of Penguin Group (USA) LLC.

Pages 71 and 188, excerpts from *Tar Baby*
By Toni Morrison, copyright © 1981 by Toni Morrison. Used by permission of Alfred A. Knopf, an imprint of Alfred A. Knopf, an imprint of Knopf Doubleday Publishing Group, a division of Random House LLC. All rights reserved. From TAR BABY by Toni Morrison. Published by Vintage. Reprinted by permission of The Random House Group Limited.

Page 73, quotation by Ray Bradbury
Bradbury, Ray. *Death Is a Lonely Business.* New York: HarperCollins, 1999. 192. Print.

Pages 82–3, Tables 3.1 to 3.3
From personal email correspondence between Monique O'Neill (Writing Department, York University) and Duncan Koerber.

Page 84, quotation by James Michener
Moore, Dinty W. *Crafting the Personal Essay: A Guide for Writing and Publishing Creative Nonfiction.* Cincinnati: Writer's Digest Books, 2010. 219. Print.

Chapter 4

Page 95, quotation by Sydney J. Harris
Andrews, Robert, ed. *The Columbia Dictionary of Quotations.* New York and Chichester, West Sussex: Columbia University Press, 1993. 16. Print.

Page 100, quotation by William Strunk and E.B. White
Strunk Jr., William and E.B. White. *The Elements of Style Illustrated.* New York: The Penguin Press, 2005. 33–34. Print.

Page 101, quotation by William Zinsser
Zinsser, William. *On Writing Well: The Classic Guide to Writing Nonfiction.* 7th ed. New York: HarperCollins, 2006. 67. Print.

Page 102, quotation by Roy Peter Clark
Clark, Roy Peter. *Writing Tools: 50 Essential Strategies for Every Writer.* New York: Little, Brown and Company, 2006. 24. Print.

Page 104, quotation by George Orwell
Orwell, George. *A Collection of Essays.* New York: Harcourt Books, 1981. 170. Print.

Page 105, quotation by Roy Peter Clark
Clark, Roy Peter. *Writing Tools: 50 Essential Strategies for Every Writer.* New York: Little, Brown and Company, 2006. 26. Print.

Page 111, quotation by Barbara Tuchman
Tuchman, Barbara W. *Practicing History: Selected Essays.* Random House, 2011. 16. Print.

Page 113, quotation by William Zinsser
Zinsser, William. *On Writing Well: The Classic Guide to Writing Nonfiction.* 7th ed. New York: HarperCollins, 2006. 170. Print.

Chapter 5

Page 124, quotation by C.S. Lewis
Lewis, C.S. *The Collected Letters of C.S. Lewis, Volume III: Narnia, Cambridge, and Joy 1950–1963.* Ed. Walter Hooper. New York: HarperCollins, 2007. 766. Print.

Page 126, quotation by Roy Peter Clark
Clark, Roy Peter. *Writing Tools: 50 Essential Strategies for Every Writer.* New York: Little, Brown and Company, 2006. 72. Print.

Page 130, quotation by Ernest Hemingway
Hemingway, Ernest, *Death in the Afternoon.* London: Vintage, 2000. 168. Print.

Page 133, quotation by Donald Hall and Sven Birkerts
Hall, Donald and Sven Birkerts. *Writing Well.* 8th ed. New York: HarperCollins College Publishers, 1994. 320. Print.

Pages 135–7, 190, 220, 223, excerpts from *The Devil Problem: And Other True Stories*
By David Remnick. Used by permission of Random House, an imprint and division of Random House LLC All rights approved.

Page 139, quotation by Stephen King
King, Stephen. *On Writing: A Memoir of the Craft: 10th Anniversary Edition.* New York: Scribner, 2010. 215. Print.

Page 140, quotation by Harriet Ottenheimer
Ottenheimer, Harriet Joseph. *The Anthropology of Language: An Introduction to Linguistic Anthropology.* Belmont, CA: Wadsworth Publishing, 2012. 340. Print.

Chapter 6

Page 154, quotation by Ezra Pound
Alexander, Michael. *The Poetic Achievement of Ezra Pound*. Berkeley and Los Angeles: University of California Press, 1981. 19. Print.

Page 155, quotation by Samuel Goldwyn
Shapiro, Fred R., ed. *The Yale Book of Quotations*. Yale University Press, 2006. 317. Print.

Page 162, quotation by George Orwell
Orwell, George. *A Collection of Essays*. New York: Harcourt Books, 1981. 165. Print.

Page 163, quotation by Ernest Hemingway
Hemingway, Ernest. *Death in the Afternoon*. London: Vintage, 2000. 47. Print.

Page 164, quotation by W. Somerset Maugham
Maugham, W. Somerset. *The Painted Veil*. New York: Penguin Books, 2007. 24. Print.

Page 164, excerpts from TV commercials.
Permission granted by the NHL.

Page 165, quotation by James Stephens
Dictionary of Quotations. 3rd ed. Ware, Hertfordshire: Wordsworth Editions Ltd., 1998. 410. Print.

Page 168, quotation by Rhys Alexander
Shepherd, Margaret and Sharon Hogan. *The Art of the Personal Letter: a Guide to Connecting Through the Written Word*. New York: Broadway Books, 2008. 88. Print.

Page 169, quotation by Orson Scott Card
Card, Orson Scott. *Alvin Journeyman*. New York: Tom Doherty Associates, 1996. 33. Print.

Page 170, quotation by George Lakoff and Mark Johnson
Lakoff, George and Mark Johnson. *Metaphors We Live By*. 2nd ed. Chicago: University of Chicago Press. 5. Print.

Page 173, quotation by Robert Fulford
Fulford, Robert. "Observer: a Real Writer Wouldn't be Caught Dead at this Orgy." *Globe and Mail,* 4 Dec. 1996: C1. Print.

Page 176, lyrics from PUSH
Words and music by Robert Thomas and Matthew Serletic. © 1996 EMI April Music Inc., EMI Blackwood Music Inc., U Rule Music and Melusic Publishing. All rights on behalf of EMI April Music Inc., EMI Blackwood Music Inc., U Rule Music. Sony/ATV Music Publishing LLC, 424 Church Street, Suite 1200, Nashville, TN 37219. All rights reserved. Used by permission.

Chapter 7

Page 183, quotation by C.H. Sisson
"Biography of C.H. Sisson." *Carcanet*. Carcanet Press, n.d. Web. 1 Nov. 2013. www.carcanet.co.uk/cgi-bin/scribe?showdoc515;doctype5biography

Page 184, excerpts from Martin Luther King
Reprinted by arrangement with The Heirs to the Estate of Martin Luther King Jr., c/o Writers House as agent for the proprietor New York, NY. Copyright © 1963 Dr. Martin Luther King Jr. © renewed 1991 Coretta Scott King.

Page 185, quotation by Laurence Cossé
Cossé, Laurence. *A Novel Bookstore*. New York, Europa Editions, 2010. 33. Print.

Page 188, quotation by Chip Heath
Heath, Chip and Dan Heath. *Made to Stick: Why Some Ideas Survive and Others Die*. New York: Random House, 2008. 64. Print.

Page 189, quotation by Mark Twain
Smith, Ronald D. *Becoming a Public Relations Writer*. 4th ed. New York: Routledge, 2012. 26. Print.

Page 201, quotation by Jim Lehrer
Rothstein, Betsy. "PBS's Judy Woodruff, Jim Lehrer reflect on prior presidential races." *The Hill*. 8 Sept. 2008. Web. 5 Nov. 2013. http://thehill.com/homenews/news/16222-pbss-judy-woodruff-jim-lehrer-reflect-on-prior-presidential-races

Page 202, excerpts from transcript
Courtesy of Charlie Rose.

Page 203, quotation by William Hazlitt
Hazlitt, William. *The Plain Speaker: Opinions on Books, Men, and Things*. London: George Bell & Sons, 1890. 50. Print.

Page 203, quotation by Brenda Ueland
Ueland, Brenda. "Tell me more: On the true art of listening." *Utne Reader* (Nov.–Dec. 1992): 104–109. Print.

Chapter 8

Page 215, quotation by Gustave Flaubert
Flaubert, Gustave. *The Letters of Gustave Flaubert: Volumes I & II, 1830–1880*. Ed. Francis Steegmuller. London: Picador, 2001. 228. Print.

Page 216, quotation by Charles Baudelaire
Moore, Fabienne. *Prose Poems of the French Enlightenment: Delimiting Genre*. Surrey, England: Ashgate Publishing, 2009. 4. Print.

Page 220, quotation by Jean Rostand
Andrews, Robert, ed. *The Columbia Dictionary of Quotations*. New York and Chichester, West Sussex: Columbia University Press, 1993. 45. Print.

Page 223, quotation by Theodor Geisel (Dr. Seuss)
Lamb, Sandra E. *How to Write It: A Complete Guide to Everything You'll Ever Write*. Berkeley, CA: Ten Speed Press, 2006. 371. Print.

Page 224, quotation by E.L. Doctorow
Campbell, James. "The Long View." *The Guardian* 14 January 2006. Web. 5 Nov. 2013. www.theguardian.com/books/2006/jan/14/featuresreviews.guardianreview28

Page 225, quotation by Barry Hannah
Hannah, Barry. Interview by Lacey Galbraith. *The Paris Review*. n.d. Web. 1 Nov. 2013. www.theparisreview.org/interviews/5438/the-art-of-fiction-no-184-barry-hannah

Page 228, quotation by Richard Rodriguez
Ehrhard, Michelle, ed. *The Portable MFA*. New York: The New York Writers Workshop, 2006. 83. Print.

Page 229, quotation by Virginia Woolf
Meltzer, Tom and Paul Foglino. *Cracking the CLEP*. 4th Ed. New York: Princeton Review Publishing, 2000. 45. Print.

Page 229, quotation by Susan Sontag
Levy, Daniel, Max Pensky, and John Torpey, eds. *Old Europe, New Europe, Core Europe*. London and New York: Verso, 2005. 218. Print.

Page 230, quotation by Bill McKibben
McKibben, Bill. *Bill on activism*. n.d. The Library of America. Web. 10 Jan. 2014. http://americanearth.loa.org/writer.mov.html?bw5640&bh5396

Page 230, quotation by Edward Tufte
Moore, Dinty W. *Crafting the Personal Essay: A Guide for Writing and Publishing Creative Nonfiction*. Cincinnati: Writer's Digest Books, 2010. 208. Print.

Pages 231-2, excerpts from *The David Suzuki Reader*
By David Suzuki and Bill McKibbben, published in 2004 by Greystone Books Ltd. Reprinted with permission from the publisher.

Page 234, quotation by Oscar Wilde
Wilde, Oscar. *Oscar Wilde: The Major Works*. Oxford: Oxford University Press, 2000. 485. Print.

Page 235, quotation by Peter Singer
Singer, Peter. *Writings on an Ethical Life*. New York: HarperCollins, 2000. xix. Print.

Works Cited

Allen, Guy. "The 'Good Enough' Teacher and the Authentic Student." *A Pedagogy of Becoming*. Ed. John Mills. Amsterdam and New York: Rodopi, 2002. 141–176. Print.

Al-Solaylee, Kamal. "Too Poor to Send Flowers." *The Best Canadian Essays 2009*. Eds. Alex Boyd and Carmine Starnino. Toronto: Tightrope Books, 2009. 3–6. Print.

American Psychological Association. *Publication Manual of the American Psychological Association*. 6th ed. Washington, DC: American Psychological Association, 2009.

Barber, John. "Judge's unsparing censure of municipal sleaze wildly exceeds expectations." *Globe & Mail* 13 Sept. 2005: A1. Print.

Barkas, Vaia. "South of Assiniboia." *Make It New: Creative Nonfiction by New Writers For New Writers*. 2nd ed. Ed. Guy Allen. Toronto: Life Rattle Press, 2008. 161–165. Print.

Belcher, Wendy Laura. *Writing Your Journal Article in 12 Weeks: A Guide to Academic Publishing Success*. Thousand Oaks, CA: SAGE Publications, 2009. Print.

Bellamy, Denise E. *Toronto Computer Leasing Inquiry/ Toronto External Contracts Inquiry: Report Volume 1: Facts and Findings*. Toronto: City of Toronto, 2005. Web. 12 May 2013. www.toronto.ca/inquiry/ inquiry_site/report/pdf/TCLI_TECI_Report_Facts_ Findings.pdf

Blatchford, Christie. "The Hazel McCallion Show: Still a Hit." *The Globe & Mail* 21 Sept. 2010: A6. Print.

Bloom, Harold, ed. *Bloom's Modern Critical Interpretations: Ernest Hemingway's A Farewell to Arms*. New York: Infobase Publishing, 2009. Print.

Bond, Jon R. and Kevin B. Smith. *The Promise and Performance of American Democracy*. 9th edition. Boston, MA: Wadsworth Cengage, 2010. Print.

Brenner, Athalya. *I am . . .: Biblical Women Tell Their Own Stories*. Minneapolis: Fortress Press, 2005. Print.

Butler, Judith. "Further Reflections on Conversations of Our Time." *Diacritics* 27.1 (1997): 13–15. Print.

Burrows, Petura. "I wear my too-black skin with pride." *Toronto Star* 20 Feb. 2011: IN2. Print.

Carey, James. *Communication as Culture: Essays on Media and Society*. New York: Routledge, 2009. Print.

———. *James Carey: a Critical Reader*. Eds. Eve Stryker Munson and Catherine A. Warren. Minneapolis, MN: University of Minnesota Press, 1997. Print.

Carr, E.H. *What is History?* London: Macmillan, 1986. Print.

Chartier, Roger. *The Order of Books*. Stanford, CA: Stanford University Press, 1992. Print.

Chow, Olivia. *My Journey*. Toronto: HarperCollins, 2014. Kindle file.

Clark, Elizabeth. "The Stovepipe Hole." *Make It New: Creative Nonfiction by New Writers For New Writers*. 2nd ed. Ed. Guy Allen. Toronto: Life Rattle Press, 2008. 88–92. Print

Clark, Roy Peter. *Writing Tools: 50 Essential Strategies for Every Writer*. New York: Little, Brown and Company, 2006. Print. 72

Coyle, Jim. "Judge Eviscerates Old Civic Guard." *Toronto Star* 13 Sep. 2005: A01. Print.

Coyne, Andrew. "Liberal Obama dons his gloves; Post-partisanship out as inaugural rallies Democrats." *National Post* 22 Jan. 2013: A1. Print.

Darnton, Robert. "Toward a History of Reading." *Media in America: The Wilson Quarterly Reader*. Ed. Douglas Gomery. Washington, D.C.: The Woodrow Wilson International Center Press, 1998. 3–20. Print.

Davidson, Emily. "Put a Hole in It, Won't You?" *Make It New: Creative Nonfiction by New Writers For New Writers*. 2nd ed. Ed. Guy Allen. Toronto: Life Rattle Press, 2008. 24–26. Print.

Dillard, Annie. *Pilgrim at Tinker Creek*. New York: Harper Perennial Modern Classics, 2013. Print.

Doyle, Charles Clay, Wolfgang Mieder, and Fred R. Shapiro, comps. *The Dictionary of Modern Proverbs*. Yale University Press, 2012. Print.

Geary, James. *I Is an Other: The Secret Life of Metaphor and How It Shapes the Way We See the World*. New York: HarperCollins, 2011. Print.

Gerard, Philip. *Researching and Crafting the Stories of Real Life*. Long Grove, IL: Waveland Press, 2004. Print.

Giles, Adam. "Christine." *Make It New: Creative Nonfiction by New Writers For New Writers*. 2nd ed. Ed. Guy Allen. Toronto: Life Rattle Press, 2008. 116–119. Print.

Gutkind, Lee. *The Art of Creative Nonfiction: Writing and Selling the Literature of Reality*. New York: John Wiley & Sons, 1997. Print.

Gwyn, Richard. "The Contender: the Appeal of Justin Trudeau's Emotional Intelligence." *The Walrus* July/ Aug. 2013: 26–30. Print.

Harris, Michael. "Martin Dumps on Poor Kids." *Fact.on.ca*. *The Toronto Sun*. 2 May 1999. Web. 23 June 2013.

Henderson, Eric. *The Active Writer: Strategies for Academic Reading and Writing*. 2nd ed. Oxford University Press, 2011. Print.

Kahn, Seth and Jong Hwa Lee. *Activism and Rhetoric: Theories and Contexts for Political Engagement*. New York: Routledge, 2011. Print

Kallis, Laurie. "Willy Lavigne." *Make It New: Creative Nonfiction by New Writers For New Writers*. 2nd ed. Ed. Guy Allen. Toronto: Life Rattle Press, 2008. 56–58. Print.

King, Stephen. *On Writing: A Memoir of the Craft: 10th Anniversary Edition*. New York: Scribner, 2010. Print.

———. "Why We Crave Horror Movies." *From Idea to Essay: A Rhetoric, Reader, and Handbook*. 12th ed. Eds. Jo Ray McCuen-Metherell and Anthony C. Winkler. Boston, MA: Wadsworth Cengage, 2009. 410–411. Print.

Koerber, Duncan. "Constructing the Sports Community: Canadian Sports Columnists, Identity, and the Business of Sport in the 1940s." *Sport History Review*. 40.2 (2009): 126–142. Print.

———. "Early Political Parties as Mediated Communities." *Media History*. 19.2 (2013): 125–138. Print.

———. "The Role of the Agent in Partisan Communication Networks of Upper Canadian Newspapers." *Journal of Canadian Studies*. 45.3 (2011): 137–165. Print.

Kolln, Martha, and Robert Funk. *Understanding English Grammar*. 9th ed. Boston: Pearson, 2012. Print.

Lakoff, George and Mark Johnson. *Metaphors We Live By*. 2nd ed. Chicago: University of Chicago Press. Print.

Lamott, Anne. *Bird by Bird: Some Instructions on Writing and Life*. Anchor Books, 1995. Print.

Laurence, Margaret. *The Stone Angel*. Chicago: University of Chicago Press, 1993. Print.

Layton, Jack. "A Letter to Canadians from the Honourable Jack Layton." *NDP.ca*. 20 Aug. 2011. Web. 1 Nov. 2013. www.ndp.ca/letter-to-canadians-from-jack-layton

Lee, Jennifer. "Going to Chinese School." *Make It New: Creative Nonfiction by New Writers For New Writers*. 2nd ed. Ed. Guy Allen. Toronto: Life Rattle Press, 2008. 48–51. Print.

Lehuu, Isabelle. *Carnival on the Page: Popular Print Media in Antebellum America*. Chapel Hill: The University of North Carolina Press, 2000. Print.

"Let's follow through on Bellamy's blast." Editorial. *Globe & Mail* 14 Sept. 2005: A20. Print.

Livia, Anna. *Pronoun Envy: Literary Uses of Linguistic Gender*. New York: Oxford University Press, 2001. Print.

McCain, Michael. "Maple Leaf Recall." 23 Aug. 2008. *Maple Leaf Foods*. Web.

McCarthy, Cormac. *All the Pretty Horses*. New York: Vintage, 1993. Print.

McLuhan, Marshall and Wilfred Watson. *From Cliché to Archetype*. New York: Viking Press, 1970. Print.

Michelangelo, Julie. "My Mom and Bramalea." *Make It New: Creative Nonfiction by New Writers For New Writers*. 2nd ed. Ed. Guy Allen. Toronto: Life Rattle Press, 2008. 10–13. Print.

Modern Language Association. *MLA Handbook for Writers of Research Papers*. 7th ed. New York: The Modern Language Association of America, 2009. Print.

Mount, Nick. "The Return of Beauty." *The Best Canadian Essays 2009*. Eds. Alex Boyd and Carmine Starnino. Toronto: Tightrope Books, 2009. 67–78. Print.

Morrison, Toni. *Tar Baby*. New York: Plume, 1982. Print.

O'Neill, Dominique. "Re: hand-outs." Message to Duncan Koerber. 8 Nov. 2013. E-mail.

Ong, Joyce. "Two Hard Years." *Make It New: Creative Nonfiction by New Writers For New Writers*. 2nd ed. Ed. Guy Allen. Toronto: Life Rattle Press, 2008. 251–255. Print.

Orwell, George. *A Collection of Essays*. New York: Harcourt Books, 1981. Print.

Palladini, Peter. "Cell Phone." *Make It New: Creative Nonfiction by New Writers For New Writers*. 2nd ed. Ed. Guy Allen. Toronto: Life Rattle Press, 2008. 77–79. Print.

Ramadi, Eric. "Two Weeks at Notre Dame Hospital." *Make It New: Creative Nonfiction by New Writers For New Writers*. 2nd ed. Ed. Guy Allen. Toronto: Life Rattle Press, 2008. 211–213. Print.

Remnick, David. *The Devil Problem: And Other True Stories*. New York: Vintage Books, 1997. Print.

"research, n.1". *OED Online*. Sept. 2013. Oxford University Press. Web. 28 Nov. 2013

"research, v.1". *OED Online*. Sept. 2013. Oxford University Press. Web. 28 Nov. 2013

Steinbeck, John. *Of Mice and Men*. New York: Penguin Books, 1993. Print.

Suzuki, David. "Global Warming." *The David Suzuki Reader*. Vancouver: Greystone Books, 2004. 60–65. Print.

———. "London in My Life." *The David Suzuki Reader*. Vancouver: Greystone Books, 2004. 14–17. Print.

———. "Why We Must Act on Global Warming." *The David Suzuki Reader*. Vancouver: Greystone Books, 2004. 66–69. Print.

Twain, Mark. *Great Short Works of Mark Twain*. New York: Perennial Classics, 2004. Print.

Waterman, Laurel. "Sesame Street." *Make It New: Creative Nonfiction by New Writers For New Writers*. 2nd ed. Ed. Guy Allen. Toronto: Life Rattle Press, 2008. 5–7. Print.

Wolff, Jonathan. "Literary Boredom." *The Guardian* 4 Sept. 2007. Web. 5 Nov. 2013. www.theguardian.com/education/2007/sep/04/highereducation.news

Woolf, Virginia. *A Room of One's Own*. Oxford: Oxford University Press, 2008. Print.

Zinsser, William. *On Writing Well: The Classic Guide to Writing Nonfiction*. 7th ed. New York: HarperCollins, 2006. Print.

———. *Writing about Your Life: A Journey into the Past*. New York: Marlowe and Company, 2004. Print.

INDEX

48–49, 61; thickeners, 47–48, 49, 61; -tion suffixes and, 129; types of, 61; unclear pronouns and, 152

word order, 96, 121–22; *see also* active voice; passive voice

works, documentation of: multiple-author, 251, 253–54; multiple by single author, 251–52, 254; single-author, 251, 253

Works Cited, 255–59; APA style, 257–59; MLA style, 24, 255–57

would, 74–75

writers (of personal essays), 246; as activists, 230–32; as cultural observers, 229

writing: effective, 36–37; learning, 1–3; practising often, 2, 32; reading and, 3, 32; short assignments and, 2, 32; "in the moment," 60; in positive settings, 3; recursive approach, 7, 8, 26, 32, 262; sequence approach to, 7–8, 32, 262; starting, 3–4; taught in school, 1, 32

writing groups, 121

Zabara, Nick, 239; "Saints and Monsters: The Psychology of Altruism and Malice," 240–43

Zinsser, William, 31, 65, 68, 101, 113